Effective Management of Nonprofit Organizations

Effective Management of Nonprofit Organizations: Leading Relationships with Stakeholders provides practical information, rooted in organizational behavior theory, for the effective and successful management of nonprofit organizations and key stakeholder groups. The book enables the reader to identify the ways in which application of management principles and theory varies between nonprofit and for-profit organizations. It also offers a path to develop the skills necessary to lead a nonprofit, enact organizational change, and create strategic plans, as well as recognize and engage with revenue mechanisms. Using case studies and narrative examples, the book provides the basis for the key skills, including marketing, accounting, entrepreneurship, governance, fundraising, and of course leadership and management. Structured around the key themes of staff, volunteers, donors, and community, topics include diversity, ethics, decision-making, culture, conflict, volunteer engagement, fundraising and stewardship, grants, foundations, PR, lobbying and government relations, and others.

This book is ideal for college students undertaking a nonprofit management course.

Melissa Newman is Associate Professor, Educator of Management at the University of Cincinnati's Lindner College of Business.

Effective Management of Nonprofit Organizations

Leading Relationships with Stakeholders

Melissa Newman

Routledge
Taylor & Francis Group
LONDON AND NEW YORK

Designed cover image: Getty Images

First published 2024
by Routledge
4 Park Square, Milton Park, Abingdon, Oxon OX14 4RN

and by Routledge
605 Third Avenue, New York, NY 10158

Routledge is an imprint of the Taylor & Francis Group, an informa business

British Library Cataloguing-in-Publication Data
A catalogue record for this book is available from the British Library

ISBN: 978-1-032-46083-3 (hbk)
ISBN: 978-1-032-46087-1 (pbk)
ISBN: 978-1-003-38003-0 (ebk)

DOI: 10.4324/9781003380030

Typeset in Sabon
by Deanta Global Publishing Services, Chennai, India

To my friends and family and especially my babies, Hannah and Abby, for filling my life with love, purpose, and meaning. And a perpetually messy kitchen.

To my Bearcats for bringing me happiness and fulfillment at work.

To the hundreds of volunteers and donors I've encountered in my nonprofit career who have taught me firsthand all the joys, and struggles, of the sector.

And this book is for all the do-gooders who give and sacrifice so much to nonprofits while never giving up on the dream of making the world a better place.

Contents

Figures

Figures

Photos

Preface

Why Did I Decide to Write This Text?

In 2020, I achieved a long-term career goal, which was to develop and implement a new course at the University of Cincinnati that combines two of my passions, management in business and nonprofit work. Throughout my career in academia, I have always found it interesting that many institutions of higher learning separate out these two activities, often housing academic majors in nonprofit work in colleges of arts and sciences or social work. On the college of business side, much of the curriculum emphasizes the commercial sector, with little-to-no emphasis on nonprofit work. Throughout my career, I've encountered hundreds of business students who aspire to impact the world through nonprofit work, so I designed my class with these students in mind.

In implementing the course, I then faced a new dilemma – I was unable to find a textbook that fit the spirit of the course. Many texts were focused on the "do-gooder" nature of nonprofits or were exclusive to service delivery rather than the business side, others were too specialized on facets of nonprofit work like social justice, while others served more as "nonprofits 101" primers. As a professor who focuses on organizational behavior, I then set out to write a textbook that covers one of the most important aspects of nonprofit leadership, which is managing the many varied stakeholder relationships in these organizations.

Who is This Book For?

While this text was originally designed for use in my nonprofit management class in a college of business, my hope is that it is broad-reaching and can be used not just in other classrooms, but that it can also serve as a valuable resource for nonprofit practitioners. The role of a nonprofit leader is *hard*, a topic covered in Chapter 4, and executive directors and board presidents are often thrust into these important leadership roles without the proper tools to succeed. I hope that this book provides both an overview of the key stakeholder groups in nonprofits, but also a deep dive into what it takes to specifically manage relationships with these groups.

My experience in nonprofits is unique, as I have served both as a nonprofit staff leader for most of my career, including over a decade as an executive director, but also as a volunteer, as I now serve on multiple nonprofit boards. As a management professor, I also tend to approach nonprofit work from an academic perspective, with the goal of integrating academic theory into practice.

As I always tell my students, you don't have to *work* in a nonprofit to make an impact in the sector. There are numerous volunteer opportunities that can provide not just personal growth and fulfillment, but also provide tremendous professional development and networking opportunities. Regardless of a person's interest in nonprofits, be it a staff or volunteer role, the learnings from this text apply.

What This Book is Not

This book is generally focused on nonprofits in the United States and, while it emphasizes the diverse nature of nonprofit agencies, it focuses most on charitable nonprofit organizations. As a management text, the emphasis is on leadership, with little discussion around topics such as accounting or finance, aside from fundraising as an activity in managing relationships with donors. It also is presented from a business lens, which can be a controversial take as there are some who criticize the "businessification" of nonprofits, a topic addressed in Chapter 2.

How Is the Book Organized?

As discussed in Chapter 1, nonprofit leaders must manage relationships with many stakeholder groups. There are too many stakeholders to cover in just one text, so I organized this text to categorize four of the most important: Staff, volunteers, donors, and the community. The framework of how this book is organized is reflected in Figure 0.1.

Part 1 provides an overview of nonprofit work, covering not only the nonprofit basics, but also the foundation of nonprofits, which is mission, strategic planning, and measuring effectiveness. It also emphasizes ethics as a cornerstone of nonprofit management.

Part 2 moves on to address the staff stakeholder group, describing the various staff positions in nonprofits and the importance of the volunteer-staff partnership, and drawing upon academic theory to suggest practical ways leaders can manage and motivate their teams, design effective organizations, implement sound leadership practices, and make good, rational decisions.

Part 3 addresses a stakeholder group that is practically unique to the sector, which is volunteers. Managing volunteer relationships can present its own set of challenges for leaders, as these are unpaid positions. This part includes topics around the role of the board and nonprofit governance, methods to engage volunteers, and approaches to the formation of teams, managing conflict, and navigating a diverse group of individuals with differing personalities.

Part 4 provides a discussion around the donor stakeholder group, using academic theory and sales practices to suggest effective approaches to fundraising and stewardship. It takes a look at nonprofit marketing from the business perspective, suggesting ways that leaders can most effectively "sell hope" in their organizational mission. It also addresses other sources of funding, such as grants, corporate giving, and other funding.

Part 5 brings the text home with a discussion around the other important stakeholder group, the community. This includes approaches to advocacy, delivery of programs, services, and events in executing on mission efforts to serve constituents and beneficiaries, and the topic of global impact and diversity.

Figure 0.1 Managing Stakeholder Relationships in Nonprofits

The order of these four stakeholder groups is strictly random, and their order of presentation in this book does not indicate that any is more important than other. In a way, this is representative of the challenge that nonprofit leaders face in having to simultaneously and equally balance the diverse and ever-changing needs of each group in managing these critical relationships.

Part 1

Nonprofits

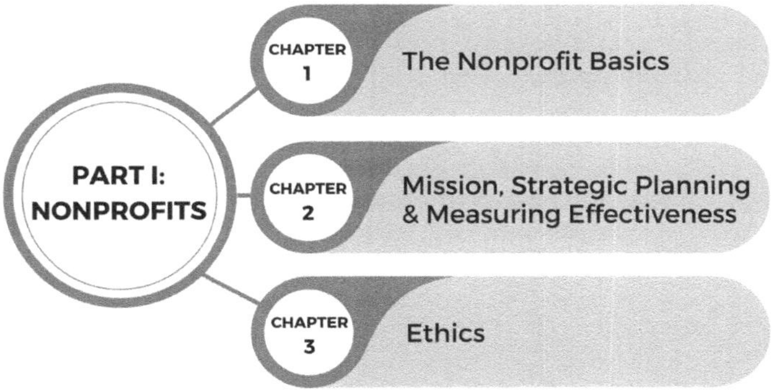

1 The Nonprofit Basics

Learning Outcomes

After reading this chapter, you should be able to:

LO 1-1: Define nonprofits and describe how they positively impact the economy.
LO 1-2: Summarize the distinctions between nonprofit and for-profit organizations.
LO 1-3: Distinguish between direct-service agencies and advocacy organizations.
LO 1-4: Describe the four general types of nonprofit organizations.
LO 1-5: Identify the key stakeholder groups in nonprofit organizations.
LO 1-6: Explain nonprofit innovation and how mission impacts innovativeness.
LO 1-7: Categorize the traits of high-impact nonprofits.

Nonprofits

Ask any person on the street to describe a nonprofit organization and you'll likely get several different answers, from "charity" to "soup kitchen" to "NGOs." In fact, take a moment yourself, consider this question, and formulate your own response. How would *you* describe a nonprofit? Since you are reading this book, you have at least some sort of passing interest in nonprofit work, and perhaps you even have experience volunteering or working for a nonprofit, either past or present. Nonprofits are complex organizations, with various classifications and legal designations, along with confusing tax treatment, and therefore tend to be misunderstood.

Nonprofit Designations

Simply defined, **nonprofits** are organizations that advance a social cause for public benefit, are not independently owned, and do not generate a profit for owners or investors. Nonprofits are sometimes referred to as nonprofit organizations (NPOs), not-for-profit organizations (NFPOs), nongovernmental organizations (NGOs), or "non-business entities." While

DOI: 10.4324/9781003380030-2

there can be some specific nuances between and among these terms, they are generally used interchangeably. There are also variations in spelling, such as nonprofit, non-profit, and non profit. It's confusing, right?

Another distinction that can generate confusion is around the term "charity." A **charity** is a *type* of nonprofit that engages in activities to assist people in need, but not all nonprofits are charities. Rather, "nonprofit" as a broad category encompasses a vast array of organizations, beyond just those that exist to assist people in need. While all charities are nonprofits, not all nonprofits are charities. Some also use the US Internal Revenue Service (IRS) classification "501(c)(3)" as synonymous with nonprofits, but, as discussed later in this chapter, not all nonprofits are classified in this way.

The nonprofit sector is often misunderstood, not due to a lack of available data, but rather because the definitions used to define its scope are vague and lacking in precision (Salamon 1992). With so many ways to describe, classify, and name nonprofits, it is no surprise that many are confused about these organizations. For the sake of simplicity and uniformity, and to prevent you from throwing this book out of a window in frustration, the expression and spelling "nonprofit" is employed consistently within this book to describe organizations that advance a cause for public benefit and do not generate a profit for private owners or investors.

> LO 1-1: Define nonprofits and describe how they positively impact the economy.

Economic Impact of Nonprofits

Think about the people in your personal and professional network. Chances are good that you know at least one person who works for a nonprofit organization. The United States has nearly 1.8 million nonprofits, with over 12 million employees ("Nonprofit Impact Matters" 2019), and these employees account for over 10% of all private jobs, making nonprofits the third-largest workforce (Salamon 2019), with payrolls exceeding those of most other US industries, including construction, transportation, and finance ("Downloadable").

Not only are nonprofit organizations major employers in the US, but they contribute significantly to economic growth in countries throughout the world. In a recent study drawing on data from 16 countries, the global nonprofit workforce, comprising both paid and volunteer workers, made up 7.4% of the total workforce, placing it ahead of major industries such as transportation and finance (Salamon 2019). From a broader perspective, the nonprofit sector accounts for an average of 4.5% of the gross domestic product in the studied countries (Fischer 2019).

> LO 1-2: Summarize the distinctions between nonprofit and for-profit organizations.

Distinctions of Nonprofit Organizations

Not only are nonprofits misunderstood based on various identifiers, but many also understandably misinterpret "nonprofit" as meaning "does not try to earn a profit." Contrary to the name, however, nonprofit organizations *do* seek to make a profit, as defined in the business sense of generating an excess of gross earnings over expenses (Hopkins 2012). Indeed, a nonprofit executive director who consistently cannot generate a net profit would likely find him or herself out of a job.

The distinction of a nonprofit, however, is *where* the profit goes, with the one common condition being that these organizations do not pay out profits to shareholders or individuals: hence the term "nonprofit." Instead, revenues are put toward achievement of the organization's goals, namely working toward the mission. Nonprofits are formed to benefit the public, not private interests.

While they clearly differ in some notable ways, such as the distribution of profits, nonprofits share several similarities with for-profit businesses. Both types of organizations require effective management of organizational design, financial operations, marketing strategy, people resources, and others. They also both require effective management of stakeholder relationships, which is the emphasis of this book. Running a nonprofit organization as an executive director is no different, really, than running a for-profit organization as its CEO, and in fact can prove even more challenging, given the added tasks of managing volunteers and engaging in fundraising. Effective nonprofit management requires a diverse skill set, education, and experience that sometimes is discounted because of the nature of the work.

While nonprofits and for-profit organizations are similar in many ways, Figure 1.1 highlights some of their distinctions. Unlike for-profit businesses, nonprofit organizations have no ownership. There are no investors, owners, or stockholders, and they are governed by a board of directors and, in most cases, staff managers, including an executive director. Regarding the board, nonprofit directors are typically uncompensated, serving in a volunteer capacity only. Although there is no federal-level regulation that forbids nonprofits from offering compensation to board members, certain states have rules against such compensation within nonprofit boards.

	NONPROFIT ORGANIZATIONS	FOR-PROFIT ORGANIZATIONS
OWNERSHIP	NONE	OWNERS/ SHAREHOLDERS
PURPOSE	PUBLIC OR MUTUAL BENEFIT	PROFIT FOR OWNERS
TAX TREATMENT	TAX EXEMPT (if certain criteria are met)	SUBJECT TO TAXATION
WORKFORCE	PAID STAFF & VOLUNTEERS	PAID STAFF
REVENUE SOURCES	DONATIONS, DUES, GRANTS, ETC.	PRODUCT SALES, INVESTMENTS
OVERSIGHT	UNPAID BOARD OF DIRECTORS	PAID BOARD OF DIRECTORS

Figure 1.1 Distinctions between Nonprofit and For-Profit Organizations

Nonprofits exist for the benefit of public interest, whereas for-profit organizations exist to generate profit for owners. Depending upon their classification (more on that in the next section), nonprofits do not pay federal income tax on their qualifying income, and their donors can typically deduct their contributions on their own taxable income.

For-profit organizations depend solely on paid staff as a labor force, whereas nonprofits benefit from the power of volunteer manpower in addition to staff. Staff as a stakeholder group is covered in Chapter 4, where it is noted that some nonprofits, particularly small or newly formed ones, rely solely on a volunteer workforce. Rather than selling a traditional product or service, nonprofits are in the business of selling hope, or a belief in the organizational mission, and rely on contributions from supporters in the form of donations, grants, sponsorships, dues, etc. as revenue sources, rather than product sales.

IRS Classifications

As noted in Figure 1.1, a primary distinction between nonprofit and for-profit organizations is that most nonprofits are tax-exempt. From a formation standpoint, nonprofits in the United States are formally organized as corporations but are designated specifically as *nonprofit* corporations with the IRS. These are referred to as "501(c)" organizations and there are 29 categories of these. Each classification represents a specific category of tax-exempt organizations, and they are distinguished by the subsection number following 501(c). The application of IRS tax treatment to nonprofits gets complex, and is beyond the scope of this book, but note that there are 29 various 501(c) designations. Figure 1.2 lists seven of the most common ones.

501(c)(3) Charitable, Religious, and Educational Organizations
501(c)(4) Civic leagues and social welfare organizations
501(c)(5) Labor/agricultural/horticultural organizations
501(c)(6) Business and professional leagues
501(c)(7) Social and recreational clubs
501(c)(8) Fraternal beneficiary societies
501(c)(9) Veterans organizations

Figure 1.2 IRS Nonprofit Classifications

Figure 1.3 501(c)(3) Classifications

While there are several 501(c) designations, of the 1.8 million nonprofits in the United States, most of them (72%) are classified as **501(c)(3) organizations,** which are nonprofit entities recognized by the IRS for their tax-exempt status ("Public" 2023). Several (but not all) of the other 501(c) nonprofit classifications are also tax-exempt, but the 501(c)(3) designation is so common because it encompasses two broad categories: public charities and private foundations. These two categories are discussed in depth in the next section. Among these two, the public charities category represents the vast majority (91%) of 501(c)(3) organizations, as depicted in Figure 1.3. 501(c)(3) organizations must meet a strict set of IRS criteria, such as required annual disclosures, to earn and maintain their tax-exempt status ("Downloadable").

LO 1-3: Distinguish between direct service agencies and advocacy organizations.

Nonprofit Categories

Regardless of their IRS classification, nonprofits as a collective are often broadly categorized across two dimensions: **direct service agencies**, providing programs in local communities or directly to the stakeholders they are intended to serve, and **advocacy organizations** that raise public awareness and push for policy reform (Hopkins 2012). While advocacy is not the central activity of direct-service agencies, many of them do engage in some degree of advocacy work, a topic discussed further in Chapter 13.

There are hundreds of nonprofit types, both in the nature of their work and how they are designated for legal and tax purposes, but, generally speaking, nonprofits can be categorized into four categories: private foundations, public charities, non-charitable nonprofits, and political organizations, as represented in Figure 1.4 (Rudder 2022). As noted in the prior section, private foundations and public charities are 501(c)(3) organizations, and they represent two of the four categories. Nonprofits that fit within one of the many other IRS designations can generally be categorized as two of the other four categories: non-charitable nonprofits or political organizations.

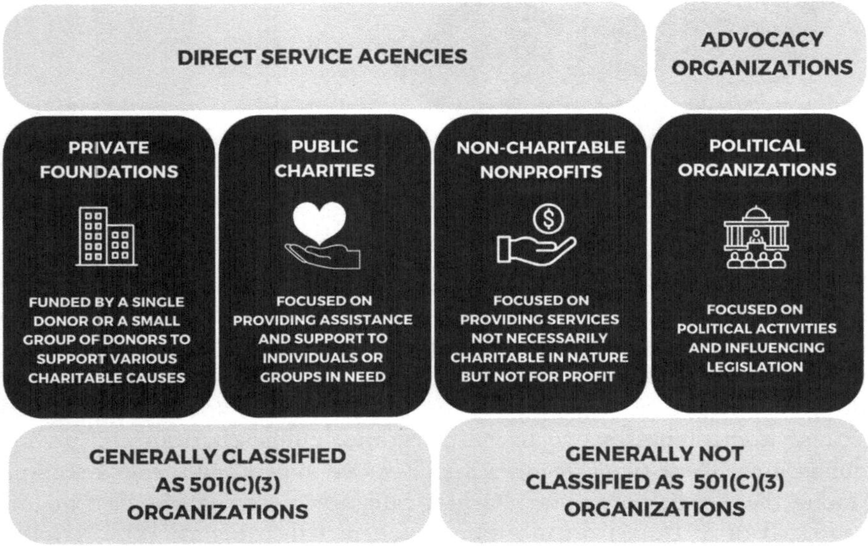

Figure 1.4 General Nonprofit Categories

LO 1-4: Describe the four general types of nonprofit organizations.

Private Foundations

Private foundations are nonprofits established exclusively for charitable purposes. In contrast to a public charity, which depends on fundraising from the general public to sustain its efforts, a private foundation usually derives its financial support from a sole individual, a family, or a corporation ("What Is" 2012). Foundations are covered in more detail within Chapter 12. A private foundation may engage in delivery of direct services, such as programs and community initiatives, but their main purpose is to fund other nonprofit organizations. They are generally classified as tax-exempt 501(c)(3) organizations.

It is important to note that an organization that includes the term "foundation" in their name is not necessarily a private foundation. The Susan G. Komen Foundation and Make-a-Wish Foundation, for example, are public charities, *not* private foundations, despite their names. The distinction is the source of funding. In the case of these two agencies, they both receive most of their funding through public support, not a single individual, family, or corporation ("What Is" 2012). Examples of private foundations include The Coca-Cola Foundation, The Walton Family Foundation, and the Bill and Melinda Gates Foundation.

Public Charities

Charitable nonprofits, or public charities, encompass a wide range of organizations and are generally the category of organization people think about when they refer to "nonprofits." **Public charities**, or charitable nonprofits, provide direct services to individuals and groups in need and comprise a broad category encompassing many types of nonprofits. They are typically classified as 501(c)(3) tax-exempt organizations and, as such, face specific restrictions around application of assets, lobbying, political activity, and individual benefits to their members ("Public" 2023).

The public charities category is a broad one, including a wide array of organizations such as hospitals, churches, colleges and universities, museums, and others, along with organizations formed to address various social needs like poverty, education, homelessness, and others (IRS). This category also includes national public foundations, such as United Way, and community foundations serving a certain geographic region.

This may seem confusing, as private foundations exist as their *own* category of nonprofits. The distinction, however, is that unlike private foundations, public foundations raise funds from the public, rather than receiving

Figure 1.5 Most Influential Nonprofits

private funding, and they support a wide range of charitable causes, not just the specific interests of private funders. Therefore, public foundations are classified as public charities.

Public charities as a category is not just diverse, but sizeable, as well, with many of the world's biggest and most influential nonprofits falling into this classification. In one ranking of the most influential nonprofits, based on a formula that measures social media engagement, web traffic, and other factors, nine out of ten of the top-ranked nonprofit organizations (noted in Figure 1.5) are 501(c)(3) public charities. The only one that is not, Human Rights Campaign (HRC), is classified as a 501(c)(4) political organization because of its advocacy work, but has a separate offshoot organization, the HRC Foundation, which is classified as a 501(c)(3). These organizations are listed in Figure 1.5 (Richards 2016).

Non-Charitable Nonprofits

The next category is non-charitable nonprofits. The term "non-charitable nonprofit" might sound like a complete contradiction but recall that not all nonprofits are charities. Some organizations exist to provide direct services on a not-for-profit basis, but these services are not charitable in. Some categories of non-charitable nonprofits include:

- **Social welfare organizations** or civic associations, which are organizations primarily focused on the common welfare of a community but that are not necessarily limited to charitable activities. Examples include the American Association of Retired Persons (AARP) and League of Conservation Voters (Noncharitable Nonprofit Organizations, 2019).

- **Trade associations** are nonprofits that represent the interests of businesses, professional groups, or even entire industries. Examples include the Association of Realtors (NAR), American Medical Association (AMA), and Home Builders Associations (HBAs).
- **Social and recreational clubs**, which are not operated for-profit, but also do not engage in charitable services. Instead, they are operated for the benefit of their membership and must be primarily supported by such membership. Examples include fraternities, sororities, country clubs, amateur sporting associations, hobby clubs, and others.

There are dozens of other examples of nonprofit organizations that fit in the non-charitable nonprofits category, including pension funds, labor unions, agricultural organizations, credit unions, and employee benefits programs. Many of these categories have their own IRS classifications, rather than 501(c)(3); some of which are detailed in Figure 1.2.

Political Nonprofits

The fourth general category of nonprofit organizations is **political nonprofits,** which focus on political activities and strive to influence legislation. Examples of political nonprofits are the American Civil Liberties Union (ACLU), Moveon.org, Emily's List, and the National Rifle Association (NRA). These are considered advocacy organizations, as their central focus is policy reform and awareness, rather than providing direct services to beneficiaries.

Political nonprofits are typically classified as 504(c)(4) organizations and do not enjoy the tax-exemption benefit, as they are engaged in political campaign activity (more on that in Chapter 13). Many political nonprofits, however, choose to establish separate foundations that are *not* engaged in political activity in order to take advantage of different tax classifications for those foundations, such as the 501(c)(3) designation. One example, which was noted above, is the Human Rights Campaign, a 501(c)(4) political nonprofit with a separate HRC Foundation, classified as a 501(c)(3) charitable nonprofit.

Affiliate Organizations

Larger nonprofits with broad geographic reach sometimes choose to operate through an interconnected network of multiple agencies. These are commonly referred to as **affiliate organizations**, which are referred to as chapters, branches, or affiliate offices. Affiliate organizations exist as separate legal entities, connected with a larger nonprofit organization, referred to as the parent organization or "headquarters." Affiliates share a common mission, purpose, or goals with the parent organization, but may have distinct operations, governance structures, and sometimes geographic locations.

Cancer Support Community (CSC), for example, uses an affiliate model in its organizational structure. CSC is the largest, professionally-led, nonprofit network of cancer support worldwide, with 190 locations worldwide, including 52 licensed affiliates and healthcare partnerships ("CSC"). Its headquarters (parent organization) is based in Washington, DC, and while they share the overarching mission and brand, local CSC affiliates have their own advisory boards, staff, and fundraising efforts tailored to the needs of their respective local communities. This structure enables CSC to provide grassroots support and resources to patients and families in various regions and engage stakeholders at the grassroots level. **Grassroots support** is a term common to the nonprofit sector that refers to activities that originate from and are driven by community members and local volunteers rather than top-down organizational structures or external authorities.

Nonprofits not only vary in type, but also in size. While the large, well-known agencies like American Red Cross and United Way are typically the

Photo 1.1 Cancer Support Community. *The executive director and a board member of the Cancer Support Community Greater Cincinnati-Northern Kentucky affiliate participate in a community event hosted by the organization. Photo by Gretchen Ramstetter.*

most visible, most nonprofits are relatively small. According to the National Council for Nonprofits, 92% of nonprofits operate on a budget of less than $1 million per year ("Nonprofit Impact" 2019).

LO 1-5: Identify the key stakeholder groups in nonprofit organizations.

Stakeholders

To work toward mission fulfillment, nonprofit leaders must engage in a diverse array of activities, and these specific activities may vary depending on the organization's mission and focus. A central part of nonprofit leadership, however, that is universal to all organizations is *managing stakeholder relationships*, the topic of this text.

Stakeholders are individuals, groups, or entities with an interest or concern in a particular organization and can influence or be influenced by the actions and outcomes related to that agency. There are many stakeholder groups, but four of the most important ones in the nonprofit sector are staff, volunteers, donors, and the community, depicted in Figure 1.6. To organize the information in this text, it is divided into specific parts to address the unique needs for each of these four key stakeholder groups.

Managing stakeholder relationships in nonprofits can be a difficult endeavor, as leaders face specific challenges and conflicting priorities. A common challenge is the fact that stakeholders often have diverse and sometimes conflicting interests, making it difficult to meet the expectations of all parties simultaneously. Staff, for example, may have needs of greater pay and benefits, whereas donors may have the conflicting priority of wanting to channel as much of the organization's revenues as possible into direct services and work toward mission rather than increasing payroll costs.

Nonprofit agencies are generally known for operating with limited resources, and the lack of sufficient resources may hinder their ability to fully address demands from all stakeholder groups. The demanding job of a nonprofit executive director, for example, is addressed in Chapter 4 and highlights some of the challenges these leaders face in balancing multiple tasks and priorities. Compounding the issue is the fact that stakeholder priorities aren't static. Rather, they constantly change and evolve over time, requiring ongoing monitoring and adaptation. One tool nonprofit leaders use to achieve this is strategic planning, a topic covered in the next chapter.

LO 1-6: Explain nonprofit innovation and how mission impacts innovativeness.

Figure 1.6 Nonprofit Stakeholders

Innovation

When challenged to identify some of the world's most innovative companies, nonprofit organizations likely do not immediately come to mind for most people. Increasingly, though, nonprofit leaders are starting to embrace the concept of innovation, as it can bolster positive outcomes. In the for-profit sector, for instance, innovativeness drives superior organizational performance (Deshpande 1993) and effectiveness in achieving a vision or long-term mission (Hurley 1998).

Innovativeness is an organization's ability to offer new products and services and to keep abreast of advances in technology and practices (McDonald 2007). It plays a vital role within any organization, as noted by "the father of modern management" Peter Drucker when he categorized it as one of the fundamental functions of a business enterprise, alongside marketing (Drucker 2002).

An interesting finding from organizational behavior research is that the primary driver of nonprofit innovativeness is something incredibly simple: *the organizational mission* (McDonald 2007). The value of a strong, clear, and motivational mission is a common thread woven throughout virtually every chapter of this text, as it can impact nearly every single aspect of nonprofit work and all stakeholder groups. The impact of mission on a nonprofit's innovativeness is no exception. Innovations are more likely to emerge, gain acknowledgment, and be embraced when an organization's core values and actions prioritize its mission (McDonald 2007).

Nonprofit leaders can foster a culture of innovation by allowing for staff and volunteers to take calculated risks and encouraging exploration of new ideas and approaches. Not only should leaders permit innovativeness, but they should proactively encourage it as a vital component to realizing the organization's mission. New concepts or ideas should be evaluated in alignment with the mission's objectives, ensuring that only those in alignment with the mission are pursued (McDonald 2007).

Social Entrepreneurship

Another aspect of innovation in nonprofits is **social entrepreneurship**, which refers to individuals who use their entrepreneurial skills and innovative approaches to solve social needs through the nonprofit sector.

Another innovative approach that is employed by both for-profit and nonprofit organizations is **social enterprise**, which typically refers to for-profit organizations prioritizing not just profits, but doing so while balancing social needs like sustainability and positive social or environmental impact. A related element of social enterprise is corporate social responsibility, or CSR, a topic addressed further in Chapter 12.

While these activities are admirable and important, they are not the focus of this text. All the elements of managing stakeholder relationships, however, are certainly just as applicable to innovative nonprofit ventures as they are to traditional ones.

> LO 1-7: Categorize the traits of high-impact nonprofits.

Traits of Highly Effective Nonprofits

The next chapter will introduce the importance of mission and strategic planning, including discussion of common methods used to measure nonprofit effectiveness, which is typically through key performance indicators and other quantifiable metrics like efficiency ratios. It also touches upon the struggle of nonprofit leaders to balance business performance with social impact. Most nonprofits tend to be evaluated based on performance metrics, but the notion of what makes a nonprofit great is up for considerable debate. Rather than

Photo 1.2 Rusty Fish Roatan. *Rusty Fish Roatan is a craft market in Honduras that operates a social enterprise. It is a certified member of Social Enterprise UK, as its business model involves sustainability by making and selling artwork out of recycled materials on the island of Roatan, The Bay Islands, Honduras. Photo by author.*

focusing exclusively on metrics, or revenue generation, perhaps it is useful to also consider practices that can be employed to maximize social change.

In one in-depth, two-year study, authors Leslie R. Crutchfield and Heather McLeod Grant sought to do just that. Their book, *Forces for Good: The Six Practices of High-Impact Nonprofits* summarized the *traits* of highly effective nonprofits, with "highly effective" not referring to just the best-marketed nonprofits, or those with the higher revenues or lowest overhead. Instead, they chose to study organizations that have created real social change and presented innovative solutions to social problems.

The six practices of high-impact nonprofits are all addressed in various sections of this text and include the following: advocate and serve, make markets work, inspire evangelists, nurture networks, adapt, and share leadership (Crutchfield 2008).

- **Advocate and Serve:** High-impact nonprofits effectively combine advocacy for systemic change with direct service to individuals and communities. They recognize that addressing root causes and policy issues is as important as providing immediate assistance. Chapter 13 touches upon the concept of advocating and serving.
- **Make Markets Work:** Effective nonprofits find innovative ways to leverage the power of markets and business practices to achieve their mission. They create and participate in partnerships with the private sector, government, and other nonprofits to drive social change. The power of partnerships is addressed in Chapter 12.
- **Inspire Evangelists:** High-impact nonprofits have a strong focus on building a passionate and committed base of supporters and volunteers. They understand the importance of engaging individuals who become enthusiastic advocates for the organization's cause. Mechanisms to engage this important stakeholder group is covered in the volunteer section, specifically Chapter 8.
- **Nurture Networks:** Successful nonprofits actively collaborate and share resources with other organizations to amplify their impact. They recognize that collective action and collaboration are often more effective than working in isolation. The concept of coalitions is addressed in Chapter 13, and networking in Chapter 12.
- **Adapt:** These nonprofits are agile and responsive, adapting their strategies and programs as circumstances change. They are willing to learn, experiment, innovate, and evolve. Innovation is a concept addressed in the preceding section of this chapter.
- **Share Leadership:** High-impact nonprofits distribute leadership throughout the organization and involve stakeholders in decision-making. They empower staff, volunteers, and beneficiaries to take ownership of the mission and contribute to its success. The idea of balanced partnerships and the dynamics of the volunteer-staff relationship are discussed in Chapter 8.

Adoption and implementation of these six practices can aid nonprofit leaders in their efforts to advance the organizational mission.

Takeaways

LO 1-1: Nonprofits are organizations that advance a social cause for public benefit, are not independently owned, and do not generate a profit for owners or investors. They contribute to the economy by creating jobs and generating revenue, all while driving social impact.

LO 1-2: Nonprofits and for-profit organizations share some similarities, but there are also some distinctions; namely, nonprofits are not privately owned and are formed to benefit the public rather than private interests. Unlike for-profit organizations, many nonprofits are tax-exempt, are governed by a board of directors that is uncompensated, earns revenues through supporter contributions, and is powered by a combination of staff and volunteer labor.

LO 1-3: Direct service agencies provide programs in local communities or directly to the stakeholders they are intended to serve, whereas advocacy organizations primarily raise public awareness and push for policy reform.

LO 1-4: The four general types of nonprofit organizations include private foundations, public charities, non-charitable nonprofits, and political organizations.

LO 1-5: There are numerous nonprofit stakeholder groups, but four of the most important ones to most agencies are staff, volunteers, donors, and the community.

LO 1-6: Innovation refers to an organization's ability to offer new products and services and to keep abreast of advances in technology and practices, and innovativeness in nonprofits can be driven by the organizational mission. Innovation can also refer to practices of social entrepreneurship.

LO 1-7: The six practices of high-impact nonprofits include the following: advocate and serve, make markets work, inspire evangelists, nurture networks, adapt, and share leadership.

Bibliography

Crutchfield, Leslie R., Heather M. Grant, and Fuqua School of Business (Duke University). *Center for the Advancement of Social Entrepreneurship. Forces for Good: The Six Practices of High-Impact Nonprofits*. Jossey-Bass, San Francisco, 2008.

"CSC Find a Location Near You." *Cancer Support Community*, www.cancersupportcommunity.org/find-location-near-you. Accessed 29 Sept. 2023.

Deshpande, R., J.U. Farley, and F.E. Jr. Webster. "Corporate Culture, Customer Orientation, and Innovativeness in Japanese Firms: A Quadrad Analysis." *Journal of Marketing*, vol. 57, 1993, pp. 23–38.

"Downloadable Charts & Figures." *National Council of Nonprofits*, www.nonprofitimpactmatters.org/data/downloadable-charts/#:~:text=Nonprofits%20by%20the%20Numbers,%2Dbased%2C%20serving%20local%20needs. Accessed 8 Jun. 2023.

Drucker, Peter F. "The Discipline of Innovation." *Harvard Business Review*, vol. 80, no. 8, 2002, pp. 95–102.

Fischer, Michael S. "Nonprofits: A Global Economic Powerhouse." *Think Advisor*, 15 Mar. 2019, www.thinkadvisor.com/2013/03/15/nonprofits-a-global-economic-powerhouse/. Accessed 9 Jun. 2023.

Hurley, R., and G. T. M. Hult. "Innovation, Market Orientation, and Organizational Learning: An Integration and Empirical Examination." *Journal of Marketing*, vol. 62, 1998, pp. 42–54.

McDonald, Robert E. "An Investigation of Innovation in Nonprofit Organizations: The Role of Organizational Mission." *Nonprofit and Voluntary Sector Quarterly*, vol. 36, no. 2, 2007, pp. 256–281.

"Noncharitable Nonprofit Organizations." *NGO Source*, 18 Aug. 2023, www.ngosource.org/blog/noncharitable-nonprofit-organizations#:~:text=The%20term%20encompasses%20nonprofit%20organizations,individual%20benefits%20to%20their%20members. Accessed 6 May 2023.

"Nonprofit Impact Matters: How America's Charitable Nonprofits Strengthen Communities and Improve Lives." *National Council of Nonprofits*, Fall 2019, www.nonprofitimpactmatters.org/site/assets/files/1/nonprofit-impact-matters-sept-2019-1.pdf. Accessed 3 Jun. 2023.

"Public Charities." *Internal Revenue Service*, 5 Jun. 2023, www.irs.gov/charities-non-profits/charitable-organizations/public-charities. Accessed 30 Jun. 2023.

Richards, William. "The 50 Most Influential Nonprofits." *The Street*, 10 May 2016, www.thestreet.com/investing/stocks/the-50-most-influential-nonprofits-html#gid=ci02572880900326 87&pid=10-planned-parenthood. Accessed 8 Jun. 2023.

Rudder, Alana, and Kelly Main. "32 Types of Nonprofits: The Complete List." *Forbes Advisor*, 21 Dec. 2022, www.forbes.com/advisor/business/types-nonprofits/. Accessed 3 Jun. 2023.

Salamon, Lester M., and Helmut K. Anheier. "In Search of the Non-Profit Sector II: The Problem of Classification." *Voluntas (Manchester, England)*, vol. 3, no. 3, 1992, pp. 267–309.

Salamon, Lester M., and Chelsea Newhouse. "The 2019 Nonprofit Employment Report." *Johns Hopkins Center for Civil Society Studies*, Jan. 2019, ccss.jhu.edu/wp-content/uploads/downloads/2019/01/2019-NP-Employment-Report_FINAL_1.8.2019.pdf. Accessed 9 Jun. 2023.

"What Is a Nonprofit Organization?" *Starting and Managing a Nonprofit Organization*. Edited by Bruce R. Hopkins. John Wiley & Sons, Inc, Hoboken, NJ, 2012.

"What Is a Private Foundation?" *Foundation Source*, foundationsource.com/what-is-a-privatefoundation/#:~:text=Although%20they%20typically%20make%20grants,disaster%20relief%20and%20hardship%20assistance. Accessed 4 Jun. 2023.

2 Mission, Strategic Planning, and Measuring Effectiveness

Learning Outcomes

After reading this chapter, you should be able to:

LO 2-1: Emphasize the importance of mission statements in nonprofits.
LO 2-2: Describe the concept of mission drift and measures to prevent it.
LO 2-3: Explain the purpose of organizational vision, values, and principles.
LO 2-4: Articulate the benefits of strategic planning.
LO 2-5: Identify the elements of an effective strategic plan and illustrate the ways nonprofit leaders develop strategic plans.
LO 2-6: Describe how nonprofits measure effectiveness and apply commonly used KPIs.
LO 2-7: Examine the criticism around the commercialization of nonprofit work.

> LO 2-1: Emphasize the importance of mission statements in nonprofits.

Nonprofit Mission

A **mission statement** expresses the purpose of the organization and describes how it meets the needs of its stakeholders. It is important for any organization, but is particularly critical in nonprofits, as it serves as a guide for decision-making, goal-setting, and resource allocation. In addition, it communicates the objective of the cause to which donors are providing their support.

As discussed in the prior chapter, research shows that a strong nonprofit organizational mission can drive innovation (McDonald 2007), but it can also serve as a source of competitive advantage (Harrison 2010), bolster employee commitment (Baker 1999), and provide clear direction for the organization and its stakeholders (Sinkula 1997).

DOI: 10.4324/9781003380030-3

Effective Nonprofit Mission Statements

Effective nonprofit mission statements share four traits: They should be simple, clear, accurate, and inspirational ("Four" 2022). Once established, nonprofit leaders should take care to frequently communicate the mission to stakeholders.

In terms of *simplicity*, mission statements should be written with plain and necessary language that avoids jargon, synonyms, and technical terms and focuses only on what's essential. A good mission makes *clear* who the organization serves and communicates the values and beliefs that underpin the organization's work to the wider community. It also needs to provide an *accurate* description of the nonprofit's activities, refraining from hyperbole or embellishment. Finally, while it should be succinct, it needs to be *inspirational*, inspiring hope and evoking emotion. Figure 2.1 highlights these four key features of an effective nonprofit mission statement.

A recurring theme throughout this text is the importance of organizational mission, as it underpins nearly *every* facet of nonprofit work. Mission statements are important drivers of strategic planning and goal-setting and serve to clarify the purpose of the organization, which is a critical aspect of gaining stakeholder support.

LO 2-2: Describe the concept of mission drift and measures to prevent it.

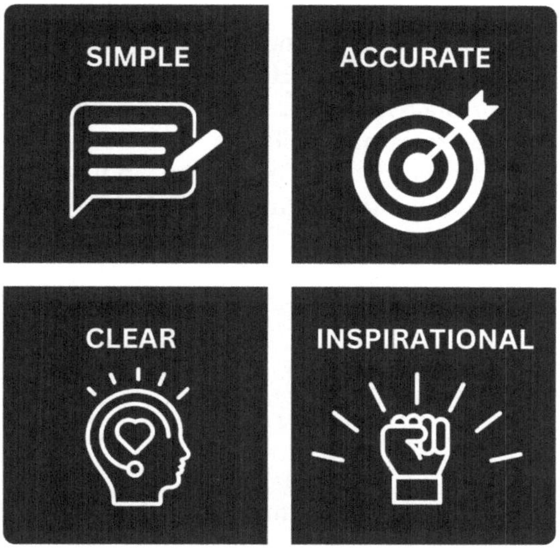

Figure 2.1 Traits of Effective Mission Statements

Mission Drift

Mission drift, sometimes called "mission creep," occurs when an organization loses focus on its original mission and begins to pursue unrelated activities. Mission drift poses a risk to any organization and is especially detrimental to nonprofits, as it can result in internal tensions (Battilana 2010), lack of stakeholder support (Dart 2004), and eventually jeopardize their survival (Battilana 2006).

Mission drift often occurs gradually and may go unnoticed until the organization's effectiveness is negatively impacted. It can occur due to a variety of factors, such as changes in leadership, external pressures, or a lack of clarity in the organization's mission ("Mission Drift"). Leaders of nonprofit organizations must actively work to prevent mission drift, and strategies to do so include regularly reviewing their mission and ensuring that all activities align with it (Kohm 2013) and engaging in good organizational design (Binder 2017).

Mission Review

If there have been legitimate changes to the organization's purpose, nonprofit leaders should examine and update their mission statement accordingly, and this can be accomplished with a **mission review.** Conducting a mission review involves engaging in discussions with staff, board members, and other key stakeholders in examining the mission statement to ensure that it aligns with the organization's values, goals, and objectives ("Leadership" 2023). A mission review can occur as part of an organization's strategic planning process, which is detailed further in this chapter.

As one example of a mission change, in recent years the American Cancer Society made a significant change to its mission statement, shifting from a focus on "eliminating cancer" to "eliminating suffering and death from cancer." The change resulted from stakeholder feedback, and reflected a broader approach to cancer, recognizing that while the ultimate goal of eliminating cancer remains, the organization also needed to address the impact of cancer on individuals and communities ("American" 2022).

> LO 2-3: Explain the purpose of organizational vision, values, and principles.

Vision

Another element that can help articulate a nonprofit's goals, but does so while looking more toward the future, is an organizational vision. A **vision statement** outlines the long-term aspirations and goals of an organization, describes the desired future state of the organization, and provides a clear picture of what the organization hopes to achieve in the long run (Kirkpatrick 2016). While this might sound like mission, there are some distinctions between the two. Think of organizational mission as who the organization is *today*, whereas the vision as where they want to be *in the future*. The mission and vision are often seen as complementary and interconnected.

A vision statement is meant to be aspirational and to inspire and motivate stakeholders, including staff, volunteers, donors, and the community, to work toward a common goal and create a positive impact in the world. As previously stated, some organizations do not create a distinct vision statement; instead, they integrate the aspirational vision element into their mission statement. Make-A-Wish Foundation is one example of a nonprofit that has a mission statement without an accompanying vision statement. Their mission is straightforward: "Together, we create life-changing wishes for children with critical illnesses" ("Our Mission" 2023).

Values

In addition to a mission and/or vision, some nonprofit organizations also choose to define the convictions that direct their actions and decision-making, which are organizational **values**. These values are important, because they serve as the foundation of the organization's culture and establish the framework for its engagement with various stakeholders (Bourne 2013). It is recommended that organizations aim to define a set of no more than 3–7 values to stay focused on core priorities and make it easier for everyone within the organization to understand and remember them.

Values can also impact employee outcomes, as research shows that employees who perceive that their personal values are in alignment with their organization's values experience greater job satisfaction and organizational commitment (Agard 2011).

Principles

Some agencies may opt to take this a step further and specify their principles, alongside their values. A **principle**, sometimes called a core or guiding principle, is a behavior and mindset standard in the workplace that reflects an action-oriented response to a core value. Think of values as the fundamental belief or characteristic of an organization, and a guiding principle as something that serves as a practical expression of that value. A summary of mission, vision, values, and principles, and the questions they address, is illustrated in Figure 2.2.

Nearly all nonprofit organizations have a mission, but the decision of whether to also include a vision statement, values, and principles varies among organizations. Some opt for only a mission, while others incorporate

Figure 2.2 Mission, Vision, Values, and Principles

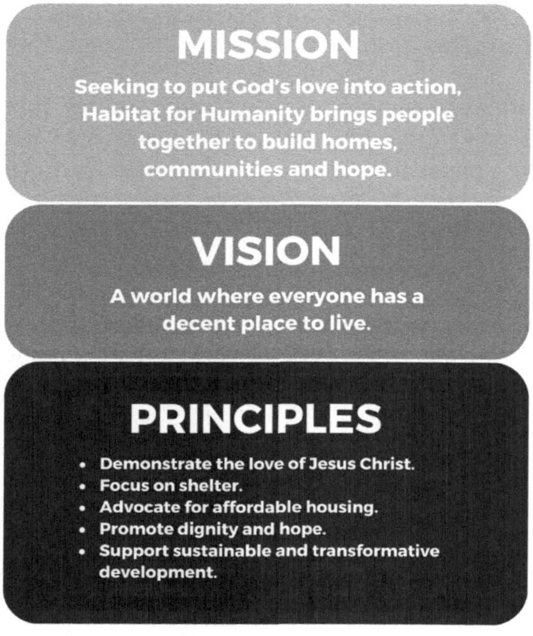

Figure 2.3 Habitat for Humanity's Mission, Vision, and Principles

one, two, or all three of the additional elements alongside their mission. When it comes to values and principles, some nonprofits publicize them for external audiences, whereas others use them more as internal mechanisms.

As illustrated in Figure 2.3, Habitat for Humanity is a global nonprofit organization that chooses to use a mission, vision, and principles (and publicize them) to guide their organization ("Our Vision" 2023).

While there are many ways that nonprofit leaders can choose to convey their mission, vision, values, and principles, the important thing is that some combination of these are used as the overarching objectives for the organization.

LO 2-4: Articulate the benefits of strategic planning.

Strategic Planning

Strategic planning is a broad term that encompasses approaches used to steer decision-making in an organization (McHatton 2011). The outcome of strategic planning is a **strategic plan**, which is comprehensive, high-level document that outlines an organization's long-term goals and the methods it intends to use to achieve them.

Benefits of Strategic Planning

While used in all sectors of the business world, it can be especially useful for nonprofit organizations, as it can assist in strategic allocation of limited resources through the use of efficient processes that align with organizational objectives (Mara 2000). Furthermore, nonprofit leaders tend to prioritize immediate needs without initially considering the broader goals of their organization, and a well-developed strategic plan can facilitate improved alignment in this regard (Craft 2006). It also serves as a systematic way to monitor progress, and typically covers a 3–5-year time period. A challenge of nonprofit leadership is balancing the diverse needs of several stakeholder groups, and the strategic planning process can aid with gaining consensus, buy-in, and collaboration from these various groups (Moxley 2003).

Given the benefits of strategic planning, one might expect most or all nonprofits to have one, but a recent study reveals that nearly half (49%) of nonprofits operate without one (Sargeant 2024). A reason that some leaders neglect to engage in strategic planning is the fact that it is an ambitious undertaking that requires a significant amount of time for development, implementation, and monitoring (McHatton 2011).

Strategic plans are forward-looking, intended to set long-range goals and strategic direction for a long period, typically three to five years. These plans serve as a roadmap for an organization, guiding its actions and decisions over the specified period. The strategic planning approach used by nonprofit leaders will vary, but most plans contain some common elements, such as mission and vision, goals and strategies, action plan steps, and performance metrics.

> LO 2-5: Identify the elements of an effective strategic plan and illustrate the ways nonprofit leaders develop strategic plans.

Elements of a Strategic Plan

Strategic plans often begin with the fundamental purpose of the organization, its *mission*, and clear articulation of the organizational *vision*, if it has one. From there, *goals* are established to identify specific, measurable, and achievable objectives that an organization aims to accomplish over the specified time covered in the strategic plan. The plan then details overarching *strategies* the organization will employ to reach its goals, and *action plans* to specify the tactical steps and initiatives that support the strategic strategies. They outline what needs to be done, who is responsible, and when these actions should be completed.

Many plans also include *performance metrics*, used to evaluate success against the defined goals set forth in the plan. These metrics help organizations track their performance and adjust strategies as needed. While strategic plans are by design a structured framework, nonprofit leaders should allow for flexibility in order to adapt to changing circumstances and unforeseen challenges. Once developed, these plans should be communicated broadly throughout the organization to demonstrate transparency and accountability and engage stakeholders.

Figure 2.4 provides a general framework for how many nonprofits choose to structure their strategic plans.

Strategic Plan Development

As noted above, developing a strategic plan can be a labor- and time-intensive endeavor, as it is intended to be a collaborative process that involves various stakeholders within the organization. In the nonprofit organization, this typically includes the executive director, board of directors, staff and volunteers, donors, and others. Involving so many people requires a series of meetings, workshops, and discussions where these stakeholders collaborate on developing the plan. The benefit is that, due to the long lifespan of a strategic plan, the strategic planning process typically only occurs every 3–5 years.

Figure 2.4 Nonprofit Strategic Plan Framework

Comprehending the business landscape is at the core of strategic planning, and one of the key instruments for fostering this understanding is the SWOT analysis (Hill 1997). A **SWOT analysis** is a commonly used method in the early stages of strategic planning that helps leaders analyze an organization's resources and environment across four dimensions: strengths, weaknesses, opportunities, and threats (Samejima 2006). Strengths and weaknesses are both internal factors, controllable by the organization, that either support or hinder the organization's efforts to achieve mission (Wilson 2023). Opportunities and threats are external, uncontrollable factors that enable or disable organizations from accomplishing their mission (Dyson 2004). When stakeholders work together to brainstorm and identify the factors within these four dimensions, the organization can build an effective strategic plan.

LO 2-6: Describe how nonprofits measure effectiveness and apply commonly used KPIs.

Measuring Effectiveness

Strategic plans are not just beneficial in setting goals and ensuring alignment with mission, but they are also valuable control mechanisms. In addition to the mission, goals, and strategy, strategic plans also include methods for evaluating performance. One way to evaluate performance, either through strategic planning or outside of it, is the use of **key performance indicators**, or

KPIs. KPIs are measurable values that focus on the aspects of organizational performance that are the most critical for the current and future success of the organization (Dominguez 2019), and in the nonprofit sector they can be set for the organization overall, for individual employees, and even for board members and volunteers.

Efficiency Margin

Nonprofit organizations can use a variety of KPIs to measure their effectiveness, impact, and overall performance. The specific KPIs a nonprofit chooses to track will depend on its mission, goals, and activities. There are hundreds of KPIs, but common ones used by most nonprofit agencies include efficiency margin, donor retention rate, cost per dollar raised, fundraising ROI, and salary productivity ratio.

Nearly all nonprofits measure and track their efficiency margin, which is sometimes referred to as efficiency ratio, program expense ratio, mission allocation, or program efficiency. **Efficiency margin** calculates the percentage of expenses allocated to programs and services compared to administrative and fundraising expenses. A higher efficiency margin indicates that a larger portion of the organization's budget goes directly toward fulfilling its mission (Coupet 2019).

An organization with an efficiency margin of 91%, for instance, means that for every dollar donated to the organization, 91 cents go toward its organizational mission. While there is no central standard for what is considered a "good" efficiency margin, most nonprofits benchmark their efficiency margins against peer agencies in their industry or use a general threshold of at least 75% (Pare 2023).

Fundraising KPIs

Other common KPIs used to measure fundraising performance include **donor retention rate** to evaluate the percentage of donors who continue to support the organization over time; **fundraising efficiency** to determine "cost per dollar raised," which refers to what it costs the organization to raise one dollar in donations; and **fundraising return on investment (ROI)** to assess the effectiveness of fundraising campaigns by comparing the amount of money raised to the cost of fundraising activities ("Donorbox" 2019).

Staff and Volunteer KPIs

A frequently used KPI to assess efficiency of staff management is **salary productivity ratio**, which measures the efficiency of staff compensation by comparing the total payroll expenses to the organization's overall expenses (Moore 2021). KPIs related to volunteer management include **volunteer retention** to measure the percentage of volunteers who continue to volunteer over time and **volunteer engagement**, which assesses the impact of volunteer work. There are additional KPIs to assess board performance, which is covered in Chapter 7.

Program Impact KPIs

Measuring the impact of programs and services can sometimes prove difficult, for while it is relatively easy to quantify certain aspects of this work, it is more challenging to assess impact on mission as a qualitative measure. **Program impact metrics** attempt to do both by assessing metrics like number of beneficiaries served, percentage of program goals achieved, or beneficiary outcomes like improvements in the quality of life for service recipients.

These are just a few examples of way nonprofit leaders use KPIs to track and evaluate performance, but there are dozens of other examples. To aid in the effective use of KPI metrics, many nonprofits have invested in **business intelligence (BI) dashboards**, often referred to simply as "BI dashboards," which are data visualization tools used to present important information like KPIs in a visual and easily digestible format (Weiner 2020).

> LO 2-7: Examine the criticism around the commercialization of nonprofit work.

Doing Well vs. Doing Good

Nonprofit leaders are facing increasing pressure to achieve results and deliver on KPIs, challenged with the notion that success, and even survival, requires that nonprofits function operate more like for-profit organizations, seeking competitive advantage (Dart 2004). "Doing well" and "doing good," however, are two different measures of success that are often used to evaluate the effectiveness of an organization's work, and it also underscores a prevalent critique of the commercialization of nonprofit undertakings.

Doing well refers to a nonprofit's ability to operate successfully as a business and involves effective stakeholder management, which is the primary topic of this book. Doing well is often measured in financial performance. Each year, for instance, *Forbes* magazine publishes a list of America's Top 100 charities, using in the evaluation private donations, total revenue, fundraising efficiency, and charitable commitment percentage. The *Forbes* top five nonprofits as of 2022, based on private donations, appears in Figure 2.5 (Barrett 2023). A notable omission in the calculation of these "top nonprofits," however, is assessment of any measure of whether these agencies are successfully delivering on mission, or *doing good*.

Figure 2.5 America's Top Five Nonprofits

Doing good refers to an organization's ability to create a positive social impact and contribute to the greater good. Nonprofits that are doing *good* are typically able to address societal challenges and make a positive difference in the lives of individuals and communities. Quantifying the impact of doing good is typically more challenging than measuring the success of doing well, as the former often involves qualitative factors, but can be done through evaluation of program impact KPIs.

The Commercialization of Nonprofit Work

While both measures of success are important, some argue that doing good should take precedence over doing well in the nonprofit sector. This perspective emphasizes the social impact of an organization's work and suggests that nonprofits should prioritize their mission and values over financial performance. There are conflicting realities, though, in that nonprofit leaders are facing increasing pressure to achieve results and deliver on KPIs, challenged with the notion that success, and even survival, requires that nonprofits operate more like for-profit organizations (Goerke 2003).

This tension between doing well versus doing good has led some critics to speak out against the "businessification" or commercialization of nonprofit work, which refers to the application of business principles to the nonprofit sector. Robert L. Payton, one of the leading scholars and critics of the commercialization of the nonprofit sector, says, "The fundamental question is whether the spread of commercialization in the nonprofit sector is leading to the corruption of the sector's essential nature and undermining its effectiveness in addressing society's needs. Nonprofit organizations exist to express and act upon the ethical values of a society. If they adopt the business model uncritically, they risk losing that focus on values and mission that is their unique strength" (Weisbrod 1998).

Ultimately, the balance between doing well and doing good will vary depending on the organization's goals, mission, and demands of their stakeholder groups. As Payton cautions, adopting the business model must be done critically, without losing focus on mission and values. Effective strategic planning is one tool that nonprofit leaders can use to keep mission, values, and goals in alignment with business performance, balancing the need to both do well *and* do good.

While financial sustainability is critical for long-term success, nonprofit organizations must also prioritize their impact and social value to remain relevant and successful in their work. Effective leaders must both run a business, while also enacting positive social impact. Pursuing both objectives simultaneously can sometimes generate tensions and conflicting priorities and is just one of the many unique challenges of effective management of nonprofit organizations.

Takeaways

LO 2-1: A mission statement expresses the purpose of the organization and describes how it meets the needs of its stakeholders. It is important for any organization, but is particularly critical in nonprofits, as it serves as a guide for decision-making, goal-setting, and resource allocation.

LO 2-2: Mission drift happens when an organization loses focus on its original mission and begins to pursue unrelated activities, and can result in internal tensions, lack of stakeholder support, and jeopardize survival. Nonprofit leaders can regularly review the mission to ensure alignment and engage in good organizational design as measures to prevent mission drift.

LO 2-3: In addition to a mission statement, some nonprofit leaders opt to also establish an organizational vision, values, and/or principles. Whereas the mission clarifies what the organization stands for now, vision is more forward-looking, explaining what the nonprofit *wants to be*. Values articulate what the organization stands for, and principles are the behaviors the organization uses to express those values.

LO 2-4: Strategic planning in nonprofits provides many benefits. A strategic plan serves as a guiding document for goal achievement, helps leaders in decision-making and adapting to environmental changes, and functions to monitor progress.

LO 2-5: While the format of strategic plans varies by agency, most nonprofit organizations include the following elements: mission, goals, strategies, action plans, and performance metrics. Strategic planning involves collaborating with stakeholders through a series of meetings, workshops, and discussions. Many organizations also include a SWOT analysis as part of the process.

LO 2-6: Nonprofits use KPIs, either as an element of a strategic plan and/or outside of it, to measure performance across different dimensions, such as fundraising, staff and volunteer management, and program impact. One of the most important KPIs is efficiency margin, which calculates the percentage of expenses allocated to programs and services compared to administrative and fundraising expenses.

LO 2-7: Nonprofit leaders must balance the sometimes-conflicting tasks of doing well versus doing good, ensuring that they achieve goals efficiently and effectively while also creating positive social impact and contributing to the greater good. The increasing emphasis on leaders to *do well* at the expense of *doing good* has drawn criticism of the commercialization of nonprofit work.

Bibliography

Agard, Kathryn A. *Leadership in Nonprofit Organizations: A Reference Handbook.* SAGE Publications, Thousand Oaks, CA, 2011.

"American Cancer Society Unveils Rebrand." *Nonprofit Times*, 17 Nov. 2022, thenonprofittimes.com/news/american-cancer-society-unveils-rebrand-mission-statement/. Accessed 8 Aug. 2023.

Baker, W.E., and J.M. Sinkula. "The Synergistic Effect of Market Orientation and Learning Orientation on Organizational Performance." *Journal of the Academy of Marketing Science*, vol. 27, 1999, pp. 411–427.

Barrett, William P. "America's Top 100 Charities 2022." *Forbes, Forbes Magazine*, www.forbes.com/lists/top-charities/?sh=ba35d265f501. Accessed 28 Sept. 2023.

Battilana, Julie, and Silvia Dorado. "Building Sustainable Hybrid Organizations: The Case of Commercial Microfinance Organizations." *Academy of Management Journal*, vol. 53, no. 6, 2010, pp. 1419–1440.

Battilana, Julie, and Matthew Lee. "Advancing Research on Hybrid Organizing - Insights from the Study of Social Enterprises." *The Academy of Management Annals*, vol. 8, no. 1, 2014, pp. 397–441.

Binder, Amy. "For Love and Money: Organizations' Creative Responses to Multiple Environmental Logics." *Theory and Society*, vol. 36, no. 6, 2007, pp. 547–571.

Bourne, Humphrey, and Mark Jenkins. "Organizational Values: A Dynamic Perspective." *Organization Studies*, vol. 34, no. 4, 2013, pp. 495–514.

Coupet, Jason, and Jessica L. Berrett. "Toward a Valid Approach to Nonprofit Efficiency Measurement." *Nonprofit Management & Leadership*, vol. 29, no. 3, 2019, pp. 299–320.

Craft, Ralph C., and Ronald G. Benson. "Needed: A Better Grasp of Strategic Planning." *Nonprofit World*, vol. 24, no. 5, 2006, pp. 24.

Dart, Raymond. "Being 'Business-Like' in a Nonprofit Organization: A Grounded and Inductive Typology." *Nonprofit and Voluntary Sector Quarterly*, vol. 33, no. 2, 2004, pp. 290–310.

Domínguez, Eladio, et al. "A Taxonomy for Key Performance Indicators Management." *Computer Standards and Interfaces*, vol. 64, 2019, pp. 24–40.

Donorbox. "9 Essential Nonprofit KPIs for Measuring Success." *NonProfit Pro (Online)*, 2019. https://www.nonprofitpro.com/article/9-essential-nonprofit-kpis-for-measuring-success/.

Dyson, Robert G. "Strategic Development and SWOT Analysis at the University of Warwick." *European Journal of Operational Research*, vol. 152, no. 3, 2004, pp. 631–640.

Manning & Napier. "Four Key Elements of Effective Mission Statements." *Nonprofit Communications Report*, vol. 20, no. 6, 2022, p. 7.

Goerke, J. "Taking the Quantum Leap: Nonprofits Are Now in Business. An Australian Per-Spective." *International Journal of Nonprofit and Voluntary Sector Marketing*, vol. 8, 2003, pp. 317–327.

Harrison, Jeffrey S., Douglas A. Bosse, and Robert A. Phillips. "Managing for Stakeholders, Stakeholder Utility Functions, and Competitive Advantage." *Strategic Management Journal*, vol. 31, no. 1, 2010, pp. 58–74.

Hill, Terry, and Roy Westbrook. "SWOT Analysis: It's Time for a Product Recall." *Long Range Planning*, vol. 30, no. 1, 1997, pp. 46–52.

Kirkpatrick, Shelley, and Inc Ebrary. *Build a Better Vision Statement: Extending Research with Practical Advice*. Lexington Books, Lanham, 2016.

Kohm, Amelia, and David La Piana. *Strategic Restructuring for Nonprofit Organizations: Mergers, Integrations, and Alliances*. Praeger, Westport, CT, 2003.

Leadership. "What Are Some Best Practices for Reviewing and Updating Your Vision and Mission Statement?" *How to Review and Update Your Vision and Mission Statements*, 17 Aug. 2023, www.linkedin.com/advice/3/what-some-best-practices-reviewing-updating-your-vision#:~:text=As%20a%20good%20practice%2C%20it,acquiring%20another%20business%2C%20rebranding%20or.

Mara, Cynthia M. "A Strategic Planning Process for a Small Nonprofit Organization: A Hospice Example." *Nonprofit Management & Leadership*, vol. 11, no. 2, 2000, pp. 211–223.

McDonald, Robert E. "An Investigation of Innovation in Nonprofit Organizations: The Role of Organizational Mission." *Nonprofit and Voluntary Sector Quarterly*, vol. 36, no. 2, 2007, pp. 256–281.

McHatton, Patricia A., et al. "Results from a Strategic Planning Process: Benefits for a Nonprofit Organization." *Nonprofit Management & Leadership*, vol. 22, no. 2, 2011, pp. 233–249.

Medley, G.J. "Strategic Planning for the World Wildlife Fund." *Long Range Planning*, vol. 21, no. 1, 1988, pp. 46–54.

"Mission Drift in US Nonprofit Organizations: Extent, Causes, and Consequences." *Nonprofit and Voluntary Sector Quarterly*, vol. 42, no. 2, pp. 332–351.

Moore, Kenneth S., and Ohio Library and Information Network. *Measuring Productivity in Education and Not-for-Profits: With Tools and Examples in R*. Springer, Cham, 2021, doi:10.1007/978-3-030-72965-3.

Moxley, David P. "Factors Influencing the Successful use of Vision-Based Strategy Planning by Nonprofit Human Service Organizations." *International Journal of Organization Theory and Behavior*, vol. 7, no. 1, 2003, pp. 107–132.

"Our Vision, Mission and Principles." *Habit for Humanity*, 1 Jan. 2023, www.habitat.org/about/mission-and-vision. Accessed 10 Sept. 2023.

"Our Mission, Vision and Values." *Make-a-Wish*, 2023, wish.org/mission. Accessed 13 Aug. 2023.

Pare, Dan. "Key Performance Indicators (KPI'S) for Nonprofit Organizations." *LGA CPA's and Business Advisors*, 19 Feb. 2023, www.lga.cpa/resources/key-performance-indicators-nonprofit-organizations/. Accessed 5 Sept. 2023.

Samejima, M., et al. *SWOT Analysis Support Tool for Verification of Business Strategy*, IEEE, 2006, doi:10.1109/ICCCYB.2006.305700.

Sargeant, Adrian PhD, and Harriet Day. "A Study of Nonprofit Leadership in the US and Its Impending Crisis." *Sustainable Philanthropy with Plymouth University*, p. 23, https://concordleadershipgroup.com/report/download/.

Sinkula, J.M., W.E. Baker, and T. Noordewier. "A Framework for Market-Based Organiza-Tional Learning: Linking Values, Knowledge, and Behavior." *Journal of the Academy of MarketingScience*, vol. 25, 1997, pp. 305–318.

Weiner, George. "Nonprofit Dashboards: The Ultimate Guide (with Examples and Templates)." *Whole Whale*, 23 Apr. 2020, www.wholewhale.com/tips/ultimate-guide-nonprofit-dashboards/#:~:text=Strategic%20or%20Business%20Intelligence%20(BI,%2C%20quarterly%2C%20or%20annual%20basis.

Weisbrod, Burton A. *To Profit or Not to Profit: The Commercial Transformation of the Nonprofit Sector*. Cambridge University Press, Cambridge and New York, NY, 1998.

Wilson, Felicia R.F. *Resource Development SWOT Analysis to Improve Organizational Sustainability for a Grassroots Nonprofit Organization*. ProQuest Dissertations Publishing, Minneapolis, MN, 2023.

3 Ethics

Learning Outcomes

After reading this chapter, you should be able to:

LO 3-1: Define ethics and identify the elements of an ethical nonprofit organization.
LO 3-2: Classify and describe the three dimensions of trustworthiness.
LO 3-3: Apply guidelines to encourage ethical conduct in nonprofit organizations.
LO 3-4: Explain how nonprofits can enact measures of transparency and accountability to foster trustworthiness.
LO 3-5: Describe the three dimensions used by nonprofits to convey organizational effectiveness.
LO 3-6: Define breach of trust, explain the moral disillusionment effect, and recommend steps nonprofits can take to respond to ethical violations.
LO 3-7: Analyze common ethical dilemmas faced by nonprofit leaders.

> LO 3-1: Define ethics and identify the elements of an ethical nonprofit organization.

Ethics in Nonprofits

Organizational ethics is a form of applied ethics that examines ethical principles and moral or ethical problems that can arise in a business environment. Maintaining high ethical standards is crucial for all organizations; however, nonprofits must pay special attention to ethical behavior, given the unique nature of their operations and functions. To achieve their mission, gain the trust of stakeholders, secure donor and funding support, and maintain their reputation and credibility, nonprofits must exhibit ethical organizational behavior by cultivating *trustworthiness* and *effectiveness* (Phillips 2023), as shown in Figure 3.1.

DOI: 10.4324/9781003380030-4

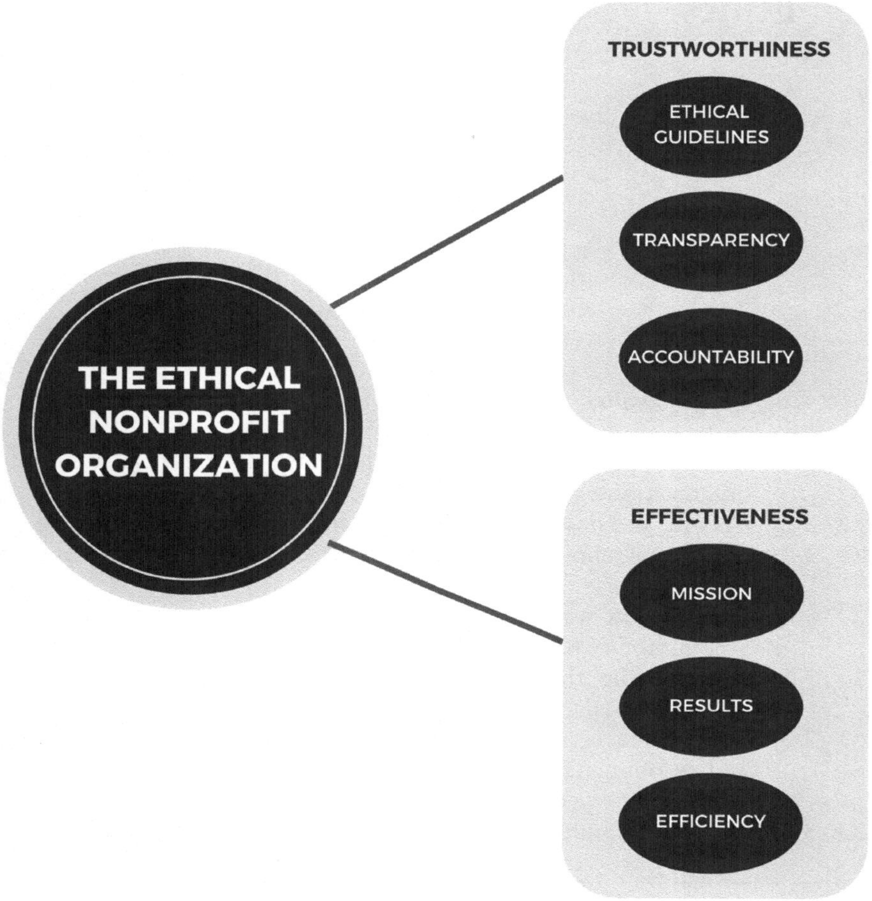

Figure 3.1 Elements of an Ethical Nonprofit Organization

LO 3-2: Classify and describe the three dimensions of trustworthiness.

Elements of an Ethical Nonprofit

For a nonprofit organization, public trust is its most valuable asset (Frederickson 2023), so nonprofit leaders need to foster a sense of trust and ensure that their organizations are considered trustworthy. They must also convey organizational effectiveness to demonstrate ethical and appropriate use of supporter funds in delivering on the promise to fulfill the agency's mission.

Trustworthiness

Trustworthiness is the quality or characteristic of being relied upon, dependable, and honest. **Organizational trustworthiness** is closely related to interpersonal trustworthiness and refers to organizations delivering on a set of personal and ethical duties, obligations, and responsibilities (Caldwell 2003). To earn and sustain trust from the public and their constituent base, nonprofits must prove themselves trustworthy through adherence to ethical guidelines, embracing of transparency, and demonstration of accountability, demonstrated in Figure 3.2.

> LO 3-3: Apply guidelines to encourage ethical conduct in nonprofit organizations.

Ethical Guidelines

Organizational ethics pose challenges, as they frequently involve situations where clear distinctions between right and wrong are not readily apparent. Maintaining high ethical standards in nonprofits is further complicated by the need to serve a diverse range of stakeholder groups, each of which may hold distinct expectations, values, and priorities (Handy 2018). Additionally,

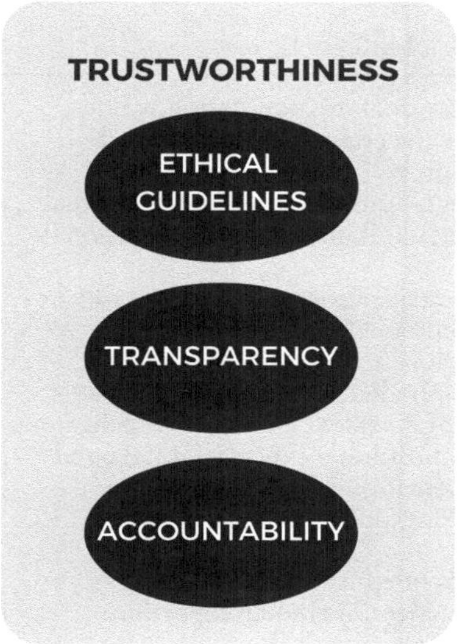

Figure 3.2 Elements of Trustworthiness of a Nonprofit Organization

the scarcity of resources commonly experienced by nonprofits can give rise to ethical dilemmas, such as the allocation of limited funds or the prioritization of services, necessitating difficult trade-offs. Nonprofit organizations can help ensure ethical conduct through the implementation and following of **ethical guidelines**, which are formal documents that provide direction and guidance for ethical conduct (Hanson 2023).

A commonly used ethical guideline in many organizations, both nonprofit and for-profit, is a **code of ethics**, which provides ethical standards that the organization expects their employees, volunteers, and stakeholders to follow in their decision-making and conduct (Rosen 2005). While specific codes may vary between organizations, they typically address the elements outlined in Table 3.1.

A **conflict of interest** refers to a situation in which a person or entity has competing or conflicting interests or loyalties that could potentially influence their ability to make fair, unbiased, or impartial decisions. Conflicts of interest can be explicit or perceived, and are not inherently unethical, as they can occur inadvertently or unavoidably in certain circumstances. Avoidance of conflicts of interest is one of the central facets of ethics in nonprofit organizations (White 2010).

Due to the ambiguity surrounding certain conflicts of interest and the significance of effectively managing them, some nonprofit organizations opt to implement a separate and distinct policy as another ethical guideline in addition to their code of ethics. A **conflict of interest policy** is a formal set of guidelines to address and manage conflicts of interest that may arise

Table 3.1 Aspects of an Effective Nonprofit Code of Ethics

Mission and Values	Specify the organizational mission, vision, values, and principles as the ethical foundation and overarching purpose.
Integrity and Accountability	Articulate the expectations of integrity, transparency, honesty, and accountability in all organizational activities.
Conflicts of Interest	Explain what the organization considers a conflict of interest and specify methods for stakeholders to identify and disclose any potential conflicts.
Respect and Non-Discrimination	Define the values embodied by the organization to foster a culture of diversity, equity, and inclusion.
Confidentiality and Privacy	Emphasize the organization's expectations around confidential information and privacy around business operations, donor information, and others.
Fundraising and Financial Practices	Highlight standards of ethical fundraising and financial practices, including reporting transparency and accountability.
Reporting and Whistleblowing	Provide provisions for reporting unethical behavior and protecting whistleblowers from retaliation.

among its stakeholders. The policy outlines the organization's expectations, procedures, and mechanisms for identifying, disclosing, and appropriately addressing conflicts of interest ("Council" 2023).

Conflict of Interest: Education in Oklahoma

In January 2023, newly elected Oklahoma State Superintendent Ryan Walters stepped down from his role as CEO of Every Kid Counts Oklahoma, a nonprofit agency that advocates for expansion of charter and private schools (Wallis 2023). Charter schools are tuition-free schools of choice that are publicly funded but independently run (Prothero 2018) and can be a divisive political issue. Critics of charter schools argue they harm traditional public schools by siphoning money from the district, causing superintendents to make difficult budget choices like cutting art classes or reducing one-on-one teaching (Morabito 2023). Walters faced questions of a potential conflict of interest, as critics questioned how a state superintendent could adequately do the job while also running a nonprofit that lobbies for substantial changes in education. Do you see a conflict here? Do you think Walters could have effectively served in both roles simultaneously?

Not only is managing potential conflicts of interest important for nonprofits to maintain trustworthiness, but US-based organizations potentially risk punishment, called "intermediate sanctions" from the Internal Revenue Service (IRS) (https://www.councilofnonprofits.org/running-nonprofit/governance-leadership/conflicts-interest), assessed both against the person who benefits, as well as against the organization ("Internal" 2023) (Council, 2023)

A good conflict of interest policy should not only require those with a conflict, or who think they may have a conflict, to disclose that potential conflict, but it also should prohibit interested board members from voting on any matter in which there is conflict ("National" 2023). Like a code of ethics, conflict of interest polices should be formal and written, and reviewed by both nonprofit staff and the board of directors.

If unethical behavior, such as violation of the conflict of interest policy, is observed, nonprofits should have provisions in place for reporting. **Whistleblowing** refers to the act of reporting or disclosing information about illegal, unethical, or wrongful activities within an organization. Individuals are protected under federal law from retaliation for "blowing the whistle" on their employer's accounting or financial management practices ("American" 2023).

Some nonprofit agencies have established formal whistleblower hotlines, where stakeholders can directly and anonymously report unethical conduct either via telephone or online channels to a designated authority in the organization who can then investigate the allegations. Ensuring the confidentiality of reporters is vital in encouraging reporting and safeguarding whistleblowers from possible retaliation. Although whistleblower policies are an important ethical guideline that can help nonprofit organizations foster trust, as of 2020 most nonprofits do not have a whistleblower policy (Eaton 2007).

The Trustworthiness Problem: A Public Decline

Recent surveys show a decline in trustworthiness of nonprofit organizations, with just 56% of Americans expressing trust in nonprofits. Worse still, the generation gaps in trust are worsening, with each successive generation expressing less trust in nonprofits than the one before it. While 67% of Baby Boomers (members of the large generation born from 1946 to 1964 ["Pew" 2023]) report feeling trust in nonprofits, less than half, 46%, of Gen Z (born 1997–2012) adults reporting the same (Berman 2022). Nonprofit leaders face many challenges, and this worrying trend is another one to tackle.

LO 3-4: Explain how nonprofits can enact measures of transparency and accountability to foster trustworthiness.

Transparency

Nonprofits also gain trust by promoting transparency through various practices and mechanisms. **Transparency** refers to refers to the practice of openness, honesty, and disclosure in the actions, decisions, and operations of an organization. Research shows that organizational trust is enhanced when honest communication, responsibility to inform, and procedural fairness all occur, which are dimensions of transparency (Caldwell 2023), with transparency being a central tenet to fostering an ethical nonprofit organization (White 2010).

Table 3.2 identifies ways that nonprofit agencies can establish a culture of3transparency by allowing stakeholders to understand the organization's financial condition, funding sources, impact on mission, and decision-making processes, among others. By implementing these transparency measures, nonprofits can foster trustworthiness, and as a result can achieve greater future contributions (Harris 2023) and obtain a source of competitive advantage with donors (Smith 2007).

Table 3.2 Transparency in Nonprofits

Financial Reporting	Regularly publish audited financial statements, annual reports, and Form 990 (or equivalent) filings. Voluntarily disclose additional information beyond legal requirements, such as program evaluations, independent evaluations, or results from external audits.
Donor Disclosure	Provide information about donors and funding sources to bolster trust, enhance transparency, and demonstrate that there are not conflicts of interest between financial backers and the organizational mission.
Governance and Board Transparency	Publicize the board of directors roster, including member names, employers, and affiliations, and publish board meeting dates, agendas, and meeting minutes.
Program and Impact Reporting	Make organizational program and impact reports publicly available and easily accessible.
Publicize Policies	Publicize the code of ethics, conflict of interest policies, and whistleblower protection policies.
Open Communication	Articulate to stakeholders their methods, avenues, and opportunities to provide feedback.

FINANCIAL REPORTING

In the United States, tax-exempt nonprofits are required, upon request, to provide copies of the three most-recently filed annual information returns, IRS Form 990, and the organization's application for tax-exemption ("National" 2023). The **Form 990** is a document designed to increase the financial transparency of nonprofit organizations and includes revenue, expenditure, and income data in addition to information used to assess whether a nonprofit aligns with federal requirements for tax-exempt status ("Form 990" 2023).

These are publicly available documents that can be found on the websites for the Secretary of State or the Attorney General where the organization is incorporated, although many charitable nonprofits choose to publish these documents on their websites to demonstrate their dedication to transparency. Other financial documents that nonprofits can proactively disclose voluntarily include audit results and monthly or quarterly financial statements.

DONOR DISCLOSURE

Publicizing donor lists provides insight into the sources of funding for the nonprofit and allows stakeholders to have visibility into the financial support received by the organization. Transparency in disclosing donor information helps to assure the public that the organization operates with integrity and is not unduly influenced by any particular donor. The topic of revealing donor information can lead to disagreement, as there is a legitimate opposing viewpoint emphasizing the importance of preserving donor anonymity. In the end, nonprofit executives must consider two conflicting ethical perspectives when determining whether to disclose donors.

GOVERNANCE AND BOARD TRANSPARENCY

The board of directors is the governing and central decision-making body of a nonprofit organization, and given this important role, it is important for nonprofit agencies to publicly disclose the membership of the board. It allows stakeholders and the public to know who is making decisions on behalf of the organization and who holds fiduciary responsibilities. Sharing information about the board members' backgrounds, expertise, and affiliations highlights the organization's credibility and the diversity of perspectives represented on the board. While public disclosure of board members is not a legal requirement in most cases, many nonprofits disclose this information voluntarily as a best practice to promote transparency and build trust (Harris 2018).

PROGRAM AND IMPACT REPORTING

Program and impact reports demonstrate accountability to stakeholders by sharing comprehensive information about program activities and outcomes (McNee 2016). These reports allow nonprofits to show that they are responsible stewards of resources and are committed to delivering on their mission ("Why Should" 2018). It assures supporters that their contributions are being used wisely and are having a positive impact on mission, improving stakeholder satisfaction and trust (Sefora-Marcela 2022).

PUBLICIZE POLICIES

Ethical guidelines, like codes of ethics and conflict of interest policies, are important tools to ensure an ethical organization, and making these policies easily accessible to the public and stakeholders can build trust. Publicizing policies demonstrates the nonprofit's commitment to ethical behavior and allows stakeholders to understand the organization's ethical standards and the principles that guide its operations. This transparency promotes accountability by providing a clear framework for expected behavior and decision-making. In addition to policies described in this chapter, other common ones include those related to executive compensation, document retention, cybersecurity, ethical fundraising practices, and others (Rhode 2009).

OPEN COMMUNICATION

Open communication promotes transparency by sharing information, updates, and decisions with stakeholders, and allowing nonprofits to actively engage with their community. It enables meaningful dialogue, feedback, and collaboration, fostering a sense of involvement, ownership, and shared responsibility. Engaging constituents and donors in more conversations, and communicating appreciation, encourages greater loyalty (Waters 2011).

Accountability

Accountability is the obligation of a nonprofit to responsibly use its resources toward its mission and to benefit the community. Accountability relationships within nonprofits are especially complex due to the expectation that they must be answerable to multiple stakeholders simultaneously. They are required to demonstrate accountability upwards to funders or patrons, downwards to clients or service recipients, and internally to themselves and their missions (Ebrahim 2016).

Accountability and transparency are interconnected concepts, and nonprofit leaders can demonstrate their accountability efforts, highlighted in Table 3.3, through the transparency efforts detailed in Table 3.2. Both are essential in fostering trust among stakeholders.

BOARD OVERSIGHT AND GOVERNANCE

A board of directors is the central governance body for a nonprofit and holds ultimate responsibility for holding the organization accountable in ensuring the organization's mission is fulfilled and its operations are conducted in accordance with fiduciary, legal, and ethical standards. Oversight is a central element of ethics in a nonprofit (White 2010), and building a strong and

Table 3.3 Accountability in Nonprofits

Board Oversight and Governance	The main purpose of a nonprofit board is to ensure accountability, so building a strong and effective board is an important accountability tool.
Stakeholder Engagement	Engaging stakeholders and not just allowing them to provide feedback (as noted in Table 3.2), but actively responding to it with action, can help nonprofits be accountable.
Program Evaluation and Impact	Measuring the effectiveness of programs and services is an important part of nonprofit work and helps hold leaders accountable in ensuring that supporter contributions are being used responsibly.
Compliance	Enact measures to ensure compliance with laws, tax requirements, ethical standards, regulations, etc.
External Validation	Seek accreditation or certification from recognized bodies in the nonprofit's field.
Internal Controls	Establish internal controls such as budgeting, expense approval, and recordkeeping policies.
Strategic Planning	Assess organizational performance and progress toward goals set forth in the strategic plan.

capable board is key to providing that oversight and ensuring accountability across these dimensions.

STAKEHOLDER ENGAGEMENT

By providing regular updates and reports, nonprofits keep stakeholders informed and provide them with a clear understanding of the organization's goals, progress, and challenges. This transparency enhances accountability and legitimacy, as stakeholders can assess whether the nonprofit is fulfilling its commitments and acting in line with its mission (Leardini 2018). Stakeholder engagement provides an avenue for stakeholders to provide feedback, suggestions, and input on the nonprofit's activities. By actively seeking and considering stakeholders' perspectives, nonprofits can make more informed decisions, address concerns, and adapt their strategies to better meet stakeholder needs (Sefora-Marcela 2022).

PROGRAM EVALUATION AND IMPACT

Figure 3.2 highlighted the importance of nonprofits being transparent in making program evaluation and impact reports available to the public, but these are also tools that play a critical role in holding the organization accountable. Program evaluations provide a mechanism to assess the performance and effectiveness of nonprofit programs, and by documenting program activities, outputs, and outcomes, nonprofits can objectively evaluate their progress in achieving their intended goals and desired impact. This measurement helps stakeholders assess whether the organization is delivering on its commitments and using resources efficiently and effectively (Sefora-Marcela 2022).

COMPLIANCE

Nonprofits are subject to legal and regulatory requirements set forth by government authorities, and compliance ensures that nonprofits adhere to these laws and regulations, including tax regulations, reporting obligations, governance standards, and operational guidelines. By complying with these obligations, nonprofits demonstrate their trustworthiness, legitimacy, and commitment to operating within the boundaries of the law in fulfilling their responsibilities as legal entities (Siddiki 2016).

EXTERNAL VALIDATION

External validation provides an independent assessment, free of bias, of a nonprofit's activities, impact, and adherence to standards. Charity evaluators and watchdog agencies such as the Better Business Bureau,

Charity Navigator, GuideStar, and others are playing an increasingly prominent role in holding nonprofit organizations accountable. These external entities, along with accrediting bodies, auditors, or certification programs, evaluate the nonprofit's performance against established criteria (Xiaoting 2019). This independent assessment ensures that nonprofits are held accountable to objective standards, rather than relying solely on self-assessment.

INTERNAL CONTROLS

Internal controls help ensure the financial integrity of a nonprofit organization. By implementing processes and procedures for financial management, for example, (such as budgeting, expense approval, and recordkeeping), internal controls minimize the risk of financial mismanagement, fraud, or embezzlement. They establish checks and balances that promote accountability and protect the organization's financial resources. Many nonprofits conduct annual internal financial audits as one type of internal control. Other internal controls seek to ensure and verify compliance with ethical guidelines, risk management assessments (Pasquale 2009), and other organizational policies.

STRATEGIC PLANNING

As covered in Chapter 2, a nonprofit's strategic plan serves as its central guiding document and can be applied as an assessment tool to measure organizational performance and progress toward goals. Using the strategic plan in this way is another approach to holding the organization accountable and bolstering legitimacy (Bryson 2010).

> LO 3-5: Describe the three dimensions used by nonprofits to convey organizational effectiveness.

Effectiveness

In addition to trustworthiness, effectiveness is the second dimension of the ethical nonprofit organization. Nonprofits make a promise to serve a societal good, and their missions are statements of that promise. Therefore, ethical nonprofit organizations are not just trustworthy, but they are also effective in making good on the promise to deliver on their stated mission. This means engaging in activities that advance the mission, demonstrating results of that work, and achieving goals and objectives efficiently, being good stewards of donor dollars (Figure 3.3).

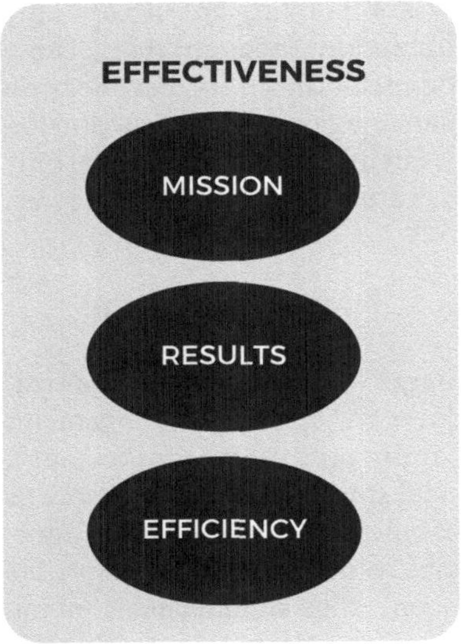

Figure 3.3 Elements of Effectiveness of a Nonprofit Organization

Mission

The importance of organizational mission was emphasized in Chapter 2 and, given that mission is the central driving force behind nonprofits, it will be a recurring concept that occurs within many other chapters of this text, including this one. Promise of mission is one of the central mechanisms associated with the public's trust in nonprofit organizations (Becker 2021) and can be used as an overarching goal to measure effectiveness of performance and social impact.

A key question for any nonprofit is "how important is your mission to society?" Determining the value that a mission, and therefore the nonprofit, adds to society is a central consideration to the ethics of an organization. Attributes of this include providing services important to society, promoting a socially worthwhile mission, and educating the public about this vision (Phillips 2023). Building awareness of organizational mission leads to more effective nonprofits.

Results

Nonprofits exist to address societal needs and achieve their stated mission; therefore, it is considered ethical for them to deliver results in exchange for the trust, time, and financial support contributed by donors. Focusing on results allows nonprofits to assess their impact and effectiveness in fulfilling their mission. By striving for measurable outcomes and results, nonprofits can ensure that their efforts translate into tangible benefits and positive change for the communities they serve. These results are often measured as key performance indicators (KPIs), a topic detailed in Chapter 2.

Efficiency

Measuring results is important, of course, but delivering results in an efficient manner is also an important factor for an ethical nonprofit. For instance, if a nonprofit agency has a mission of "feeding those who are food insecure," and they spend $1 million annually in total expenses and only serve 50 beneficiaries, are they fulfilling mission? One could argue that, yes, they are "feeding those who are food insecure," but others could feasibly argue that they are doing so at an extraordinary cost, relative to results, and therefore are not efficient. And as such, they are not acting ethically and responsibly with the dollars entrusted to them to deliver on mission. To operate ethically, nonprofits must not just deliver results that support mission, but they must do so efficiently. In other words, what is the price for the results? Several of the KPIs introduced in Chapter 2 specifically address measures of nonprofit efficiency.

LO 3-6: Define breach of trust, explain the moral disillusionment effect, and recommend steps nonprofits can take to respond to ethical violations.

Breach of Trust

Even when nonprofit leaders implement all best practices and assurances of transparency, accountability, and ethical behavior, a breach of trust can still occur. A **breach of trust** refers to a violation or betrayal of a relationship or duty in which someone fails to fulfill their responsibilities or obligations, often resulting in a loss of confidence or faith in that person or organization. A nonprofit can enact the best ethical guidelines and policies, elect the most qualified board of directors, and be completely transparent, but still run afoul of public trust or face an organizational scandal.

One example of a notable breach of trust happened with the prominent international humanitarian organization, Oxfam, which was rocked by scandal in 2018 when it came to light that the organization had covered up claims of its Haiti-based senior staff hiring prostitutes, some of them teenage girls, in the wake of the 2010 Haitian earthquake. The mission of Oxfam is to help create lasting solutions to the injustice of poverty, and prior to the 2018 scandal, the organization enjoyed a stellar reputation. Oxfam's reputation

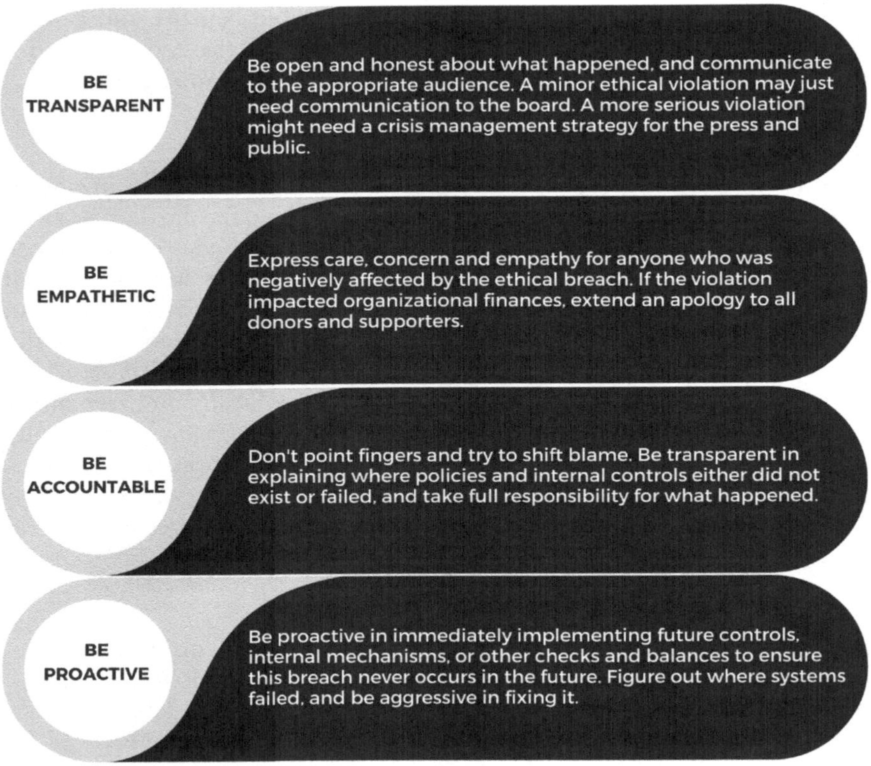

Figure 3.4 Steps to Respond to an Ethical Breach

and fundraising took a devastating hit and, even years later, the organization is struggling to regain trust (Scurlock 2020).

Further, nonprofits face a sort of double standard when it comes to ethical breaches, because the **moral disillusionment effect** tells us that nonprofits tend to be judged more harshly than for-profit organizations for the same ethical transgressions (Hornsey 2021). When faced with an ethical breach, it is critical that nonprofit leaders take quick and decisive steps, summarized in Figure 3.4, in addressing the violation. This includes *being transparent* about what happened, *being empathetic* in expressing care and concern for those impacted, *being accountable* for the incident and not shifting blame, and *being proactive* in implementing controls to prevent such a breach in the future (Gnadt 2020).

LO 3-7: Analyze common ethical dilemmas faced by nonprofit leaders.

Ethical Dilemmas

An **ethical dilemma** occurs when someone must make a choice between two or more conflicting moral principles and values. Nonprofit leaders encounter ethical dilemmas comparable to those encountered in for-profit organizations, although the nonprofit sector often introduces distinct ethical challenges.

One example of a unique ethical dilemma that nonprofits face is the question of financial integrity in deciding whether to accept donations that have any unpalatable associations or conditions (Rhode 2009). **Tainted money** refers to money of questionable origin, such as money derived from illegal or unethical activities. A **tainted donor** is a contribution received by a donor with a questionable reputation, which may be entirely unrelated to the gift's manner or means (Moody 2023).

Imagine that the American Lung Association is offered a lucrative sponsorship from Philip Morris International, a multinational tobacco company. Should it accept? On the one hand, the organization has an ethical obligation to be effective and produce results efficiently in working toward achieving its mission to save lives by improving lung health and preventing lung disease. This means raising money, and a lucrative sponsorship aligns with that. On the other hand, Philip Morris' production of cigarettes and e-vapor products, as well as their business practices in promoting the sale of these products, runs counter to that mission. Is Philip Morris a tainted donor? Is acceptance of the contribution worth the indirect costs? While this is a more extreme example, other ethical issues in nonprofits are more nuanced and difficult to address.

Another challenge in nonprofits is the matter of resource scarcity, which tends to be a more persistent problem in nonprofit organizations than in the for-profit sector. Many nonprofit leaders are put under immense pressure to demonstrate effectiveness, by delivering on mission, demonstrating results, and doing so efficiently, but they often are not provided with the adequate tools and resources to achieve these tasks. Given this scenario, research suggests that employees sometimes feel they must choose between breaking the rules and getting the job done (Cave 2005).

Breaking the rules means direct violation of established policies and ethical guidelines, but a more common occurrence is rule-bending. **Rule-bending** involves a decision to go around the formally stated obligations by not fully following a rule, requirement, procedure, or specification (Sekerka 2014). Rule-bending can be driven by self-serving motives but can sometimes occur out of the perception of necessity; the idea that that constraints are so tight, resources too scarce, and goals so difficult, that the only way to achieve what is being asked is to circumvent the formally stated rules. Rule-bending can also be motivated by intentions that rule-bending is either necessary to navigate organizational red tape or it is in the best interest of the nonprofit. In this case, rule-bending could be considered an act of **positive deviance**, which refers to a deviation from norms that may result from good intentions and even bring about positive results (Borry 2017).

One commonly bent rule in nonprofits is "spend before year-end." Some funding comes with the stipulation that it must be used prior to a certain period, such as the end of a fiscal year. If the money is not spent, it is not only lost, but the agency risks losing that money, in whole or part, in future years. This leads to a tendency to bend the rules and spend the money on other things for the nonprofit that are not precisely within the scope of the funding's purpose, but close enough, or to advance purchase for the upcoming fiscal year to "bank" resources (Sekerka 2014). Since no rules are technically directly broken, is this strategy unethical?

To minimize rule-breaking and rule-bending, nonprofit leaders and funders can take care to ensure that goals are reasonable and achievable, policies are set for a legitimate reason and that reason is effectively communicated, adequate resources are provided to achieve goals, and that some degree of flexibility is permitted in decision-making when the situation warrants it.

Takeaways

LO 3-1: Organizational ethics is a form of applied ethics that examines ethical principles and moral or ethical problems that can arise in a business environment, and the elements of an ethical nonprofit organization center on the dimensions of trustworthiness and organizational effectiveness.

LO 3-2: To foster trustworthiness, nonprofits can employ approaches within three categories: ethical guidelines, transparency, and accountability.

LO 3-3: One of the three dimensions of trustworthiness is ethical guidelines, and these consist of measures to guide ethical conduct in nonprofit organizations, including codes of ethics and conflict of interest policies.

LO 3-4: Two of the three dimensions of trustworthiness are transparency and accountability. Transparency can be fostered through various reports, open communication, and proactive disclosures. Accountability is demonstrated through measures such as oversight, program evaluation, external validation, and others.

LO 3-5: In addition to trustworthiness, demonstration of effectiveness is the second component of an ethical nonprofit organization, and this can be measured and communicated around achievement of impact on mission, results, and efficiency.

LO 3-6: A breach of trust refers to ethical violations, which can impact nonprofits more significantly than commercial organizations due to the moral disillusionment effect. Nonprofits should be transparent, empathetic, accountable, and proactive in their response.

LO 3-7: Nonprofit leaders face some unique ethical dilemmas, such as determining how to deal with tainted donations and navigating rule-bending that can occur due to resource constraints, conflicting priorities, and pressure to deliver results.

Bibliography

American Bar Association. *Nonprofits and Sarbane-Oxley*, 11 July 2023, https://www.americanbar.org/groups/center-pro-bono/resources/program-management/nonprofits_sarbanes_oxley/.

Becker, Annika. "Trust in the Nonprofit Domain: Towards an Understanding of Public's Trust in Nonprofit Organizations." *The Psychology of Trust*, edited by Martha Peaslee Levine. IntechOpen, London, 2021.

Berman, Greg. "The Chronicle of Philanthropy." *Leaders Must Confront Declining Trust in the Nonprofit World — Before It's Too Late*, 2 Aug. 2022, https://www.philanthropy.com/article/leaders-must-confront-declining-trust-in-the-nonprofit-world-before-its-too-late. Accessed 11 July 2023.

Borry, Erin. "Ethical Climate and Rule Bending: How Organizational Norms Contribute to Unintended Rule Consequences." *Public Admin*, vol. 95, no. 1, 2017, pp. 78–96.

Bryson, John M. "The Future of Public and Nonprofit Strategic Planning in the United States." *Public Administration Review, Suppl.Special Issue on the Future of Public Administration in 2020*, vol. 70, no. 1, 2010, pp. S255–S267.

Caldwell, Cam, and Stephen E. Clapham. "Organizational Trustworthiness: An International Perspective." *Journal of Business Ethics*, vol. 47, no. 4, 2003, pp. 349–364.

Cave, Damien. "Army Recruiters Say They Feel Pressure to Bend Rules." *New York Times*, 3 May 2005, p. 23.

Clolery, Paul. "NPT Study: Most Nonprofits Don't Have Whistleblower Policies." *The Non-profit Times*, Jan. 2020.

Council of Nonprofits. "Conflicts of Interest." 11 July 2023, https://www.councilofnonprofits.org/running-nonprofit/governance-leadership/conflicts-interest.

Eaton, Tim V., and Michael D. Akers. "Whistleblowing and Good Governance." *The CPA journal,* vol. 77, no. 6, June 2007, pp. 66–71

Ebrahim, Alnoor. "The Many Faces of Nonprofit Accountability." *The Jossey-Bass Handbook of Nonprofit Leadership and Management*, edited by David Renz, 4th Edition. 102–123, John Wiley & Sons, San Francisco, CA, 2016.

Frederickson, H George, and Richard K Ghere. *Ethical Challenges in Nonprofit Organizations: Maintaining Public Trust.* Routledge, New York, 2013.https://www.taylorfrancis.com/books/mono/10.4324/9781315704517/ethics-public-management-richard-ghere-george-frederickson?refId=51399328-4eaf-4705-bc9e-ca074545b50b&context=ubx.

Gnadt, Maggie. "How Nonprofit Organizations Can Get Back on Track after Bad Press." *Nonprofit MarCommunity*, 31 Jan. 2020, nonprofitmarcommunity.com/bad-press/.

Handy, Femida, and Allison Russell. *Ethics for Social Impact: Ethical Decision-Making in Nonprofit Organizations*. Springer International Publishing, Cham, 2018.

Hanson, Craig. *An Introduction to Ethics for Nonprofits and NGOs*. Springer International Publishing, New York, 2023.

Harris, Erica E., and Daniel Neely. "Determinants and Consequences of Nonprofit Transparency." *Journal of Accounting, Auditing & Finance*, vol. 36, no. 1, 2018, pp. 195–220.

Harris, Jared, Andrew Wicks, and Bidhan Parmar. "Ethical Business Decisions: The Framework." *Darden Ideas to Action*, 31 July 2015, https://ideas.darden.virginia.edu/ethical-business-decisions-the-framework. Accessed 11 July 2023.

Hornsey, Matthew, et al. "The Moral Disillusionment Model of Organizational Transgressions: Ethical Transgressions Trigger More Negative Reactions from

Consumers When Committed by Nonprofits." *Journal of Business Ethics*, vol. 172, no. 4, 2021, pp. 653–671.
Internal Revenue Service. "Form 990 Resources and Tools." 8 Feb. 2023, https://www.irs.gov/charities-non-profits/form-990-resources-and-tools. Accessed 11 July 2023.
Internal Revenue Service. "Intermediate Sanctions." 5 Jan. 2023, https://www.irs.gov/charities-non-profits/charitable-organizations/intermediate-sanctions. Accessed 11 July 2023.
Leardini, Chiara, Sarah Moggi, and Gina Rossi. "The New Era of Stakeholder Engagement: Gaining, Maintaining, and Repairing Legitimacy in Nonprofit Organizations." *International Journal of Public Administration*, vol. 40, no. 6, 2018, pp. 520–532.
McNee, Michael. "Charities Stepping Up Efforts in Impact Measurement and Reporting." *Nonprofit Business Advisor*, vol. 320, 2016, pp. 1–3.
Moody, Michael, and Michael Pratt. "Dorothy A. Johnson Center for Philanthropy." 22 Dec. 2020, https://johnsoncenter.org/blog/tainted-money-and-tainted-donors-a-growing-crisis/. Accessed 11 July 2023.
Morabito, Charlotte. "Why Charter Schools Are So Controversial." *CNBC*, 9 Sept. 2022, https://www.cnbc.com/video/2022/09/09/why-charter-schools-are-so-controversial.html. Accessed 11 July 2023.
National Council of Nonprofits. "Financial Transparency and Public Disclosure Requirements." 11 July 2023, https://www.councilofnonprofits.org/running-nonprofit/ethics-accountability/financial-transparency-and-public-disclosure-requirements.
Pasquale, Arena, and Patrick Renz. "Project Governance: Implementing Corporate Governance and Business Ethics in Nonprofit Organizations." *Journal of Management & Governance*, vol. 13, no. 4, 2009, pp. 355–363.
Pew Research Center. "Generations." 14 May 2019, https://www.pewresearch.org/religion/chart/generations/. Accessed 11 July 2023.
Phillips, Kenneth H. *Trust, Impact, and Fundraising for Nonprofits*. Abingdon: Routledge, 2023.
Prothero, Arianna. "Education Week." *What Are Charter Schools?* 9 Aug. 2018, https://www.edweek.org/policy-politics/what-are-charter-schools/2018/08. Accessed 11 July 2023.
Rhode, Deborah, and Amanda Packel. "Ethics and Nonprofits." *Stanford Social Innovation Review*, vol. 7, no. 3, 2009, pp. 29–35.
Rosen, Michael. "Doing Well By Doing Right: A Fundraiser's Guide to Ethical Decision-Making." *Journal of Philanthropy and Marketing*, vol. 10, no. 3, 2005, pp. 175–181.
Scurlock, Rebecca, Nives Dolsak, and Aseem Prakash. "Recovering from Scandals: Twitter Coverage of Oxfam and Save the Children Scandals." *Voluntas*, vol. 31, no. 1, 2020, pp. 94–110.
Sefora-Marcela, Nemteanu, et al. "Social Reporting Impact on Non-Profit Stakeholder Satisfaction and Trust during the COVID-19 Pandemic in an Emerging Market." *Sustainability*, vol. 14, no. 20, 2022.
Sekerka, Leslie C., and Roxanne Zolin. "Rule-Bending: Can Prudential Judgment Affect Rule Compliance and Values in the Workplace?" *Public Integrity*, vol. 9, 2014, pp. 225–243.
Siddiki, Saba, and Suzann Lupton. "Assessing Nonprofit Rule Interpretation and Compliance." *Nonprofit and Voluntary Sector Quarterly*, vol. 45, no. 4, 2016, pp. 156S–174S.
Smith, Pamela C., and Kelly A. Richmond. "Call for Greater Accountability wtihin the U.S. Nonprofit Sector." *Academy of Accounting and Financial Studies Journal*, vol. 11, no. 2, 2007.

Wallis, Beth. "KGOU." *Ryan Walters steps down from position at nonprofit amid conflict-of-interest concerns*, 11 Jan. 2023, https://www.kgou.org/education/2023-01-11/ryan-walters-steps-down-from-position-at-nonprofit-amid-conflict-of-interest-concerns. Accessed 11 July 2023.

Waters, Richard. "Increasing Fundraising Efficiency through Evaluation: Applying Communication Theory to the Nonprofit Organization–Donor Relationship." *Nonprofit and Voluntary Sector Quarterly*, vol. 403, no. 3, 2011, pp. 458–475.

White, D. *The Nonprofit Challenge: Integrating Ethics into the Purpose and Promise of Our Nation's Charities*. Palgrave MacMillan, New York, 2010. E-Book.

"Why Should Nonprofits Consider Impact Reporting?" *NonProfit Pro* (Online), 2018, https://uc.idm.oclc.org/login?qurl=https%3A%2F%2Fwww.proquest.com%2Ftrade-journals%2Fwhy-should-nonprofits-consider-impact-reporting%2Fdocview%2F2791548062%2Fse-2%3Faccountid%3D2909.

Xiaoting, Hao, and Daniel Neely. "The Decision to Advertise Nonprofit Accreditation Status." *Journal of Nonprofit & Public Sector Marketing*, vol. 31, no. 4, 2019, pp. 390–402.

Part 2

Staff

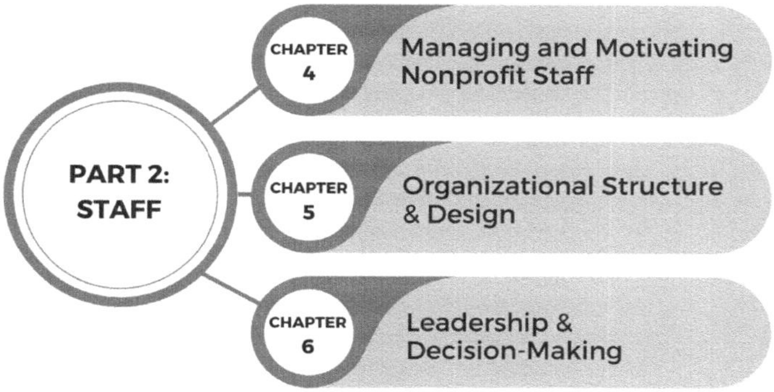
PART 2:
STAFF
CHAPTER
4
Managing and Motivating Nonprofit Staff
CHAPTER
5
Organizational Structure & Design
CHAPTER
6
Leadership & Decision-Making

4 Managing and Motivating Nonprofit Staff

Learning Outcomes

After reading this chapter, you should be able to:

LO 4-1: Describe the labor force of nonprofits, including both staff and volunteers.
LO 4-2: Explain the role, function, and importance of the nonprofit executive director.
LO 4-3: Categorize the types of staff positions within nonprofit organizations.
LO 4-4: Identify the key factors of managing nonprofit staff, such as hiring, training, and retention.
LO 4-5: Discuss employee turnover and its causes and identify types of withdrawal behaviors.
LO 4-6: Distinguish between the various performance evaluation methods.
LO 4-7: Apply the various theories of motivation to the nonprofit workplace.

> LO 4-1: Describe the labor force of nonprofits, including both staff and volunteers.

Nonprofit Staffing

A nonprofit organization is run by a combination of its board of directors, executive leadership, and staff members. The board of directors is responsible for making strategic decisions, setting policies, and overseeing the organization's overall direction. The executive leadership, often including an executive director or CEO, handles day-to-day operations, implements the board's decisions, and manages the organization's programs and activities. The staff members carry out the organization's mission and programs under the guidance of the executive leadership and the board.

A nonprofit is only as successful as the team of people driving its operation and mission, so staffing an organization with the people who carry out the

DOI: 10.4324/9781003380030-6

mission and programs is a critical component. Many nonprofits rely heavily on both volunteers (De Clerck 2021) and paid staff, with recent figures indicating a 70/30 ratio of paid staff to volunteers within international nonprofits (Ariella 2023). When it comes to paid staff, while there is a commonly held perception that nonprofit employees are paid considerably less than individuals employed in the for-profit sector, research findings are mixed. Some studies have found that a pay gap does exist (Handy 1998), while others suggest that the differences in wages are attributable to industry differences (Leete 2001). One study determined that nonprofit employees face a nonprofit pay penalty of 15.65%, or $8,895 compared to their peers in the for-profit sector (Fong 2017).

While paid staff comprise much of the labor for most agencies, the number of employees in nonprofits can vary widely depending on the size of the organization. Large nonprofits with more than $50 million in assets, for instance, have an average of 389 employees, while those with fewer than $100,000 in assets have an average of just under five employees (McKeever 2017). While small and newly established nonprofits might depend more on part-time and independent contractor labor such as consultants, most paid staff positions in nonprofits overall, around 79%, are classified as full time ("Nonprofit Pay" 2023). Of all positions in a nonprofit, the role of executive director is arguably the most influential, both in leading the organization and in hiring, motivating, and retaining the paid employees.

> LO 4-2: Explain the role, function, and importance of the nonprofit executive director.

Executive Director

The **executive director** is the highest-ranking staff position in a nonprofit and is overseen by a board of directors with shared responsibility for making staffing decisions, engaging in strategic planning, and making crucial determinations to advance the organization's mission. This is considered an "executive leadership" position within the organization.

Some organizations use the title of chief executive officer, or CEO, and a differentiating factor between the two titles is the scale of the organization they lead. Typically, smaller nonprofits tend to use the title of executive director, whereas the CEO title is more commonly employed in mid- to large-sized organizations (Nguyen 2023). Affiliate nonprofit organizations often designate the CEO title for the head of the overall larger nonprofit and assign the title of executive director to the leaders of the chapters or affiliate organizations, although this can vary from nonprofit to nonprofit.

The role of the executive director in a nonprofit organization is pivotal, and the individual in this position must assume multiple responsibilities and fulfill various roles, some of which are highlighted in Figure 4.1. This includes

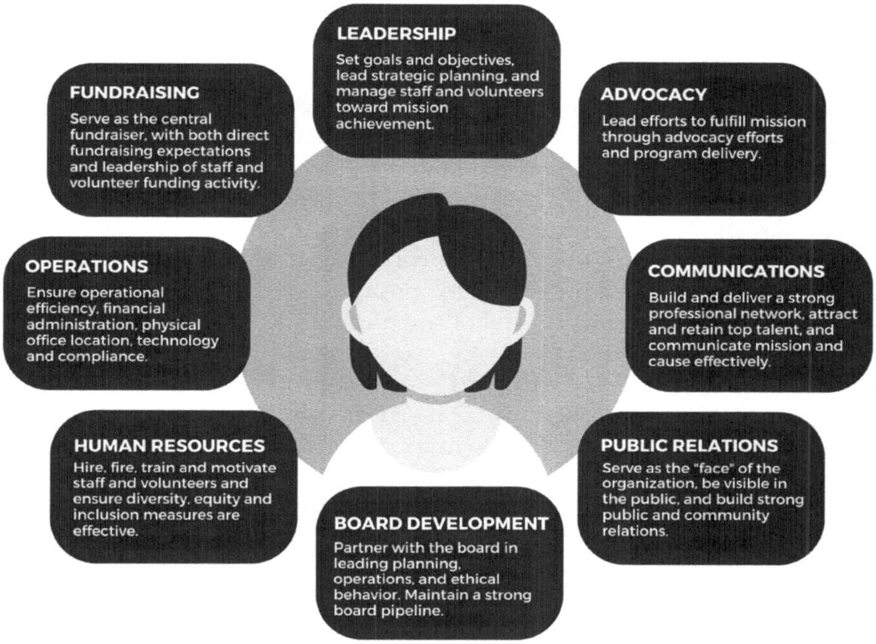

Figure 4.1 The Many Roles of a Nonprofit Executive Director

overall leadership responsibility in setting goals and objectives and leading strategic planning; serving as the lead fundraiser and "face" of the organization; managing operations and administrative functions like human resources (HR), communications, and public relations; developing the board of directors; and others. The smaller the nonprofit, the more central the executive director is in making operational decisions and, while the specific tasks of the role may vary from nonprofit to nonprofit, the executive director of a nonprofit wears many hats and must wear them equally well (Haddad 2022).

A central element to the success of an executive director is their approach to leadership, and various leadership styles – as well as ways that leaders make decisions in organizations – is addressed in Chapter 6.

LO 4-3: Categorize the types of staff positions within nonprofit organizations.

Staff Positions

Nonprofit paid staff positions can vary widely depending on the size and nature of the agency but can generally be classified as one of four categories:

management, administrative, development, and program delivery ("What Are" 2022) (Figure 4.2). It is important to note that these categories are not mutually exclusive, and in fact they often overlap. For instance, an executive director might best fit in the "management" category, but this position also performs administraive, fundraising, and program delivery work; a major gifts director is both management and development, and so on.

Management Positions – Employees in a management role often carry the word "director" or "manager" in their title, and these roles include positions like executive director, development manager, director of government relations, research director, etc. These positions require oversight of other employees and carry a higher level of responsibility.

Administrative Positions – These are positions that are generally not directly involved in either development work or program delivery, but rather exist to support those functions. This can include administrative support or roles such as human resources, marketing, accounting, legal, volunteer engagement, and others.

Development Positions – Development positions are central in raising funds for the organization and can include not just donor-facing roles, but also fundraising around grants, foundations, and corporate giving. Job titles in this category can include development coordinator, grant writer, major gifts officer, planned gifts coordinator, and others.

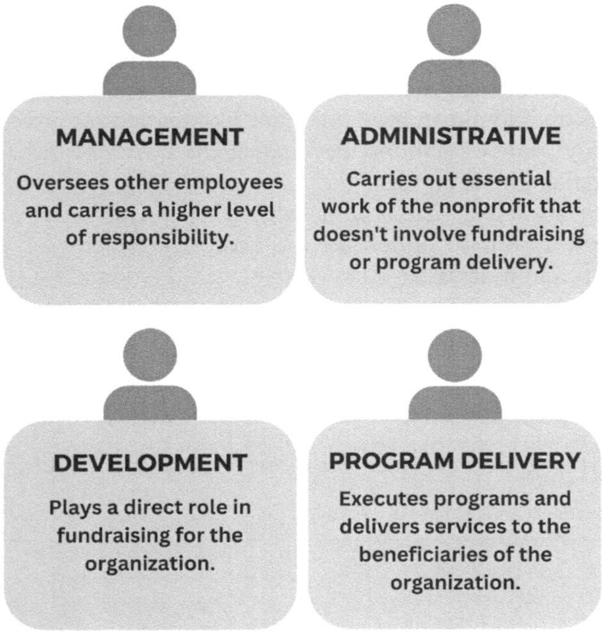

Figure 4.2 Categories of Nonprofit Positions

Program Delivery Positions – Positions that directly provide and deliver programs and services to beneficiaries of the nonprofit agency's mission fall within this category. This can include roles such as child care worker, housing coordinator, social worker, outreach coordinator, policy analyst, program officer, and others.

LO 4-4: Identify the key factors of managing nonprofit staff, such as hiring, training, and retention.

Managing Nonprofit Staff

Some of the important decisions nonprofit leaders face pertain to human resources, encompassing areas such as recruitment, retention, performance evaluation, and the motivation of both paid staff and volunteers. Chapter 9 emphasizes these aspects from the perspective of volunteers, while the current chapter delves into the considerations related to the paid staff.

Hiring

Making decisions around who to hire can be a stressful decision, as many nonprofits do not have the luxury of a large paid workforce. As noted in the introduction to this chapter, small agencies on average have fewer than five paid staff, so each hiring decision can prove critical, as just one underperforming employee can wreak havoc on a small team. Moreover, leaders face a recruitment problem, in that recent workforce shortages are hitting nonprofit agencies especially hard ("The Nonprofit" 2023). There are many reasons for this, some of which are impacting the labor market in general, but specific to the nonprofit sector, nearly four out of five (79%) nonprofit respondents to a recent National Council of Nonprofits survey reported salary competition as a key contributing factor ("The Nonprofit" 2023). Given the importance, and challenges, of hiring, retention becomes even more critical for leaders to manage. Another challenge leaders face is ensuring that the workforce is diverse, a topic analyzed in detail in Chapter 15.

Training and Onboarding

Once a hire is made, it is important for leaders to ensure that new staff are properly trained and onboarded, functions which are unfortunately sometimes neglected in nonprofits due to resource constraints. **Training** refers to the process of equipping newly hired individuals with the necessary skills, knowledge, and information to perform their job roles effectively. This may include things like teaching a new fundraising employee how to access and use the organization's donor database.

Onboarding is a process that assists new employees in acclimating into the organization, understanding the agency's culture, people, mission, and expectations, and goes beyond training the employee with job skills. This may include activities such as integrating the new hire into a team-building exercise with his or her new coworkers to foster a sense of belonging and to understand the dynamics of the team. Onboarding is important, because research shows that new employees who undergo a robust onboarding experience exhibit 50% higher productivity during their initial hiring period and tend to remain part of the organization even after three years (Haddad 2022).

LO 4-5: Discuss employee turnover and its causes and identify types of withdrawal behaviors.

Retention

Employee retention requires strategic actions by management to keep employees motivated and focused so they elect to remain employed and fully productive for the benefit of the organization ("Nonprofit Staff" 2015). While prioritizing employee retention is important for most organizations, it becomes especially key for nonprofits, as these agencies depend on their staff to cultivate long-term relationships with donors and to preserve institutional knowledge, both which are challenging if not impossible to replicate. Imagine all the inimitable donor knowledge that a major gifts officer holds after ten years on the job, for example. She's spent a decade building trust with a particular donor family, watching their families grow and expand, and cultivating a relationship with them. When she leaves the organization, that hard-earned, years-long relationship is gone, replaced with someone new who the donor family does not know and who must start from scratch. Sure, the donor family hopefully has trust in the organization and its mission, but the value and power of people and their human relationships cannot be ignored.

One way to assess retention is by evaluating employee turnover. **Turnover**, or "churn,"

measures the number of employees who leave an organization during a specified period, typically in one year (find source). This measure should be of particular concern to nonprofit managers, as the annual staff turnover for nonprofit agencies is higher than the general labor market, at 19% compared to 12% ("Managing For" 2023). Turnover is expensive, as the time and resources required to replace, train, and onboard new employees is costly.

Studies estimate that losing an employee can cost a company 1.5–2 times the employee's salary (Davis 2023). Moreover, the time investment required by managers to replace departing employees can be substantial, further adding to the already heavy workload of an executive director.

Several factors contribute to the high turnover observed within the nonprofit sector. Employees within these organizations often cite overwhelming workloads, absence of career growth prospects, inadequate pay ("Managing For" 2023), toxic work culture, and stress from unrealistic goals as key drivers behind their choice to leave (Joslyn 2019). Another reason nonprofit employees leave is **job burnout**, which is a state of physical or emotional exhaustion that also involves a sense of reduced accomplishment and loss of personal identity (Bakker 2021). Nonprofit work can also be high in **emotional labor**, which involves the efforts of workers to understand others, have empathy with their situation, and internalize their feelings (Steinberg 1990).

Nonprofit leaders can take some action to minimize turnover, like managing an organization with a strong and positive culture, setting achievable goals, and utilizing volunteer labor to alleviate some of the workload and burnout, although addressing some of the key turnover factors, like pay, are not always feasible in resource-strapped nonprofit organizations. Managers can also take care to make note of employee withdrawal behaviors, which often signal an employee at risk of leaving the organization. With early intervention, turnover can hopefully be prevented.

New Hire Turnover

A vulnerable point when an employee is at risk of departing the organization is in the early weeks of their employment, so leaders should take particular care to properly onboard and monitor a new employee and their progress easing into the organization (Caldwell 2018). **New hire turnover** is a measure of the percentage of employees who leave a company during a time period, typically within the first year on the job (Pavlou 2023). It is not uncommon (Siocon 2023), and two reasons for early turnover is misaligned expectations and culture shock.

When making a job offer, or even through the interviewing process, nonprofit hiring officials should be direct and honest with prospective new hires about the tasks and expectations of the job to avoid a misalignment between expectations and the realities of the position. For example, if an event coordinator job description specifies that the position requires "occasional night and weekend work," but the newly hired employee finds herself working her first three consecutive weekends on the job, she is likely to experience job dissatisfaction and will be at risk for early turnover.

Workplace culture, or the norms and values of the workplace, is addressed in the next chapter and can be another contributing factor to early turnover. **Culture shock** in the workplace is the discomfort an individual feels when confronted with unfamiliar work practices, values, and dynamics in a new job or organization, which can lead to turnover (Peat 2022). Screening and hiring employees based on **culture fit**, which refers to the alignment of values, beliefs, and behaviors between the employee and employer, can help prevent culture shock. Hiring leaders should be open about their organization's culture during the interview process, ask interview questions specifically to gauge alignment of the candidate's culture fit, and clearly convey their key values and norms to prospective employees.

Withdrawal Behavior

Sometimes employees will indirectly communicate their dissatisfaction and high likelihood of eventually turning over through certain actions. **Withdrawal behavior** refers to actions or behaviors that employees exhibit as a way of mentally or emotionally distancing themselves from their work responsibilities (Colquitt 2021). These behaviors are often signs of employee dissatisfaction, disengagement, or burnout.

Work withdrawal behaviors can vary in their nature and severity, but generally involve employees pulling back from active participation in their work tasks or the workplace environment. This pulling back can be either physical or psychological. **Physical withdrawal** behaviors happen when individuals physically distance themselves from their work environment and include behavior such as frequently and intentionally missing work, consistent tardiness, leaving work early, and taking frequent breaks. **Psychological withdrawal** occurs when an employee engages in actions that disengage them mentally or emotionally from their work or responsibilities, and include behaviors such as goofing off at work, daydreaming, neglecting responsibilities, and social withdrawal (Colquitt 2021).

When a leader notices withdrawal behaviors within their team, taking proactive steps to address the situation becomes essential. This approach helps foster a supportive work environment and uphold productivity levels.

LO 4-6: Distinguish between the various performance evaluation methods.

Evaluating Performance

Working in nonprofits can be difficult, as employees regularly face high performance pressure, but are not always provided with the adequate resources needed to perform successfully. As discussed in the preceding chapter, while accountability is important, leaders need to ensure that employees are treated fairly regarding performance expectations. This includes assurance that set goals are difficult, yet achievable, and that employees are provided with the resources needed to achieve their goals. Management must supply the employee with adequate resources to achieve those goals. Further, rather than setting goals unilaterally *for* employees, nonprofit leaders can better engage subordinates by collaborating to set goals together.

Chapter 2 discussed how nonprofits use key performance indicators, or KPIs, in measuring organizational performance, and these are sometimes used to gauge individual employees' performance as well. In addition to KPIs, there are numerous other performance evaluation methods, and three that are commonly used are management by objectives (MBOs), behaviorally anchored rating scales (BARS), and 360-degree appraisals.

Management by Objectives

Management by objectives, commonly abbreviated as MBOs, is a performance evaluation approach that involves setting clear, measurable goals aligned with the organization's objectives to improve performance and decision-making (Mio 2015). Like KPIs, MBOs are quantifiable and should be **SMART goals**, an acronym that means that goals should each be specific, measurable, achievable, relevant, and time-bound. MBOs are beneficial because they provide clear direction, align individual and team goals, and emphasize results.

Some goals, however, are difficult to quantify, which is one downfall of the MBO approach. For a development position, MBOs might make sense, as leaders can set specific and quantifiable fundraising goals. For a program delivery position, however, measuring performance through MBOs might prove more difficult. Objectives can include quantifiable measures such as number of beneficiaries served, but this is likely an inadequate way to measure the goal of fulfilling organizational mission. While imperfect, however, MBOs are employed by many nonprofit organizations. Figure 4.3 details some examples of nonprofit MBOs, by position.

Behaviorally Anchored Rating Scales

Behaviorally anchored rating scales (BARS) are measurement tools that assign a numeric value to specific descriptions of employee behavior. This takes the emphasis away from strict numerical ratings and instead provides a behaviorally based assessment of employee performance. In turn, employees can better understand the behaviors desired by the organization's leaders, and strive to exhibit them (McCoy 2023).

How organizations use BARS can vary, with some using a scale of seven or ten points, although five is the most common. The choice of the number of rating levels depends on the complexity of the behaviors being evaluated and ease of use for raters. An example of how BARS can be used in a nonprofit organization to measure the performance of a program delivery position (volunteer coordinator), using a five-point scale, is reflected in Figure 4.4.

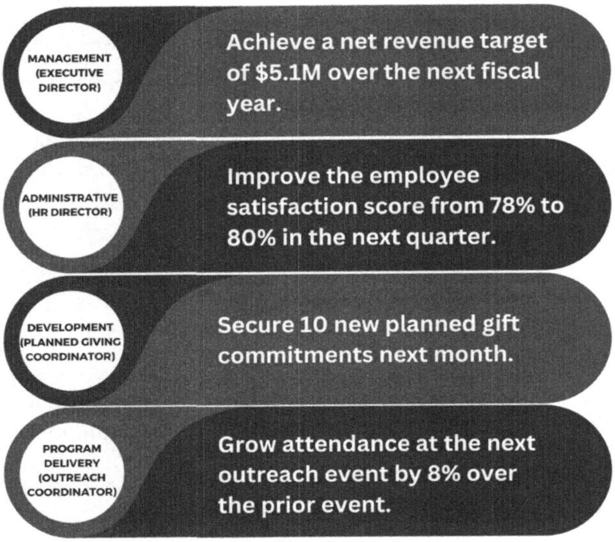

Figure 4.3 Nonprofit MBOs Examples

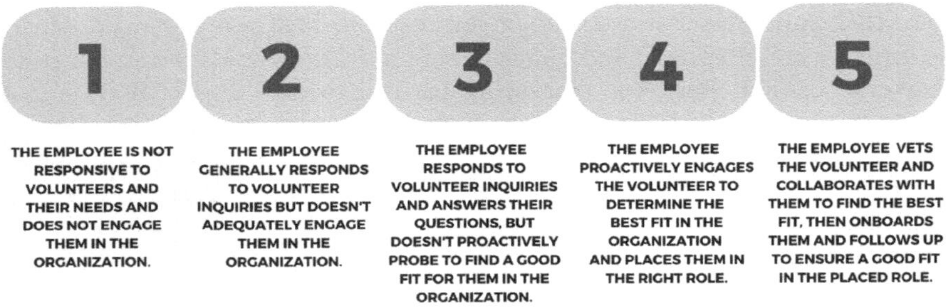

Figure 4.4 Volunteer Coordinator BARS Example

This approach is beneficial because it encourages employee behaviors that align with organizational values and principles but can be time-consuming to set up and subjective in assessment.

360-Degree Appraisal

A **360-degree appraisal** is measures performance by gathering feedback on employee performance from a wide array of individuals with whom that employee work. Just as a complete circle spans 360-degrees, this approach seeks to be well rounded in providing a comprehensive evaluation of performance from multiple sources ("Getting 360" 2014). The downside of this performance evaluation approach is that this feedback can be time-consuming to gather, and it can create conflict in organizations if an employee's coworker provides a poor rating or negative feedback about their colleague.

Regardless of the appraisal method used, evaluating performance can be a time-consuming and even costly endeavor and, as such, some nonprofit leaders only half-heartedly engage in formal performance evaluation, or do so inconsistently. Regular performance evaluations, however, are crucial for managers to provide feedback, set expectations, identify areas for improvement, and align employee goals with organizational objectives.

> LO 4-7: Apply the various theories of motivation to the nonprofit workplace.

Theories of Motivation

Ask any average person on the street what they think is the number one motivator of employees and the answer will likely be "money." While money is one motivating factor, and important one, it is not the *only* one – nor is it the most significant. In fact, according to organizational behavior research, the nature of the work is the factor most closely correlated with organizational commitment and performance (Colquitt 2021).

Motivation can be influenced by rewards, with **extrinsic rewards** referring to tangible benefits and career progression, while those that naturally come from the work itself are categorized as **intrinsic rewards**. Think of extrinsic rewards as coming from external sources, and intrinsic rewards from internal motivations. Some research suggests that nonprofit work tends to be more intrinsically motivating, and because the nature of the work is such an important factor in employee motivation, these intrinsic rewards can be just as valuable for some individuals as monetary compensation. In short, many nonprofit employees are highly motivated by their work and are even willing to accept less pay compared to a similar job in a for-profit organization (Fong 2009).

This fact probably brings a sigh of relief to nonprofit managers, most of whom do not have excess financial resources to incentivize paid staff financially. But, while many nonprofit employees end up working in the sector due to the fulfillment and passion for the nature of the work itself, that alone cannot sustain job satisfaction, performance, commitment, and motivation. Leaders must provide resources and tools to motivate employees and improve retention, which as noted above is a problem for many nonprofit organizations. While there are many well-known theories of motivation, knowing the basics of some key ones, such as equity theory, expectancy theory, and goal-setting theory, can help leaders understand the drivers of employee motivation.

Equity Theory

Equity theory suggests that motivation at work is driven primarily by the employees' perception of fairness. Whether we realize we do it or not, most individuals keep a running mental ledger that compares their *inputs* (things like time, effort, skills) to the job to the *outcomes* (things such as pay, rewards, and benefits) with those of others to gauge whether their treatment is fair and equitable, influencing their motivation and job satisfaction (Colquitt 2021).

Equity theory tells us that employees evaluate their perception of fairness of the decisions made by their managers, and they judge the fairness of how they are treated relative to others in the organization. To avoid an imbalance of the perception of equity, nonprofit leaders should enact measures to ensure fairness in employee treatment, especially around factors such as pay, rewards, and promotions. Further, they need to be transparent in communicating these outcomes, explaining how they can be earned, and following through in the fairness of the distribution of these rewards, based upon performance.

Expectancy Theory

Expectancy theory posits that people are motivated to perform when they believe their efforts will lead to successful performance (expectancy), that successful performance will lead to desired outcomes (a term called instrumentality), and that these outcomes are valuable and aligned with their goals (a term called valence). More simply stated, an employee must have confidence that their work will lead to successful performance and that performance will translate to outcomes that they value (Colquitt 2021).

The belief one has in oneself to reach specific goals is known as **self-efficacy** (Sitzman 2023). With expectancy theory, the "expectancy" part requires the employee have a high degree of self-efficacy, in believing that they have the ability, tools, and resources to achieve their workplace goals. Nonprofit leaders can help bolster their employees' self-efficacy by providing skill development and support, and cheering their subordinate on as they progress toward the goal. Leaders can also ensure that goals are SMART and, again, difficult but achievable.

Expectancy theory also requires instrumentality, the belief of the employee that their successful performance will lead to desired outcomes. This is where performance evaluations and goal-setting can also come into play. Nonprofit leaders can set clear expectations, through their selected performance evaluation method, and specifically articulate the outcomes that will result in achievement of the stated goals. Leaders must also take care to remain consistent in the goals set for the stated time period and not "move the goalpost," which refers to unfairly altering the conditions or rules of procedure during a game.

Finally, expectancy theory emphasizes the term valence, which is the value the employee places on the outcomes they will receive if they do achieve their goals. If a stated outcome for performance is, for instance, a promotion to a better job title but without an increase in pay, that's of little motivation to an employee who cares nothing about titles but does highly value financial outcomes. Leaders must ensure that the outcomes are valued by employees.

Goal-Setting Theory

In the earlier discussion around performance evaluations, we learned that goals should be SMART – specific, measurable, achievable, realistic, and time-bound – but how do we know this? **Goal-setting theory** asserts that setting specific and challenging goals leads to increased motivation, effort, and performance as individuals strive to achieve those objectives, aided by clear direction and feedback (Colquitt 2021).

That's the rudimentary definition, and as a motivational framework, goal-setting theory can get complex, so leaders can use the SMART acronym and a simple and easy-to-remember way to set goals in accordance with what we know from the theory. The one important aspect of goal-setting theory absent from the SMART acronym, however, is that goals need to also be *difficult*. It might surprise you that difficult goals can be more powerful in motivating an employee than easy ones, but the key is ensuring that they are *achievable*. That's why it is essential that leaders set SMART goals, and ones that are difficult but achievable, in employee performance evaluation and goal-setting. Goal-setting theory also emphasizes the need for leaders to provide clear direction and feedback.

Takeaways

LO 4-1: Nonprofit organizations are powered not just by paid staff, but also volunteers.

LO 4-2: The most influential staff position in nonprofit organizations is the executive director, a demanding position that requires a diverse skill set and varied job functions including leadership, fundraising, operations, human resources, board development, public relations, communications, and advocacy.

LO 4-3: Nonprofit staff positions can generally be categorized as management, administrative, development, and program delivery, although these categories are not mutually exclusive.

LO 4-4: Managing nonprofit staff requires hiring, training and onboarding, retention, and motivation.

LO 4-5: Employee retention can be a challenge for nonprofits who deal with high turnover, particularly in the early stages of new hire employment, which sometimes occurs as a result of job burnout, positions high in emotional labor, or culture shock. Employee withdrawal behaviors including psychological (daydreaming, low performance, etc.) and physical withdrawal (tardiness, absenteeism, etc.) sometimes signal potential employee turnover.

LO 4-6: Leaders should work with employees to establish SMART goals that are difficult but achievable and assess goal attainment through various performance evaluation methods such as MBOs, BARS, and 360-degree appraisal.

LO 4-7: Nonprofit leaders can apply learnings from the various theories of motivation, such as equity theory, expectancy theory, and goal-setting theory, to foster a fairer and more equitable workplace, in turn better motivating employees.

Bibliography

Ariella, Sky. "26 Incredible Nonprofit Statistics [2023]: How Many Nonprofits Are in the U.S.?" *Zippia*, 12 May 2023, www.zippia.com/advice/nonprofit-statistics/.

Bakker, Arnold B., and Juriena D. de Vries. "Job Demands-Resources Theory and Self-Regulation: New Explanations and Remedies for Job Burnout." *Anxiety, Stress, and Coping*, vol. 34, no. 1, 2021, pp. 1–21.

Caldwell, Cam, and Ray Peters. "New Employee Onboarding – Psychological Contracts and Ethical Perspectives." *The Journal of Management Development*, vol. 37, no. 1, 2018, pp. 27–39.

Colquitt, Jason, Jeffery LePine, and Michael Wesson. *Organizational Behavior: Improving Performance and Commitment in the Workplace*. McGraw Hill, New York, 2021. Print.

Davis, Kylie. "Nonprofit Burnout Statistics: The High Cost of High Turnover." *Givebutter*, 11 May 2022, givebutter.com/blog/nonprofit-burnout-statistics. Accessed 8 Jun. 2023.

De Clerck, Tom, et al. "Enhancing Volunteers Capacity in all-volunteer Nonprofit Organizations: The Role of Volunteer Leaders' Reliance on Effective Management Processes and (De)Motivating Leadership." *Nonprofit Management & Leadership*, vol. 31, no. 3, 2021, pp. 481–503.

Fong, Cecilia A. *The Nonprofit Wage Differential*. ProQuest Dissertations Publishing, Washington, DC, 2009.

"Getting 360-Degree Feedback Right." *Harvard Business Review*, 1 Aug. 2014, hbr.org/2001/01/getting-360-degree-feedback-right.

Haddad, Duke. "What Skills Does a Nonprofit Executive Director Need?" *NonProfit Pro* (Online), 2022. https://www.nonprofitpro.com/post/what-skills-does-a-nonprofit-executive-director-need/.

Handy, F., and E. Katz. "The Wage Differential between Nonprofit Institutions and Corporations: Getting More by Paying Less?" *Journal of Comparative Economics*, vol. 26, 1998, pp. 246–261.

Joslyn, Heather. "Why Fundraisers Leave, and How to Keep Them." *The Chronicle of Philanthropy*, 6 Aug. 2019, www.philanthropy.com/article/why-fundraisers-leave-and-how-to-keep-them/. Accessed 8 Jun. 2023.

Leete L. "Whither the Nonprofit Wage Differential? Estimates from the 1990 Census." *Journal of Labor Economics*, vol. 19, 2001, pp. 136–170.

Managing for Employee Retention - SHRM, www.shrm.org/ResourcesAndTools/tools-and-samples/toolkits/Pages/managing-for-employee-retention.aspx. Accessed 29 Sept. 2023.

McCoy, John W. "Behaviorally Anchored Rating Scale: A Full Guide with Examples." *AIHR*, 26 Sept. 2023, www.aihr.com/blog/behaviorally-anchored-rating-scale/#:~:text=anchored%20rating%20scale-,Behaviorally%20Anchored%20Rating%20Scale%3A%20A%20Definition,%2D%20or%20nine%2Dpoint%20scale.

McKeever, Brice, et al. "The Nonprofit Workforce: By the Numbers - Non Profit News: Nonprofit Quarterly." *Non Profit News | Nonprofit Quarterly*, 13 Jan. 2017, nonprofitquarterly.org/nonprofit-workforce-numbers/.

Mio, Chiara, Andrea Venturelli, and Rossella Leopizzi. "Management by Objectives and Corporate Social Responsibility Disclosure: First Results from

Italy." *Accounting Auditing & Accountability Journal*, vol. 28, no. 3, 2015, pp. 325–364.

Nguyen, Therese. "Being an Executive Director versus CEO in the Nonprofit Sector." *Tronvig*, 4 May 2023, www.tronviggroup.com/executive-director-versus-ceo/.

"Nonprofit Pay and Benefits: Estimates from the National Compensation Survey." *U.S. Bureau of Labor Statistics*, Jan. 2016, www.bls.gov/opub/mlr/2016/article/nonprofit-pay-and-benefits.htm. Accessed 8 Jun. 2023.

"Nonprofit Staff Retention, Part 1: Are Higher Salaries Really the Answer?" *IPM Advancement*, Jan. 2015, www.ipmadvancement.com/blog/nonprofit-staff-retention-are-higher-salaries-really-the-answer. Accessed 11 Jun. 2023.

Pavlou, Christina. "How to Reduce New Hire Turnover." *Resources for Employers*, 11 Apr. 2023, resources.workable.com/tutorial/new-hire-turnover-rate. Accessed 15 Jun. 2023.

Peat, Daniel M., and Jaclyn Perrmann-Graham. "Where do I Belong? Conflicted Identities and the Paradox of Simultaneous Stigma and Social Aggrandizement of Military Veterans in Organizations." *International Journal of Human Resource Management*, vol. ahead-of-print, no. ahead-of-print, 2022, pp. 1–29.

Siocon, Gem. "4 Steps to Calculate and Improve New Hire Turnover Rate." *Recruitee*, 11 Apr. 2023, recruitee.com/articles/new-hire-turnover-rate. Accessed 11 Jun. 2023.

Sitzmann, Traci, and Gillian Yeo. "A Meta-Analytic Investigation of the within-Person Self-Efficacy Domain: Is Self-Efficacy a Product of Past Performance or a Driver of Future Performance?" *Personnel Psychology*, vol. 66, no. 3, 2013, pp. 531–568.

Steinberg, R.J. "Labor Economics and the Nonprofit Sector: A Literature Review." *Nonprofit and Voluntary Sector Quarterly*, vol. 19, 1990, pp. 151–169.

Steinberg, R.J., and D.M. Figart. "Emotional Demands at Work: A Job Content Analysis." *Annals of the American Academy of Political and Social Science*, vol. 561, 1999, pp. 177–191.

"The Nonprofit Workforce Shortage Crisis." *National Council of Nonprofits*, Jan. 2023, www.councilofnonprofits.org/nonprofit-workforce-shortage-crisis. Accessed 8 Jun. 2023. – Council

"What Are the Job Titles in a Non-Profit Organization?" *HHCS*, 29 July 2022, hhcsonline.org/what-are-the-job-titles-in-a-non-profit-organization/.

5 Organizational Structure and Design

Learning Outcomes

After reading this chapter, you should be able to:

LO 5-1: Explain organizational structure and organizational design, highlight the differences between them, and discuss their interconnected relationship.
LO 5-2: Describe how leaders can apply the job characteristics theory, specialization, job rotation, job enrichment, and job enlargement to improve employee motivation and performance in job design.
LO 5-3: Explain the organizational structure components of job design, departmentalization, hierarchy of authority, delegation, and span of control.
LO 5-4: Recognize the various types of communications in organizations, diagram how communications flow within an organization, and explain the silo effect.
LO 5-5: Rationalize why performance-based compensation is the best approach when designing reward and recognition programs and how theories of motivation apply to this strategy.
LO 5-6: Summarize organizational culture, describe the common culture types in nonprofit organizations, and explore how leaders play a key role in shaping culture.
LO 5-7: Express the reasons why leaders restructure and explain the potential pitfalls of redesigning organizations.

> LO 5-1: Explain organizational structure and organizational design, highlight the differences between them, and discuss their interconnected relationship

Distinctions between Structure and Design

A nicely designed organization is like a tidy, well-organized closet. It is easy to get dressed when your clothes are neatly organized by type and everything is in its place, easy to access. Compare this to trying to get dressed out of

DOI: 10.4324/9781003380030-7

random piles of clothes thrown on the floor. It would take quite a while to find what you're looking for, and when you do find it, it would likely be a wrinkled mess. Like a disorganized closet, when an organization is poorly designed, it can create problems and slow decision-making, so it is imperative that leaders ensure that their organizational design is effective.

The terms organizational design and organizational structure are often used interchangeably, but although they are related concepts, they bear some distinctions. While they both pertain to how an organization is arranged, they focus on different aspects.

Organizational structure is a formal framework that refers to the hierarchy and arrangement of roles, rules, responsibilities, and reporting relationships within an organization. It serves as the static representation of the organization, can mostly be visualized in graphic form on an organizational chart, and is the foundation for organizational design (Thompson 2023).

While organizational structure is static, organizational design is the *dynamic* representation of organization since it involves an ongoing method for tweaking the systems that are no longer effective for the organization. Formally defined, **organizational design** is a step-by-step methodology which involves intentional shaping of various organizational components to align them with the organization's strategy to achieve specific goals and outcomes (Allen 2012).

To visualize the way an organization is designed and structured, one can consult the agency's **organizational chart**, as it provides a diagram that shows the structure of an organization and the relationships and relative ranks of its parts and positions/jobs (Robbins & Judge 2018). Figures 5.2 through 5.8 provide some examples of various basic organizational charts.

LO 5-2: Describe how leaders can apply the job characteristics theory, specialization, job rotation, job enrichment, and job enlargement to improve employee motivation and performance in job design.

Organizational Structure

As the basis of organizational design, organizational structure focuses on five main components: job design, departmentalization, hierarchy of authority, delegation, and span of control. Before designing a job, however leaders must first conduct a **job analysis** to investigate and identify the duties, tasks, responsibilities, skills, and knowledge, and essential qualifications for a certain job profile. After conducting a job analysis for a position, leaders can then engage in job design, using one of several approaches, such as application of the job characteristics model, job rotation, job enlargement, job enrichment, and specialization.

Job Design

The first building block of organizational structure is **job design** (Kuman 2022), which is the process of defining an individual's responsibilities at work, areas of decision-making responsibility, and expectations and goals, while motivating and rewarding the employee (Van Vulpen 2023). Once a job is designed, nonprofit leaders should create a **job description**, which is a document that outlines the elements of the job established in the job design process. The job description is a clear and concise way to convey what the job entails (Foss 2015).

Job Characteristics Theory

The **job characteristics theory** proposes that jobs designed to include certain characteristics – variety, identity, significance, autonomy, and feedback – can lead to greater motivation, satisfaction, and performance in employees (Hackman 1980). These five characteristics can be remembered with the acronym VISAF:

- **Variety:** The extent to which a job requires the use of a variety of skills and talents. Jobs that are more varied tend to be more interesting and fulfilling.
- **Identity:** The degree to which a job allows an individual to complete a whole and identifiable piece of work. Jobs that allow an employee to participate in the creation of something from start to finish, where at the end of the task they can proudly say, "Look, I did that!" tend to be more satisfying.
- **Significance:** Many nonprofit jobs are high in significance, which refers to an employees' perception of the importance and positive impact of their work. Jobs with greater significance provide employees with a sense of meaningfulness.
- **Autonomy:** The level of independence and control an individual has over their work and decision-making. Jobs with a higher degree of autonomy provide employees with more ownership over their role.
- **Feedback:** The extent to which workers receive clear and direct information about the effectiveness of their performance. Feedback can come either from a person, like a supervisor, of from the job itself. Jobs with a higher level of feedback can help bolster employee self-efficacy.

When jobs are designed with these five characteristics ingrained within them, it can result in three positive psychological states:

- **Meaningfulness of work** refers to the extent to which employees perceive their tasks as being meaningful, valuable, and contributing to a larger purpose or goal. The characteristics of *variety, identity, and significance* contribute to this psychological state.

- **Responsibility for outcomes** is the psychological state that occurs in jobs with a high degree of *autonomy* and refers to the sense of accountability an employee feels about their contribution to positive outcomes.
- **Knowledge of results** happens in jobs designed with a high degree of *feedback* and pertains to the extent to which employees receive clear and comprehensible information about the outcomes and impact of their job performance.

When leaders take care to strategically design jobs embedded with the components of job characteristics theory, employees can experience those three psychologic states and, in turn, generate many positive organizational outcomes such as high performance, motivation, job satisfaction, and others.

Human beings are complex, and there's no "one size fits all" application of anything in management and organizations, including job design, so it is important to note that in the job characteristics model, there are individual differences among employees. These variables are called moderators and they affect the strength or direction of the relationship between the other variables. These moderating variables include the knowledge and skill of the individual, their need for personal accomplishment, learning, and development (called "growth need strength"), and the context of the job (satisfaction with their managers, pay, co-workers, etc.) (Colquitt 2021).

Figure 5.1 illustrates the interaction between the five job characteristics (VISAF) and three psychological states, along with the organizational outcomes.

> LO 5-3: Explain the organizational structure components of job design, departmentalization, hierarchy of authority, delegation, and span of control.

Other Approaches to Job Design

The job characteristics model is one approach to job design, but others include specialization, job rotation, job enrichment, and job enlargement. **Specialization**, also known as division of labor, occurs when workers learn how to perform specific tasks very well rather than focusing on doing many different tasks (Hsieh 2004). While specialization is beneficial in allowing an employee to become highly skilled and efficient in completing the specific tasks, it can result in boredom and lack of skill growth, so leaders should weigh the needs of the organization and employee in job design when determining the degree of specialization. While assembly-line work in manufacturing is the prime workplace environment to deploy specialization, it can be integrated into any type of organization, including nonprofits.

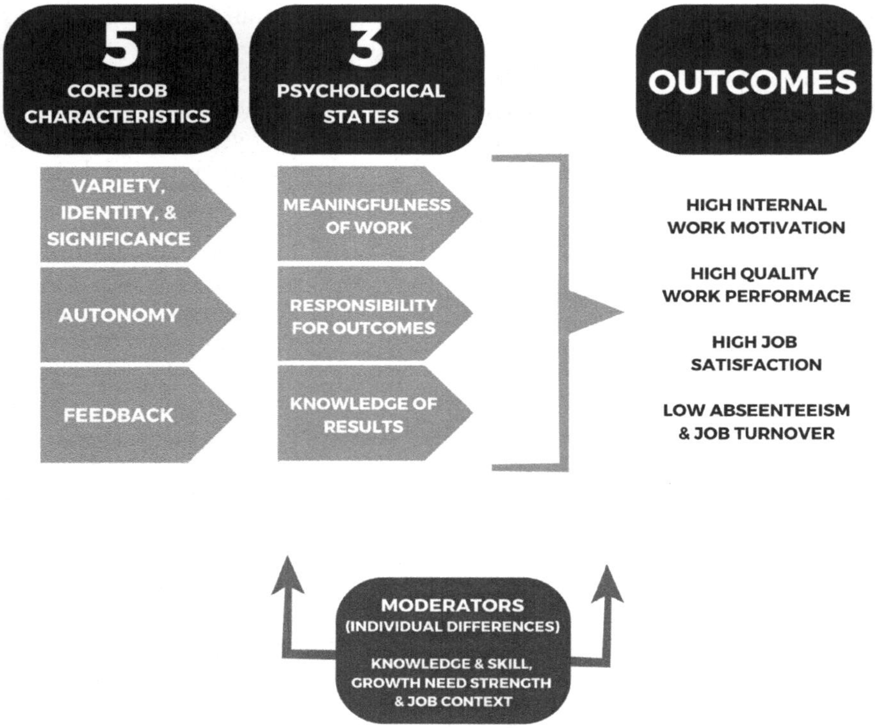

Figure 5.1 Job Characteristics Model

> Nico is development manager for Emmaus France, but finds it difficult to be jack-of-all-trades, master of none, as he is the only fundraising employee on staff. Juggling responsibilities for raising money from individuals, including major gift fundraising, annual gifts, foundations and grants, planned gifts, and corporate sponsorships, is incredibly difficult, as all of these fundraising approaches require different strategies, and he can never focus on any of them adequately. His executive director decides to expand the development team and redesign Nico's job. Nico is thrilled that his newly modified position as grants manager will allow him to specialize exclusively on his favorite form of fundraising, grants. Now that he has adequate time to focus on this one area, he becomes highly skilled and efficient at doing the work.

When work is too specialized, or an employee is long-tenured in his or her position, however, boredom and lack of fulfillment can set in. To address these issues, leaders can use job rotation, job enrichment, job enlargement in job design to provide opportunities for skill development and variety.

Job rotation is an approach where employees rotate through different roles in the organization, which provides them with more variety in their work and allows them to develop new skills. **Job enrichment** aims to enhance the depth and complexity of a job by adding qualitative tasks that require more responsibility, autonomy, and skill, making the job more challenging, interesting, and creative. **Job enlargement** seeks to decrease the boredom of performing a redundant task by expanding the scope of a job by quantitatively adding more tasks at a similar skill level (Hsieh 2004).

While job enrichment and job enlargement might sound similar, they differ in that job enrichment seeks to provide employees with more meaningful and challenging tasks, whereas job enlargement expands tasks without necessarily increasing the difficulty of them. Job enrichment generally results in positive outcomes, but job enlargement may not, as an employee who is asked to do more at work may not perceive that as a good thing.

Rachel works for London Cardiac Risk in the Young and her job is focused almost exclusively on executing the agency's annual charity gala event. After five years of working on just this one event, which she has completely mastered, she finds herself bored and unfulfilled. Her executive director could redesign Rachel's job in the following ways to address this:

- **Job rotation:** Rachel's executive director pairs her with her colleague who plans the organization's annual 5K walk fundraiser, so they rotate events every other year. So next year, instead of planning the gala, Rachel will plan the run. This allows them both to expand their skills and add variety to their work.
- **Job enrichment:** The annual gala has always had the same theme, "Fighting Cardiac Disease." Rachel's executive director knows that Rachel is a creative person, so she offers her the opportunity to start integrating different themes into the event each year, which Rachel finds challenging, interesting, and exciting.
- **Job enlargement:** Rachel's executive director asks her to plan not just the gala, but also the annual 5K fundraising walk each year to expand her number of tasks and give her more quantity and variety in her work.

Departmentalization

Organizational leaders need to not just determine what jobs are needed, and design those jobs, but they must also determine where to place these positions within the organization. **Departmentalization** is the process of grouping people, teams, or activities into departments or functions with specific objectives, goals, and outcomes to be achieved (Robbins & Judge 2018). There are several methods of departmentalization that organizations can use to group their activities and resources, and functional, product, geographic, customer, and matrix are the most common ("Understanding").

Functional departmentalization groups people into departments based on similar job functions or tasks. Some nonprofits use this approach by segmenting employees based on their job function: marketing, development, program services, finance, corporate relations, etc., visually represented in Figure 5.2.

Product departmentalization groups people into departments based on different product lines or categories, allowing specialized focus on each product's development, marketing, and sales. In the nonprofit sector, this would translate into the end "product," which might vary depending on the type of nonprofit. A social services agency that provides a variety of resources to beneficiaries of the cause might group people into departments based on the category of services provided, denoted in Figure 5.3.

National or international nonprofit organizations with numerous chapter or affiliate offices spread across a wide geographic area may benefit from **geographic departmentalization**, which groups people on the basis of territory. Figure 5.4 provides a visual example of how this might look.

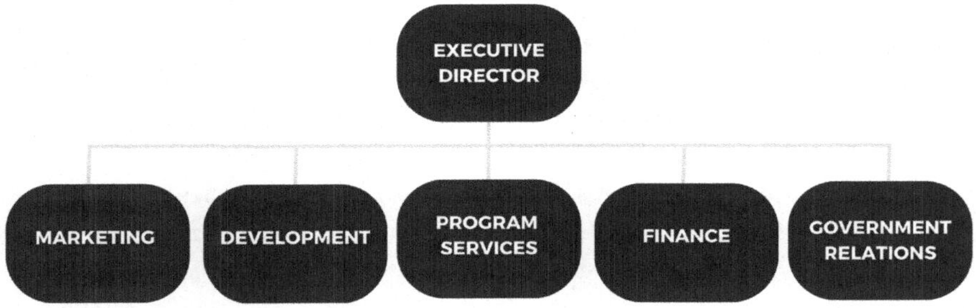

Figure 5.2 Functional Departmentalization

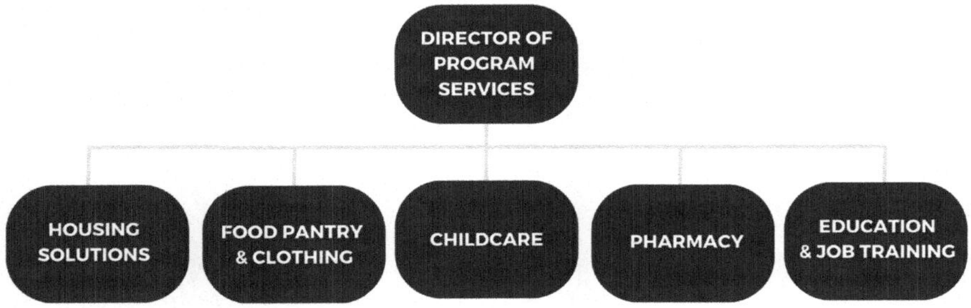

Figure 5.3 Product Departmentalization

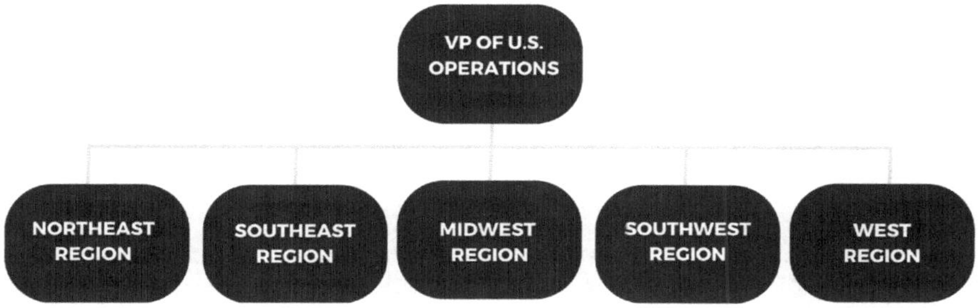

Figure 5.4 Geographic Departmentalization

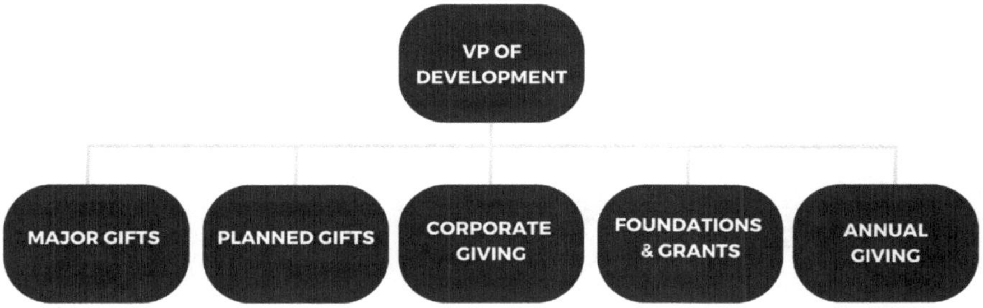

Figure 5.5 Customer Departmentalization

Customer Departmentalization organizes people into departments based on the customer segments or types that they serve, allowing departments to tailor products and services to specific customer groups. In the nonprofit sector, "customers" can refer to any number of categories, such as donors, volunteers, beneficiaries, or service recipients, etc. Figure 5.5 graphically represents how customer departmentalization could be effective in serving the service recipient "customer" in an agency that serves, tailoring the fundraising approach and organizational strategy to each donor category.

Some organizations find that none of these departmentalization options works for the nature of their business, and opt for **matrix departmentalization**, a hybrid structure in which two or more forms of departmentalization are used together. A matrix structure can get complex, however, and there's potential for ambiguity in decision-making and authority due to the dual reporting relationships that characterize a matrix organization, where employees report to more than one manager. Figure 5.6 represents a simplified matrix example of a nonprofit that uses a hybrid of geographic and customer departmentalization.

Choosing the appropriate departmentalization approach is a key decision of organizational design and should be done with care, in assessing the approach that best fits the agency and its mission and objectives.

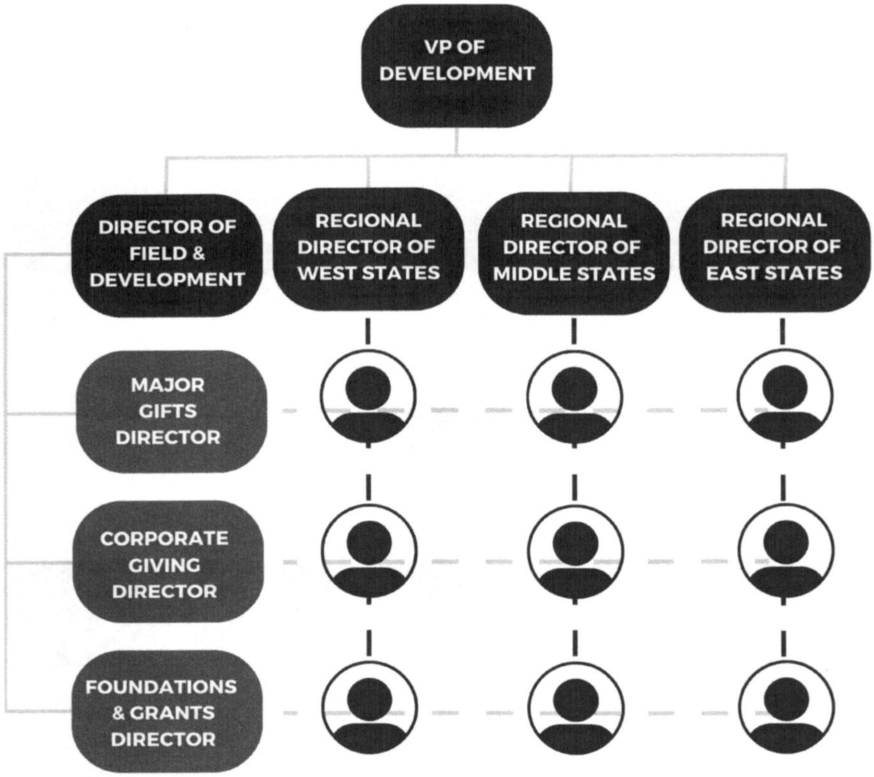

Figure 5.6 Matrix Departmentalization

Hierarchy of Authority

An organizational chart visually represents the chain of command, or reporting lines, in making it clear who reports to whom in the organization. These reporting lines are formally known as hierarchy of authority. **Hierarchy of authority** is the formal structure of levels and positions within an organization that outlines the reporting relationships and the flow of decision-making and communication. In a hierarchy of authority, each position has a specific level of autonomy and authority, with higher-level positions generally having greater degree of both (Robbins & Judge 2018).

Delegation

Departmentalization in organizational structure tells us how people in the organization are grouped and this can easily be represented visually on an organizational chart. Hierarchy of authority shows who reports to whom, and that also is easily discerned by viewing an organizational chart. More difficult to convey, however, and not readily apparent by looking at an org chart, is *how* authority is distributed from those higher in the hierarchy to those below them.

Delegation is the process of assigning authority, responsibility, and tasks from a higher-level position or manager to a subordinate or lower-level employee. Delegation can prove beneficial for the subordinate, as it can empower them to make decisions, take on tasks, and exercise control within their assigned roles, while holding them accountable for the outcomes. Delegation benefits managers, as it helps distribute workloads and promotes efficiency (Malmi 2021).

Centralized organizations are those where delegation is rare, and leaders tend to hold power and decision-making authority without distributing it to lower-level positions. In these organizations, power is held *centrally* by those management positions at the top of that hierarchy of authority seen in the organizational chart.

A **decentralized** organizational structure allows for more delegation, where lower-level positions have more decision-making authority. Instead of concentrating power centrally within managers, it is spread out throughout the organization.

Span of Control

To delegate authority to subordinates, managers must have adequate people resources; in other words, they must have capable and available direct reports to delegate decisions and authority, which is not always the case in the nonprofit sector. **Span of control**, also known as span of management, refers to the number of subordinates or employees that a manager or supervisor can effectively oversee and manage within an organization. It defines the extent to which decision-making, supervision, and communication can be efficiently handled by a single manager (Wallin 2014).

Organizations with a **flat span of control** are those where a manager supervises a relatively large number of subordinates, resulting in a wider organizational hierarchy with fewer management layers. This means that each manager has more accountability, with fewer subordinates to whom to delegate responsibility, and they may struggle in providing adequate supervision and development for a large number of subordinates. The benefit, however, is that leaders can operate efficiently, and communicate easily, with their teams since they work together directly.

Figure 5.7 provides a representation of a flat organization's organizational chart. Just looking at the chart visually makes it clear how flat (or wide) it looks in terms of number of subordinates reporting to a manager. In this example, all positions of this small nonprofit report directly to the executive director.

Organizations with a **tall span of control** are those where a manager supervises a smaller number of subordinates, leading to a narrower organizational

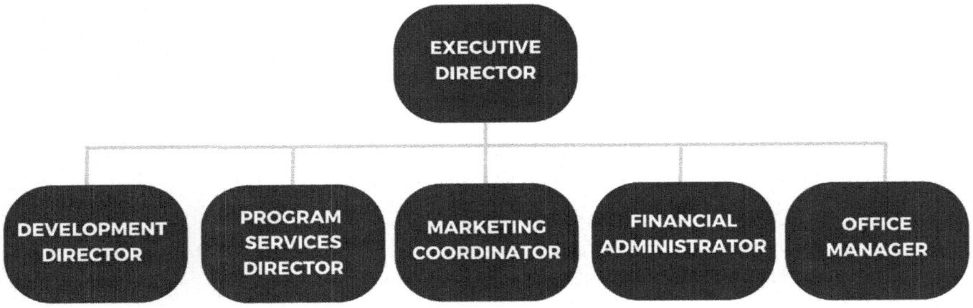

Figure 5.7 Flat Span of Control

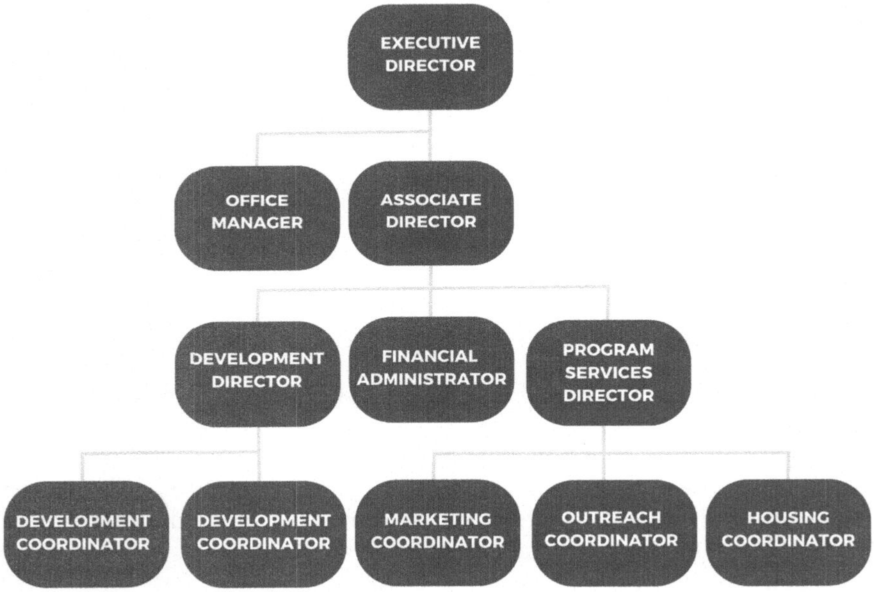

Figure 5.8 Tall Span of Control

hierarchy of authority with more management layers. Tall organizations can result in slower decision-making and communication, as there are multiple layers in which information must flow, but managers spend less time on direct supervision of subordinates, allowing them to focus their time on other priorities.

Figure 5.8 represents a sample nonprofit organizational chart for a tall organization, where there are multiple Filayers of management. In this example, the executive director only provides direct supervision to two subordinates, although the agency has 11 employees in total.

LO 5-4: Recognize the various types of communications in organizations, diagram how communications flow within an organization, and explain the silo effect.

Organizational Design

As noted in the introduction to this chapter, organizational structure is the foundation of organizational design, but design encompasses various aspects beyond structure. Organizational design requires that leaders align these components with the organization's strategy and make changes when processes in the organization are dysfunctional. There are many components of organizational design, and three notable ones are communication channels, rewards and recognition, and culture.

Communication Channels

Facilitating the flow of information within organizations is another aspect of organizational design, and this includes both formal and informal channels, internal and external communications, and varying direction of communications.

Formal communication is the flow of official information through proper, predefined channels and routes. An example might be a marketing coordinator emailing a press release to her media contacts to announce and publicize an upcoming educational program available to the community. Because in this example the communication is being sent to someone outside the organization, it is external. **External communication** involves interactions between an organization and parties outside of it, such as customers, suppliers, stakeholders, and the general public.

Informal communication flows unrestrictedly throughout the organization, often moves rapidly, and is not confined by predetermined channels or established communication pathways. After a weekend fundraising event, as one example, the nonprofit staff might engage in "watercooler talk" the Monday after to catch up and gossip about the event and all that happened. This type of conversation is also an example of **internal communication,** which refers to the exchange of information *within* an organization.

Whether formal or informal and internal or external, the direction of communication can be identified. Communication channels can be **downward,** originating from management and flowing down to lower-level employees; **upward,** flowing from employees to higher-level management; **horizontal** (or lateral), which occurs between individuals or departments on the same level in the hierarchy of authority; or **diagonal,** which cuts across different levels and functional

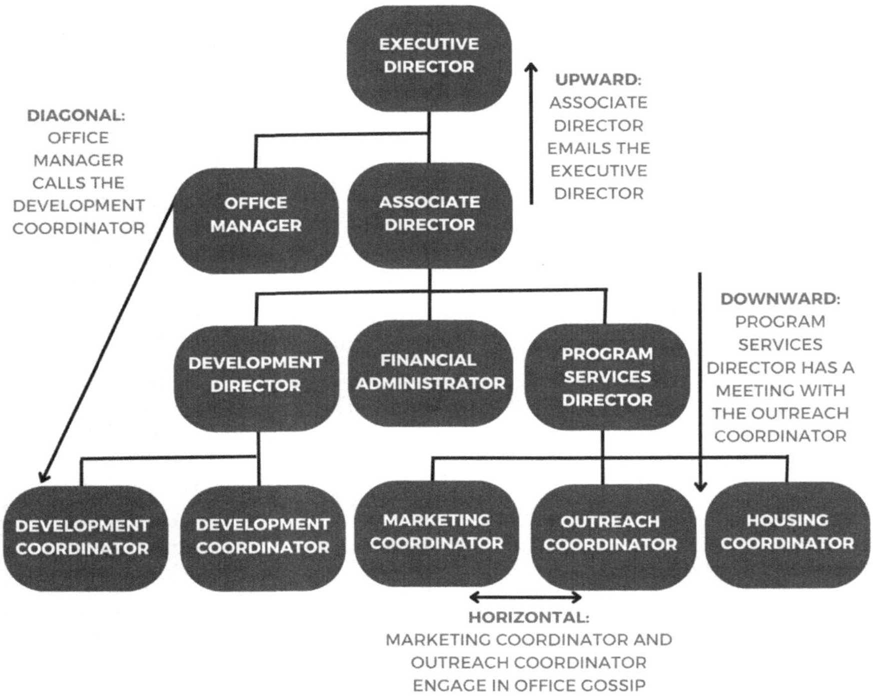

Figure 5.9 Direction of Communication in a Nonprofit

areas of the hierarchy. Unlike horizontal and vertical (upward and downward) communication, diagonal communication involves interactions between those not directly connected by reporting relationships (Robbins & Judge 2018). A depiction of the direction of communication appears in Figure 5.9.

There are numerous communication problems that can arise in organizations, one of which is the **silo effect**, which refers to the isolated and compartmentalized functioning of different departments or teams within an organization, leading to limited communication and stifled collaboration across the organization (Tett 2015). There are numerous causes of the silo effect, one of which is poor organizational structure. Leaders can engage in organizational design to address some of the structural problems that hinder the effective flow of communication, including more clearly communicating lines of authority and reporting relationships, decentralizing to allow for more autonomous decision-making, and better defining roles and responsibilities.

> LO 5-5: Rationalize why performance-based compensation is the best approach when designing reward and recognition programs and how theories of motivation apply to this strategy.

Rewards and Recognition

Another aspect of organizational design is rewards and recognition, which involves designing formal reward and recognition structures that motivate employees to achieve organizational objectives. Chapter 4 examined various theories of motivation, and leaders can take these learnings and apply them to the design of these rewards and recognition programs. Equity theory stresses the need for equitable treatment of employees in allocating outcomes and expectancy theory emphasizes the importance of providing outcomes of value to the employee. Goal-setting theory tells us that employee goals should be SMART, specifically difficult yet achievable, and leaders should provide clear direction and feedback. One simple way to achieve most of the things we know about employee motivation from academic research is to tie pay to performance.

The **performance-based compensation** approach ties organizational outcomes such as compensation, rewards, and recognition to employee performance. This ensures that outcomes are fair and equitable, employees are held accountable in terms of their performance, and employees' individual goals align with the organization's objectives (Miller 2022). Leaders can also survey employees to determine what outcomes they find of value and design the incentives of their organizational rewards and recognition programs around those. When completing performance evaluations, like MBOs, BARS, and 360-degree appraisals, leaders can clearly specify for employees how their performance is measured to set goals and allocate outcomes accordingly using the performance-based compensation approach.

> LO 5-6: Summarize organizational culture, describe the common culture types in nonprofit organizations, and explore how leaders play a key role in shaping culture.

Organizational Culture

Good organizational design has a significant impact **organizational culture,** which refers to the shared values, beliefs, norms, attitudes, and behaviors that define the collective identity and character of an organization (Carvalho 2019). Culture affects ways that employees interact and make decisions and can impact organizational effectiveness and efficiency.

Organizational structure, design, and culture are inextricably linked. The structure established through organizational design can shape and reinforce certain cultural aspects. For instance, a flat, decentralized organizational structure can promote a culture of autonomy and empowerment.

At the heart of culture is values, a topic addressed in length within Chapter 2. As discussed in that chapter, nonprofit organizations should have clear mission, vision, and values. While publishing a list of values and proclaiming their importance is a step, however, it is a different matter to genuinely embody those values through consistent behaviors. It falls upon leaders to take the initiative and ensure these values are actively practiced because, while culture is shaped through a combination of factors, one of the most influential is leadership behavior (Pun 2022).

Leaders can shape culture by leading by example, engaging in effective organizational design, and establishing recognition programs that reinforce cultural values. Organizational culture can take various forms, but some examples of culture types common in the nonprofit sector include:

- Nonprofits with a **mission-driven culture** prioritize mission above all else.
- A **community-focused culture** is one that prioritizes strong connections with local communities and the beneficiaries served by the organization.
- Agencies with a **donor-centric culture** tend to prioritize donors as a stakeholder group.
- An **inclusive culture** is one that emphasizes diversity, equity, and inclusion among all stakeholder groups.
- **Ethical cultures** prioritize ethical and moral standards.

These are just a few examples, and these are by no means mutually exclusive. In fact, many organizations exhibit a *combination* of these cultures. For example, *all* nonprofits should be mission-driven, but that does not mean they have to do so at the expense of being community-centric.

> LO 5-7: Express the reasons why leaders restructure and explain the potential pitfalls of redesigning organizations.

Organizational Restructuring

As previously stated, organizational design involves adapting to change, and in some circumstances, leaders must engage in **organizational restructuring,** which involves making significant changes to an organization's design, which can include its structure, processes, roles, and sometimes even its culture (Robbins & **Judge** 2018).

Restructuring can be relatively minor, such as realigning departments. For example, a nonprofit with a functional organizational structure has separate marketing and PR departments and opts to merge them into one unit. Or, a reporting line in the hierarchy of authority is modified, so a department now reports to a different manager. Occasionally, substantial restructuring takes place, which may involve the elimination of positions, layers of management, or even entire departments, leading to the loss of jobs or even mass layoffs.

While restructuring is sometimes necessary, leaders should approach this carefully, as the significant change resulting from an organizational restructuring can have a negative impact on stakeholders.

Workforce in Crisis: Layoffs to Shortages

The COVID-19 pandemic was financially devastating for many industries, but it hit the nonprofit sector particularly hard. Many agencies were caught completely unaware, with inadequate (or no) crisis plans in place. Many organizations that had spent years with spending policies that poured as much money as possible into mission fulfillment found that they had minimal cash reserves on hand to pay the bills, namely payroll, when in-person fundraising events and other key revenue-funding sources came to a screeching halt in the spring of 2020. As a result, massive furloughs and layoffs ensued that summer, and 18 months later, the nonprofit sector found that the pendulum had swung. After enacting significant reorganizations which included consolidation of department and elimination of large numbers of staff, now that the funding situation had improved and eliminated positions were added back, the sector now found itself in a position of not being able to fill vacant roles, with a whopping workforce shortage of 450,000 positions ("Nonprofit Workforce" 2023). When revenues unexpectedly and/or significantly drop, why is drastic reorganization often the first action of organizations? If you were a nonprofit leader and had to make difficult decisions about layoffs, which positions would you eliminate and which would you preserve? Why?

Takeaways

LO 5-1: The terms organizational design and organizational structure are related concepts that both pertain to how an organization is arranged, but they focus on different aspects. Structure is a static representation of the organization and its architecture, whereas design is a dynamic method of modifying systems that are no longer effective for the organization.

LO 5-2: When designing jobs, leaders can first conduct a job analysis and then apply various approaches to job design to optimize employee motivation and performance. This includes job characteristics theory, which suggests integrating five specific characteristics into a job to create three prime psychological states. Other approaches include specialization to allow employees to focus on a specific task and methods to alleviate employee boredom, such as job rotation, job enrichment, and job enlargement.

LO 5-3: In addition to job design, organizational structure is comprised of departmentalization, which refers to how people are grouped; hierarchy of authority, which identifies levels of positions; delegation, which is the assignment of authority and tasks to a lower-level employee; and span of control, which relates to the number of subordinates supervised by one manager.

LO 5-4: Communications in organizations can be internal or external, formal or informal, and can flow in multiple directions. Downward is from management to lower-level employees, upward is from lower-level employees to higher-level individuals, horizontal is between employees at the same level, and diagonal cuts across all different levels. The silo effect happens when the isolated and compartmentalized functioning of different departments or teams within an organization leads to limited communication and collaboration.

LO 5-5: The various theories of motivation explored previously taught us that leaders need to ensure that rewards are fair and equitable and valued by employees, and individual and organizational goals should be aligned. As such, tying pay to performance with a performance-based compensation plan is the best approach when designing reward and recognition programs.

LO 5-6: Organizational culture refers to the shared values, beliefs, norms, attitudes, and behaviors that define the collective identity and character of an organization, and it is shaped in part by the influence of the organizational leaders. Mission-driven, community-focused, donor-centric, inclusive, and ethical are common culture types in nonprofits.

LO 5-7: Given that organizational design is an ongoing and dynamic process, there is a constant need for leaders to reassess organizational structure, and this sometimes involves making changes through an organizational redesign or restructuring. This is often done in response to changing market conditions or business needs.

Bibliography

Allen, Roger K. "What Is Organizational Design?" *The Center for Organizational Design*, 2015, centerod.com/2012/02/what-is-organizational-design/. Accessed 18 Jun. 2023.

Carvalho, André M., et al. "Operational Excellence, Organisational Culture and Agility: The Missing Link?" *Total Quality Management & Business Excellence*, vol. 30, no. 13–14, 2019, pp. 1495–1514.

Colquitt, Jason, Jeffery LePine, and Michael Wesson. *Organizational Behavior: Improving Performance and Commitment in the Workplace*. McGraw Hill, New York, 2021. Print.

Foss, Nicolai J., et al. "Why Complementary HRM Practices Impact Performance: The Case of Rewards, Job Design, and Work Climate in a Knowledge-Sharing Context." *Human Resource Management*, vol. 54, no. 6, 2015, pp. 955–976.

Hackman, J.R., and Greg R. Oldham. *Work Redesign*. Addison-Wesley, Reading, MA, 1980.

Hsieh, An-Tien, and Hui-Yu Chao. "A Reassessment of the Relationship between Job Specialization, Job Rotation and Job Burnout: Example of Taiwan's High-Technology Industry." *International Journal of Human Resource Management*, vol. 15, no. 6, 2004, pp. 1108–1123.

Kuman, Anuj. "6 Approaches to Job Design." *GetUpLearn*, 17 Nov. 2022, getuplearn.com/blog/approaches-to-job-design/. Accessed 18 Jun. 2023.

Malmi, Teemu, et al. "Culture and Management Control Interdependence: An Analysis of Control Choices that Complement the Delegation of Authority in Western Cultural Regions." *Accounting, Organizations and Society*, vol. 86, 2020, p. 101116.

Miller, Stephen. "Time for Nonprofits to Revisit Performance Management and Pay Strategies." *Society for Human Resource Management*, 14 Jun. 2022, www.shrm.org/resourcesandtools/hr-topics/compensation/pages/time-for-nonprofits-to-revisit-performance-management-and-pay-strategies.aspx. Accessed 22 Jun. 2023.

"Nonprofit Workforce Shortages: A Crisis That Affects Everyone." *National Council of Nonprofits*, 22 Mar. 2023, www.councilofnonprofits.org/reports/nonprofit-workforce-shortages-crisis-affects-everyone.

"Pandemic and Workforce Shortage Relief for Nonprofits." *Council of Nonprofits*, 13 Jun. 2022, www.councilofnonprofits.org/sites/default/files/media/documents/2023/nonprofit-pandemic-workforce-shortage-relief-letter.pdf. Accessed 18 Jun. 2023. – Council letter

Pun, Elizabeth. "Why Defining Your Nonprofit's Culture Will Be the Most Important Thing You Do This Year." *Classy*, 28 June 2022, www.classy.org/blog/why-defining-your-nonprofits-culture-will-be-the-most-important-thing-you-do-this-year/.

Robbins, Stephen P., and Tim Judge. *Essentials of Organizational Behavior*. Pearson, New York, NY, 2018.

Tett, Gillian. *The Silo Effect: The Peril of Expertise and the Promise of Breaking Down Barriers*. Simon & Schuster, New York, 2015.

Thompson, Jayne. "Difference between Organizational Structure & Design." *Houston Chronicle*, 5 Mar. 2019, smallbusiness.chron.com/difference-between-organizational-structure-design-3839.html. Accessed 21 Jun. 2023.

"Understanding Organizational Structures." *Society for Human Resource Management*, www.shrm.org/resourcesandtools/tools-and-samples/toolkits/pages/understanding-organizational-structures.aspx#:~:text=Five%20elements%20create%20an%20organizational,control%20and%20chain%20of%20command. Accessed 19 Jun. 2023.

Van Vulpen, Erik. "Job Design: A Practitioner's Guide." *Academy to Innovate HR*, Jan. 2023, www.aihr.com/blog/job-design/. Accessed 3 Jun. 2023.

Wallin, Linda, et al. "Span of Control and the Significance for Public Sector Managers' Job Demands: A Multilevel Study." *Economic and Industrial Democracy*, vol. 35, no. 3, 2014, pp. 455–481.

6 Leadership and Decision-Making

Learning Outcomes

After reading this chapter, you should be able to:

LO 6-1: Describe the seven common general leadership styles.
LO 6-2: Define situational leadership and identify the four situational leadership styles.
LO 6-3: Differentiate between programmed and nonprogrammed decisions.
LO 6-4: Apply the rational decision-making model to nonprofit decision-making.
LO 6-5: Specify the various problems that can arise in the decision-making process.
LO 6-6: Identify the three ethical frameworks that can be applied to ethical decision-making in nonprofits.
LO 6-7: Employ the four-component model within the decision-making process.

> LO 6-1: Describe the seven common general leadership styles.

General Leadership Styles

As noted in Chapter 4, nonprofits are led by an executive director who is overseen by a board of directors with shared responsibility for making staffing decisions, engaging in strategic planning, and making crucial determinations to advance the organization's mission. Effective leaders impact employee satisfaction, performance, and effectiveness (Turner & Muller 2005) and contribute more to the workplace compared to any other human component of the organization (Gibson 1991).

Leadership is the use of power and influence to direct the activities of followers toward goal achievement (Colquitt 2021), and the executive director's approach to leadership can have a significant impact on the success

DOI: 10.4324/9781003380030-8

of a nonprofit. Executive directors do not just lead the organization's paid staff, but they also must manage other stakeholder relationships, including their board, volunteers, and donors, all of which may require slightly different approaches. Nonprofits are also influenced by other organizational leaders, such as the board president, who may have a different leadership approach than the one embodied by the executive director.

General leadership styles represent an overarching leadership philosophy that a leader may consistently apply across various situations, including their methods, characteristics, and behaviors, when directing their teams. Over time, researchers have identified multiple leadership styles, with some leadership taxonomies describing just three broad leadership styles (autocratic, democratic, and laissez-faire) and others expanding to many more categories. While there is no definitive, universally accepted categorization approach to identifying general leadership styles, seven of them are described below, and illustrated in Figure 6.1.

The Greek prefix auto- means "self" ("Auto"), so it should come as no surprise that **autocratic** leaders prefer to make decisions by themselves. With this style, the leader makes decisions alone without asking for the opinions or suggestions of the employees in the work unit (Colquitt 2021). This decision-making style is sometimes alternately referred to as authoritarian leadership.

Democracy refers to a rule of majority, so it makes sense that the **democratic** leadership style refers to an approach that distributes responsibility among the membership, empowers group members, and aids the group's decision-making process (Dyczkowska 2018). Unlike autocratic leaders, democratic leaders do not make decisions unilaterally, but through consensus and gaining the buy-in of others. This style is sometimes referred to as participative.

The term laissez-faire has French origins, meaning "allow to do" ("Laissez-Faire"), and the **laissez-faire** leader uses a hands-off leadership approach where the leader avoids leadership duties altogether and allows their followers to have the autonomy to make their own decisions and manage their own tasks (Colquitt 2021).

Transformational leaders motivate their teams by establishing an inspiring vision and promoting individual development. They frequently serve as role models, foster a constructive work environment, and prioritize empowering their team members to achieve their utmost capabilities. They are successful because they are capable of stimulating, mobilizing, and inspiring their employees to achieve the desired objectives (Boehm 2015).

Instead of leading by inspiring, some leaders tend to approach management as a transaction and use a system of rewards and punishments to manage their teams. This is called transactional leadership. **Transactional** leaders generally establish clear expectations, monitor performance closely, and provide rewards for meeting goals or outcomes (Eagly 2003).

A leadership style that is often described in the nonprofit sector is **servant leadership**. This style emphasizes the leader's primary role as a servant to their team or organization, rather than as a traditional authority figure, as

Figure 6.1 General Leadership Styles

they aim to serve and support their team by providing resources, removing obstacles, and fostering a collaborative environment. It is important to note that while the term is still widely used, "servant leader" is considered by some to be outdated and even problematic (Jetter 2020), and others criticize it because it denotes a lack of authority of the manager and the function of management in the organization.

Another leadership category has emerged in more recent years that depicts the leader's need to support their team, but without necessarily diminishing their role as an authority figure. **Empathetic** leadership emphasizes active listening, compassion, and creation of a supportive environment in understanding and addressing the emotions, needs, and perspectives of team members. Given the nature of nonprofit work, an empathic leadership style can prove beneficial, and studies show there is a significant relationship between empathetic leadership, job satisfaction and performance (Kock 2019), and greater goal progress (Scott 2010).

While leaders may certainly embody the characteristics of one of these leadership styles, effective leaders often blend elements from *multiple* leadership styles based on the situation, their team's needs, and their personal strengths. The situational nature of leadership is explored below.

LO 6-2: Define situational leadership and identify the four situational leadership styles.

Situational Leadership Styles

As noted above, while most nonprofit leaders' general leadership styles can fit within one of the previously identified seven categories, the when, where, how, and why of applying these different styles can vary. This is called **situational leadership.** Situational leadership styles and general leadership styles are not mutually exclusive; rather, they are complementary and can be used in conjunction with each other (Crosby 2021).

Situational Leadership Model

The **situational leadership model** was first introduced by Paul Hersey and Ken Blanchard in 1969 and proposed that effective leadership involves adjusting one's leadership style based on each unique situation, including tasks and relationships, to meet the needs of the team or team members (Thompson, Geir & Glasø 2015). It identifies four situational leadership styles: telling, selling, participating, and delegating, and is based not just on the leadership itself, but also the development level, referred to as maturity or "readiness," of the subordinate (Thompson, Geir & Vecchio 2009).

This theory proposes that leaders adjust their leadership style according to situational factors, and one of these factors is the level of readiness exhibited by their followers. **Readiness** is broadly defined as the degree to which employees have the ability and the willingness to accomplish their specific tasks (Colquitt 2021). The leadership styles introduced in the situational leadership model are telling, selling, participating, and delegating (Serrat 1993) and are noted in Figure 6.2.

As the name implies, the **telling** leadership style involves directly telling a follower what to do. This includes providing specific instruction and close supervision. This approach is effective when leading a follower with **low readiness,** which refers to a follower who is unable, unwilling, or too insecure to do the task. Telling requires a higher degree of leadership than the other styles, and the leader's clear direction is intended to build the confidence and competence of their followers.

A **selling** approach is when a leader attempts to convince a follower of their ideas by explaining task directions in a persuasive manner. The leader must emphasize the importance of the task and provide step-by-step guidance, ensuring that the follower understands what needs to be done and how to do it effectively (Thompson, Geir & Vecchio 2009). This style is aimed at ensuring that the follower understands what needs to be done and how to

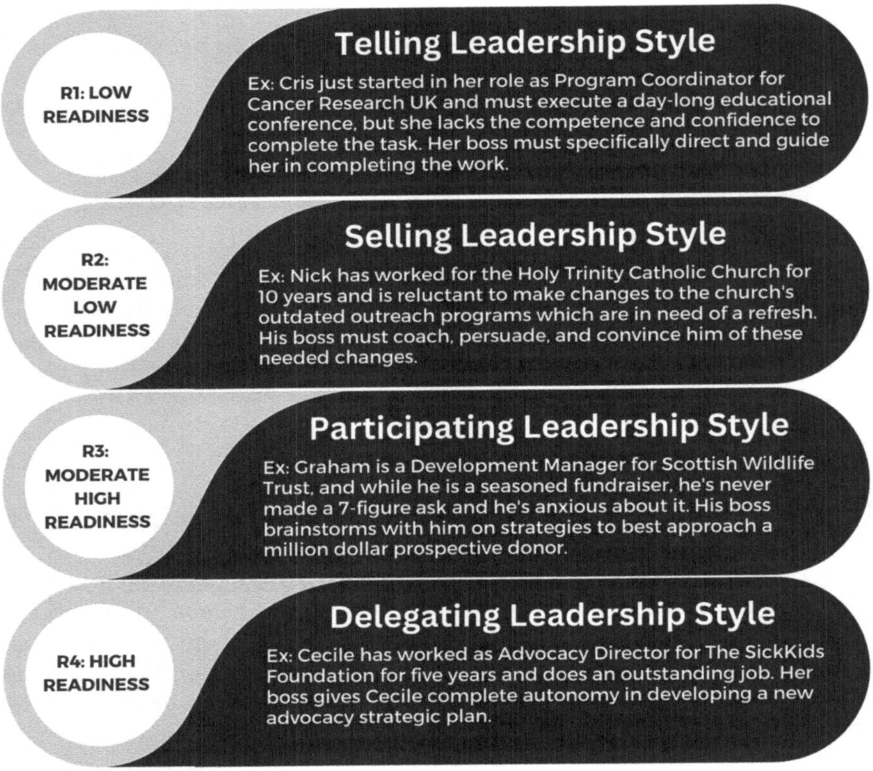

Figure 6.2 Situational Leadership in Nonprofits

do it effectively, and works when leading followers with **moderate low readiness**, which refers to a follower who is confident, but not willing or able to do the task (Hersey & Blanchard 1997).

A **participating** approach involves shared ideas and decisions to gain followers' commitment to the task and foster a sense of mutual understanding and cooperation. The leader involves the team members in discussions and provides support and encouragement, fostering a positive and empowering work environment. This style is effective when leading followers with **moderate high readiness**, which occurs when a follower is capable but not confident in doing a task (Hersey & Blanchard 1997.

Finally, the **delegating** style calls for a leader to empower their followers to take responsibility to independently complete tasks (Thompson, Gier & Vecchio2009). This approach is effective when a follower has **high readiness**, which happens when the follower is capable, confident, experienced, and needs little direction to complete the task.

This is a simplified explanation of the situational leadership theory, and it is important to note that leadership is just one variable of leadership effectiveness. Other factors that can influence leadership effectiveness include the characteristics of leaders, the characteristics of followers, and other characteristics of the situation besides leader-employee relations (Serrat 1993). The key takeaway here is to understand the frameworks that examine the styles and decision-making approaches of leaders.

LO 6-3: Differentiate between programmed and nonprogrammed decisions.

Decision-Making

Decision-making is an important component of leadership, and this is influenced by leadership style. Good leaders are decisive and make decisions based on facts and removed from bias. Nonprofit leaders must make countless decisions daily, from significant to minor ones, and these decisions are generally made without the leader putting much thought into the process behind their decision-making. Understanding the formalized process of decision-making, and being cognizant of it, however, can help leaders in making better decisions.

What are typically considered easy decisions are **programmed decisions**, as these are made automatically with little consideration because of prior knowledge that allows for immediate recognition of the situation and course of action to be taken. **Nonprogrammed decisions**, however, are more complex and are made when a problem is new, complex, or not recognized (Colquitt 2021).

LO 6-4: Apply the rational decision-making model to nonprofit decision-making.

Not surprisingly, staff in management positions are more often faced with having to make more of the complex nonprogrammed decisions than those who are not in leadership roles. When challenged with a difficult or nonprogrammed decision, decision-makers can turn to the **rational decision-making model** as a step-by-step approach to the decision-making process that allows them to use facts and information to maximize outcomes by examining all available alternatives (Uzonwanne 2015). While there are multiple models that outline differing steps, most can be generalized into six basic steps, listed below and represented in Figure 6.3.

The first step is to *identify the problem* that requires a solution, which may involve a **gap analysis** to get a better handle on the difference that exists between

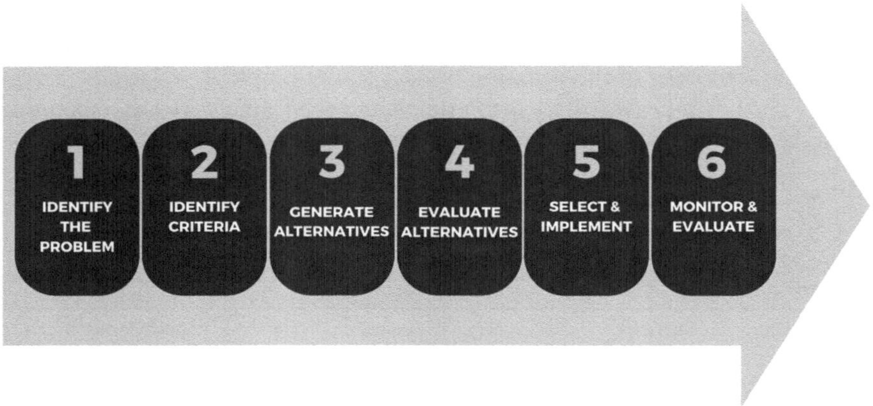

Figure 6.3 Rational Decision-Making Model

current and desired states (Hanna 2021). Next, decision-makers should *identify criteria* for what success will look like at the end of the process in closing that gap. The third step is to *generate alternatives* that might be potential solutions. During this step, leaders should avoid evaluating these alternatives, and instead focus on identifying as many potential solutions as possible.

Once potential solutions are determined, decision-makers should then, and only then, *evaluate alternatives* by gathering and using facts to assess each alternative against criteria they previously defined. This includes analyzing the potential outcomes, risks and benefits, and costs of each outcome. After completing this evaluation, leaders can then *select and implement* the best possible option and take action. The final step is to *monitor and evaluate* the implementation and measure outcomes to ensure that the chosen option is proving successful in closing the identified gap (Colquitt 2021).

One big assumption of the rational decision-making model is that it gives the benefit of the doubt to decision-makers that they are rational. Problems can occur, however, when applying the model to real-world applications and considering the human beings making the decisions (Campitelli 2010). Some of these issues are that problems cannot always be clearly defined; individuals are not always capable of recognizing and articulating the problem; and that there are real-life constraints related to time, financial resources, or other factors that might hinder the implementation of the decision. Furthermore, human beings, being fallible, can be susceptible to various decision-making issues.

LO 6-5: Specify the various problems that can arise in the decision-making process.

Decision-Making Problems

When making decisions, particularly those more complex nonprogrammed decisions, individuals should take care to avoid some common decision-making problems such as bounded rationality, satisficing, analysis paralysis, decision avoidance, decision fatigue, projection bias, stereotyping, and escalation of commitment.

The rational decision-making model calls for decision-makers to evaluate information by gathering facts, but sometimes decisions are made with incorrect or limited information. **Bounded rationality** is the concept that human decision-makers are limited in their ability to fully process information and make fully rational choices due to cognitive constraints and time limitations (Schwarz 2022). Leaders, especially in resource-strapped nonprofits, are often pressed to make decisions quickly, without the luxury of time to fully engage in a decision-making process, including gathering facts. **Satisficing** occurs when decision-makers select the first acceptable alternative considered (Colquitt 2021) and is another problematic potential byproduct of time-pressed, resource-constrained nonprofit leaders making decisions.

While time constraints can create decision-making problems around making decisions too impulsively, paradoxically, excessive time spent on deciding can be another problem. **Analysis paralysis** arises when excessive scrutiny or overthinking of options prevents an individual or a group from reaching a decision (Talbert 2017). **Decision avoidance** happens when an individual avoids making a choice by postponing it or by seeking an easy way out that involves no action or no change (Anderson 2003). This can happen for several reasons, one of which is fear of making the wrong choice or facing potential consequences. Both analysis paralysis and decision avoidance can occur in nonprofits due to immense scrutiny and pressure to efficiently manage scarce resources and be good stewards of donor contributions.

Nonprofit leaders face a multitude of decisions, which can result in **decision fatigue**, a state where the limited reserve of stamina for making decisions becomes drained (Polman 2016), potentially leading to impulsive or suboptimal decisions.

Sometimes decision-making problems arise due to faulty perceptions. This includes **projection bias**, which occurs when people project their own thoughts, motives, and attitudes on other people (Colquitt 2021), and **stereotyping**, which happens when assumptions are made about others on the basis of their membership in a social group (Ashforth 1989).

The final type of decision-making problem occurs when a decision starts to go wrong. **Escalation of commitment** occurs when individuals continue to invest in a decision or project, even in the face of negative outcomes, to avoid admitting failure or losing face. Another way of thinking of this is "throwing good money after bad" (Ross 1993).

These represent only a selection of the numerous decision-making challenges that may emerge. Decision-making constitutes a crucial aspect of leadership, and successful leaders adhere to a data-driven decision-making approach while remaining mindful of potential obstacles, making every effort to prevent their occurrence.

> LO 6-6: Identify the three ethical frameworks that can be applied to ethical decision-making in nonprofits.

Ethical Decision-Making

Some decisions are further complicated by presenting an ethical dilemma. Chapter 3 provided an overview of ethics in nonprofits and touched upon some of the common ethical dilemmas in the nonprofit sector. Given the unique ethical challenges that can occur within nonprofits, coupled with the many decisions that nonprofit leaders must make each day, it is helpful for these leaders to consider formalized approaches and guidelines to ethical decision-making. **Ethical frameworks** are structured systems of principles and values that guide individuals in making moral decisions and evaluating right and wrong ("What Are").

While there are many approaches posited by ethicists and organizational behavior researchers, three common frameworks employed by nonprofit leaders to guide ethical decision-making include: Association of Fundraising Professionals (AFP) Guidelines, the four-component model, and the mission test. These guidelines may be used individually, or in concert with one another.

AFP Guidelines

The AFP, founded in 1960, is a nonprofit organization with the mission to empower individuals and organizations to practice ethical fundraising through professional education, networking, research, and advocacy ("AFP Vision" 2018). The organization provides several **AFP guidelines**, available at no cost to nonprofit fundraising professionals, including the Donor Bill of Rights, which outlines ten rights of donors that should be fulfilled by the beneficiary organization, and the AFP Code of Ethical Standards ("The Donor" 2019). Consulting these guidelines can be useful when making decisions, particularly those that present as an ethical dilemma or decision.

The Mission Test

When pressed for a quick decision or ethical dilemma, one rudimentary approach nonprofit leaders can easily apply is the "**mission test**," which involves simply asking "Which course of action aligns most effectively with and supports the organizational mission?" Naturally, this approach is not perfect; as mentioned earlier, it can result in the rationalization of bending rules to better fulfill the mission. However, recognizing the mission as a pivotal element in decision-making is of utmost importance.

In addition to the mission test, some also use the "mirror test," which challenges leaders to ask themselves the question, "could I look myself in the mirror and feel good about myself after making this choice?" (Kouchaki 2023), or the "publicity test," which asks leaders to consider, "could I defend this choice if it made the front page of the newspaper tomorrow?" (Harris 2014).

A more sophisticated approach to ethical decision-making in nonprofits involves applying the mission test as part of the four-component model, described below, and illustrated in Figure 6.4.

> LO 6-7: Employ the four-component model within the decision-making process.

Four-Component Model

The **four-component model of ethical decision-making** is another approach to ethical decision-making and is drawn from research in social psychology (Colquitt 2021). This theory, illustrated in Figure 6.4, argues that when confronted with a moral dilemma, individuals move through a multistage, interactive sequence of psychological processes: moral awareness, moral judgment, moral intention, and moral action. Any failure during the process

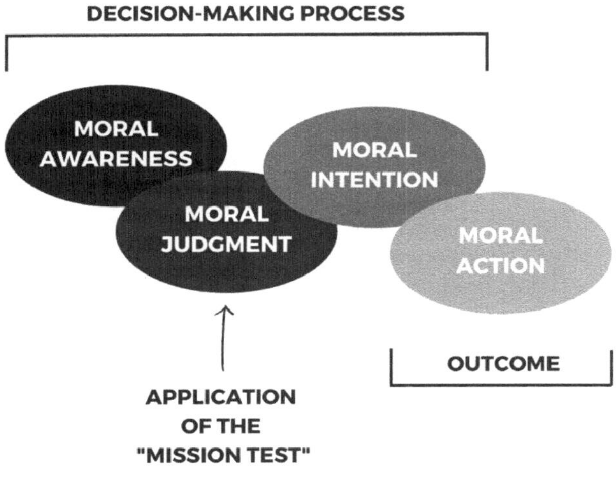

Figure 6.4 Four-Component Model in Nonprofits

can result in an unethical decision and ultimately lead to unethical behavior (Lincoln 2010).

Moral awareness is the recognition that a moral issue exists and the ability to discern the ethical dilemma in a problematic scenario and is the first step of the four-component model (Reynolds 2006). The next step is **moral judgment**, which moves beyond simple recognition of a moral issue and involves the evaluation of choices and outcomes to explore which action is morally justified (Brown 2023). It is at this point that nonprofit leaders can apply the mission test. This means that while evaluating the various choices, leaders need to carefully consider the question, "Of these choices, which aligns most effectively with and supports the organizational mission?"

The third step of the process is **moral intention**, which refers to the desire of the decision-maker to *want* to commit to the moral course of action, meaning that they are willing to prioritize moral values over their personal values (Wren 2010). And the final step is **moral action**, which refers to the actual behavior in the situation and outcome of the process (Rest 1999). While some leaders end up engaging in these steps without even being aware of the process, mindful attention to following the four-component model can assure a greater likelihood of ethical decisions.

Takeaways

LO 6-1: There are several categories to describe general leadership styles, and some of the common ones include autocratic, democratic, laissez-faire, transformational, transactional, servant, and empathetic.

LO 6-2: The situational leadership model calls for leaders to adjust their leadership style based on each unique situation, including tasks and relationships, to meet the needs of the team or team members. In addition to the general leadership styles, there are four situational leadership styles, including telling, selling, participating, and delegating.

LO 6-3: Programmed decisions are made automatically with little consideration because prior knowledge allows for immediate recognition of the situation and course of action to be taken. In contrast, nonprogrammed decisions are more complex and are made when a problem is new, complex, or not recognized.

LO 6-4: The rational decision-making model helps leaders make more informed decisions through implementation of six steps: identify the problem, identify criteria, generate alternatives, evaluate alternatives, select and implement, and monitor and evaluate.

LO 6-5: Common decision-making problems include bounded rationality, satisficing, analysis paralysis, decision avoidance and fatigue, projection bias, stereotyping, and escalation of commitment.

LO 6-6: Three common ethical guidelines used in the nonprofit sector are the AFP guidelines, the mission test, and the four-component model to ethical decision-making.

LO 6-7: The four-component model provides four steps of ethical decision-making: moral awareness, moral judgment, moral intention, and moral action.

Bibliography

"AFP Vision, Mission and Guiding Principles." *Association of Fundraising Professionals*, 3 Sept. 2018, afpglobal.org/afp-vision-mission-and-guiding-principles.

Anderson, Christopher J. "The Psychology of Doing Nothing: Forms of Decision Avoidance Result from Reason and Emotion." *Psychological Bulletin*, vol. 129, no. 1, 2003, pp. 139–167.

Ashforth, Blake E., and Fred Mael. "Social Identity Theory and the Organization." *The Academy of Management Review*, vol. 14, no. 1, 1989, pp. 20–39.

"Auto-." *Etymology*, www.etymonline.com/word/auto-. Accessed 28 July 2023.

Boehm, S.A., Dwertmann, D.J.G., Bruch, H. and Shamir, B. "The Missing Link? Investigating Organizational Identity Strength and Transformational Leadership Climate as Mechanisms That Connect CEO Charisma with Firm Performance." *The Leadership Quarterly, Elsevier*, vol. 26, no. 2, 2015, pp. 156–171.

Brown, Étienne, and EBSCOhost. *Moral Judgement: An Introduction through Anglo-American, German and French Philosophy*. Rowman & Littlefield, Lanham, 2023.

Campitelli, Guillermo, and Fernand Gobet. "Herbert Simon's Decision-Making Approach: Investigation of Cognitive Processes in Experts." *Review of General Psychology*, vol. 14, no. 4, 2010, pp. 354–364.

Colquitt, Jason, Jeffery LePine, and Michael Wesson. *Organizational Behavior: Improving Performance and Commitment in the Workplace*. McGraw Hill, New York, 2021. Print.

Crosby, Gilmore. "Lewin's Democratic Style of Situational Leadership: A Fresh Look at a Powerful OD Model." *The Journal of Applied Behavioral Science*, vol. 57, no. 3, 2021, pp. 398–401.

Dyczkowska, Joanna, and Tomasz Dyczkowski. "Democratic Or Autocratic Leadership Style? Participative Management and its Links to Rewarding Strategies and Job Satisfaction in SMEs." *Athens Journal of Business & Economics (Online)*, vol. 4, no. 2, 2018, pp. 193–218.

Eagly, Alice H., Mary C. Johannesen-Schmidt, and Marloes L. van Engen. "Transformational, Transactional, and Laissez-Faire Leadership Styles: A Meta-Analysis Comparing Women and Men." *Psychological Bulletin*, vol. 129, no. 4, 2003, pp. 569–591.

Gibson, J.L., Donnelly, J.H., and Ivancevich, J.M. *Organizations: Behaviour, Structure, Processes*. Business Publications, Plano, TX, 1991.

Hanna, Katie Terrell, and Francesca Sales. "What Is Gap Analysis and How Does It Work?" *CIO, TechTarget*, 29 Oct. 2021, www.techtarget.com/searchcio/definition/gap-analysis.

Harris, Jared D., Brian T. Moriarty, and Andrew C. Wicks eds. *Public Trust in Business*, Cambridge University Press, Cambridge, England, 2014.

Hersey, Paul, and Kenneth H. Blanchard. "Situational leadership." *Dean's Forum*. Vol. 12, no. 2, 1997.

Jetter, Rick. "The Problem with Servant Leadership." *Plug-In, plug-in*, 6 July 2020, www.rickjetter.com/single-post/the-problem-with-servant-leadership.

Kock, Ned, et al. "Empathetic Leadership: How Leader Emotional Support and Understanding Influences Follower Performance." *Journal of Leadership & Organizational Studies*, vol. 26, no. 2, 2019, pp. 217–236.

Kouchaki, Maryam, et al. "Are You as Ethical as You Think You Are?" *Greater Good*, greatergood.berkeley.edu/article/item/are_you_as_ethical_as_you_think_you_are. Accessed 29 June 2023.
"Laissez-Faire Definition & Meaning." *Merriam-Webster*, www.merriam-webster.com/dictionary/laissez-faire. Accessed 28 July 2023.
Lincoln, Sarah H., and Elizabeth K. Holmes. "The Psychology of Making Ethical Decisions: What Affects the Decision?" *Psychological Services*, vol. 7, no. 2, 2010, pp. 57–64.
Polman, Evan, and Kathleen D. Vohs. "Decision Fatigue, Choosing for Others, and Self-Construal." *Social Psychological & Personality Science*, vol. 7, no. 5, 2016, pp. 471–478.
Rest, James R., et al. "DIT2: Devising and Testing a Revised Instrument of Moral Judgment." *Journal of Educational Psychology*, vol. 91, no. 4, 1999, pp. 644–659.
Reynolds, Scott J. "Moral Awareness and Ethical Predispositions: Investigating the Role of Individual Differences in the Recognition of Moral Issues." *Journal of Applied Psychology*, vol. 91, no. 1, 2006, pp. 233–243.
Ross, Jerry, and Barry M. Staw. "Organizational Escalation and Exit: Lessons from the Shoreham Nuclear Power Plant." *Academy of Management Journal*, vol. 36, no. 4, 1993, pp. 701–732.
Schwarz, Gary, Tom Christensen, and Xufeng Zhu. "Bounded Rationality, Satisficing, Artificial Intelligence, and Decision-Making in Public Organizations: The Contributions of Herbert Simon." *Public Administration Review*, vol. 82, no. 5, 2022, pp. 902–904.
Scott, Brent A., et al. "A Daily Investigation of the Role of Manager Empathy on Employee Well-being." *Organizational Behavior and Human Decision Processes*, vol. 113, no. 2, 2010, pp. 127–140.
Serrat, Olivier. "Review of Situational Leadership® After 25 Years—A Retrospective (Blanchard, Zigarmi, & Nelson, 1993)." *Leading Solutions*. Springer, Singapore.
Talbert, Bonnie. "Overthinking and Other Minds: The Analysis Paralysis." *Social Epistemology*, vol. 31, no. 6, 2017, pp. 545–556.
"The Donor Bill of Rights." *Association of Fundraising Professionals*, 23 Jan. 2019, afpglobal.org/donor-bill-rights.
Thompson, Geir, and Lars Glasø. "Situational Leadership Theory: A Test from Three Perspectives." *Leadership & Organization Development Journal*, vol. 36, no. 5, 2015, pp. 527–544.
Thompson, Geir, and Robert P. Vecchio. "Situational Leadership Theory: A Test of Three Versions." *The Leadership Quarterly*, vol. 20, no. 5, 2009, pp. 837–848.
Turner, J.R. and Muller, R. "The Project Manager's Leadership Style as a Success Factor on Projects: A Literature Review." *Project Management Journal*, vol. 36, no. 2, 2005, pp. 49–61.
Uzonwanne, Francis. "Leadership Styles and Decision-Making Models among Corporate Leaders in Non-Profit Organizations in North America: Leadership Styles and Decision-Making Models." *Journal of Public Affairs*, vol. 15, no. 3, 2015, pp. 287–299.
"What Are Ethical Frameworks?" *Plone Site*, aese.psu.edu/teachag/curriculum/modules/bioethics-1/what-are-ethical-frameworks. Accessed 29 June 2023.
Wren, Thomas E., and Thomas E. Wren. *Moral Obligations: Action, Intention, and Valuation*. Transaction Publishers, New Brunswick, NJ, 2010.

Part 3

Volunteers

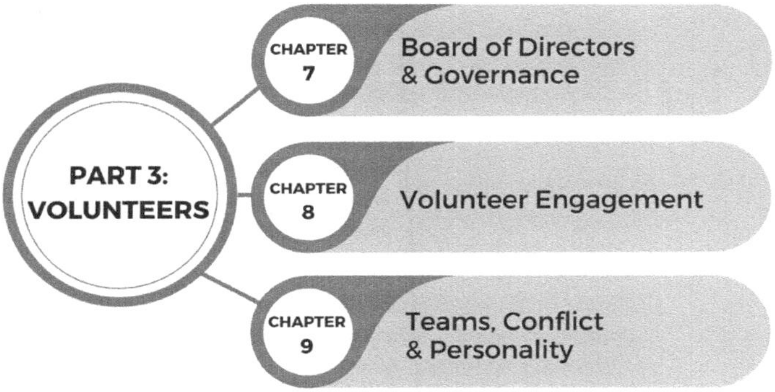

7 Board of Directors and Governance

Learning Outcomes

After reading this chapter, you should be able to:

LO 7-1: Describe the concept of nonprofit governance and explain the role that a board of directors plays.
LO 7-2: Summarize the core legal responsibilities and obligations of a non-profit board of directors.
LO 7-3: Distinguish between the two primary types of nonprofit boards.
LO 7-4: Categorize the common types of nonprofit advisory boards and explain when, how, why, and for how long they are established.
LO 7-5: Describe nonprofit board leadership positions, explain their relationship with staff, and discuss how board members are selected.
LO 7-6: Evaluate how nonprofit boards of directors make decisions.
LO 7-7: Explain ways nonprofit leaders evaluate board performance and engagement.

> LO 7-1: Describe the concept of nonprofit governance and explain the role that a board of directors plays.

The Role of the Board

Nonprofit governance refers to the system of policies, practices, and processes that guide the management and decision-making within a nonprofit organization. It encompasses the structure and mechanisms through which a nonprofit's leadership, including its board of directors, executive leadership, and management, work together to ensure the organization's mission is carried out effectively and ethically ("Good Governance"). While corporate governance is a well-studied area, research and development of theory into nonprofit governance is underdeveloped (Coule 2015).

DOI: 10.4324/9781003380030-10

Nonprofit governance refers not just to people, but also practice and policy such as mission and values, accountability, ethical practices, and performance evaluation, much of which was covered in Section 1 of this book. The *people* aspects of governance, such as executive leadership and staff, were also addressed in Section 1. This chapter, however, addresses the other critical people component of governance, the nonprofit board of directors.

In most cases, nonprofit organizations are legally required to have a board of directors. A **board of directors** is a group of individuals elected or appointed to provide oversight, make strategic decisions, and guide the activities of an organization, ensuring that the nonprofit operates in accordance with its mission and relevant laws (Trower 2013). This is a general definition, but it is important to note that there are two different types of nonprofit boards, governing and advisory, covered in detail below. Some of what is discussed in this section applies specifically to governing boards.

Many of the components to a nonprofit's structure are set forth in their **bylaws**, which are a written set of rules and regulations that outline the internal structure, governance, and operations of the organization, including details about board composition, decision-making processes, and key policies. The specific requirements for the composition and responsibilities of a nonprofit's board dictated in the bylaws can vary based on the laws of the jurisdiction in which the organization is registered, as well as the specific needs of the nonprofit. However, having a board is a common and fundamental aspect of nonprofit governance and accountability. Unlike most corporate boards, nonprofit board members are typically *not* compensated ("Board Roles") but serve as volunteer leaders of the organization.

While the matter of compensation between the two differs, the role of a nonprofit board is the same of that of a for-profit corporate board. Board members are the fiduciaries who steer the organization toward a sustainable future by adopting sound, ethical, and legal governance and financial management policies, as well as by making sure the nonprofit has adequate resources to advance its mission. A **fiduciary** refers to a legal or ethical relationship of trust and confidence where one party (the fiduciary) is obligated to act in the best interests of another party, putting the other party's needs and interests ahead of their own ("Fiduciary Duty" 2022).

Another distinction of nonprofit boards is that they generally tend to get more involved in the organization's operations, which can lead to tensions around perceived micromanagement and blurring of the lines between the roles of senior staff versus board leaders (Trower 2013). The importance of the volunteer-staff partnership, and finding ways to strike a balanced relationship, is a topic covered in the next chapter.

> LO 7-2: Summarize the core legal responsibilities and obligations of a nonprofit board of directors.

Board Duties and Responsibilities

Legal Responsibilities

According to the Council of Nonprofits, a nonprofit board has three primary legal duties, known as the "duty of care," "duty of loyalty," and "duty of obedience," represented in Figure 7.1 ("Board Roles"). **Duty of care** means that a board "takes care" of the organization by ensuring prudent use of all resources, encompassing facilities, personnel, and the nonprofit's reputation. **Duty of loyalty** is the set of obligations to ensure that no conflicts of interest exist, the interests of the nonprofit are put ahead of any individual, and that work is always conducted in a manner to advance the organizational mission. **Duty of obedience** refers to the compliance of relevant laws and regulations and ensures that the organization is committed and focused on its mission, vision, and values and adheres to its own stated bylaws. Note that legal obligations of boards can vary by country, and what is presented here is representative of the United States.

Other Obligations

While these three obligations encompass the core legal and fiduciary duties of a nonprofit board, the expectations and obligations extend further to encompass what can be categorized as obligations to lead, fund, and advocate, represented in Figure 7.2.

Obligation to lead refers to the leadership role that boards play in overseeing the organization and its strategic direction, and includes one of its

Figure 7.1 Legal Responsibilities of the Board

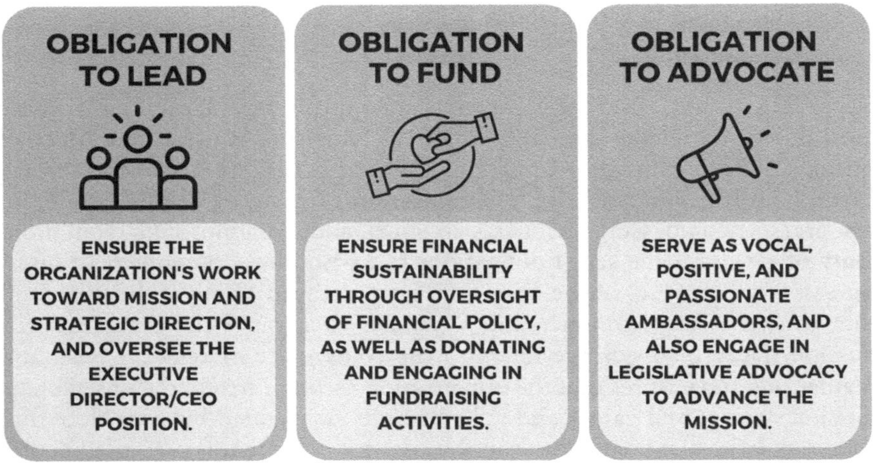

Figure 7.2 Additional Board Obligations

most important responsibilities, which is to hire and set the compensation for the CEO/executive director position and supervise and evaluate that person. **Obligation to fund** is the responsibility that the board has around ensuring financial sustainability of the organization, including not just financial policy oversight, but also fundraising responsibilities, both in making direct personal contributions and in raising funds from other sources. **Obligation to advocate** refers to responsibility of board members to serve as vocal, positive, and passionate ambassadors of the organization to be cheerleaders of the mission, and advocate for legislative policy that advances the nonprofit's mission.

LO 7-3: Distinguish between the two primary types of nonprofit boards.

Types of Nonprofit Boards

The position of a nonprofit board member carries significant duties and obligations; however, it is important to differentiate between different types of nonprofit boards, as the role of a board member can differ accordingly. While there are many types of nonprofit boards, discussed further below, the two primary categories are governing boards and advisory boards. Most nonprofits have both – a governing board to lead, and an advisory board (or multiple advisory boards) to assist with operations.

Governing vs. Advisory Boards

A nonprofit **governing board** has a legal fiduciary responsibility and authority for overall governance and strategic direction and makes high-level decisions, sets policies, and ensures the organization is fulfilling its mission. An **advisory board**, on the other hand, provides expertise, guidance, and recommendations to the organization but typically does not have the decision-making authority. Nonprofits are required to have a governing board, and most opt to also utilize one or more advisory boards (Haddad 2016).

Typically, when someone mentions a nonprofit board of directors in general, they are referring to the primary governing board. Some nonprofits refer to their advisory boards as advisory committees to avoid confusion. Some of the key differences between governing and advisory boards are denoted in Figure 7.3.

Unlike a governing board, an advisory board does not have a legal obligation, and while they also provide guidance and advice, advisory boards lack the formal decision-making power of a governing board. Advisory board member positions are also typically not elected; rather they are assigned to interested and qualified volunteers. Nonprofits are not legally required to have advisory boards, but many choose to establish and utilize them, as they can be a great resource in providing manpower and support in achieving the mission of an organization (Jowdy 2018).

Another key difference between governing and advisory boards is that one of the responsibilities of a governing board is to hire and oversee the CEO/

	GOVERNING BOARDS	ADVISORY BOARDS
DECISION-MAKING	HAS AUTHORITY TO MAKE DECISIONS	PROVIDES ADVICE, BUT HAS NO AUTHORITY
STAFF SUPERVISION	HIRES AND OVERSEES THE CEO/ EXECUTIVE DIRECTOR	HAS NO AUTHORITY OVER CEO/EXECUTIVE DIRECTOR OR STAFF
FORMATION	ELECTED IN ACCORDANCE TO BYLAWS	TYPICALLY APPOINTED
RESPONSIBILITY	HAS A LEGAL, FIDUCIARY RESPONSIBILITY	NOT LEGALLY RESPONSIBLE
REQUIREMENT	REQUIRED BY LAW	OPTIONAL
OVERSIGHT	OVERSEES FINANCES, MANAGEMENT, & PERFORMANCE	CAN PROVIDE ADVICE, BUT NO OVERSIGHT AUTHORITY

Figure 7.3 Differences Between Governing and Advisory Boards

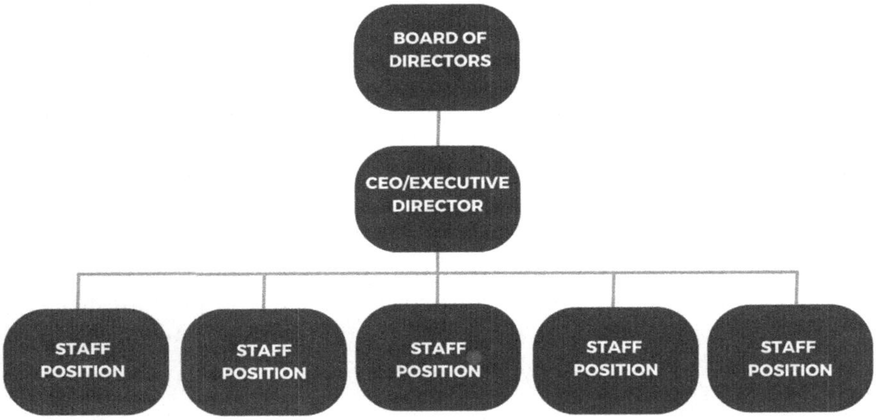

Figure 7.4 Hierarchical Relationship for a Governing Board

executive director, whereas advisory boards have no supervisory relationship with the executive director or any other staff position ("Board Roles"). Figure 7.4 provides a general sample nonprofit organizational chart to demonstrate the hierarchical reporting relationship of an executive director position and governing board. Although not all board member responsibilities noted in the previous section apply to advisory boards – such as the legal duties – many of them still apply. For example, advisory boards are expected to serve as ambassadors for the cause, advance the mission, and behave ethically.

LO 7-4: Categorize the common types of nonprofit advisory boards and explain when, how, why, and for how long they established.

Categories of Advisory Boards

Although advisory boards lack the authority to make decisions, the guidance they offer can impact organizational choices, rendering them an essential asset for nonprofits. Further, they can provide valuable people resources for smaller nonprofits that lack sufficient paid staff capacity. Due to the valuable insights and volunteer labor they provide, nonprofits commonly employ one or more of them, which include the following categories ("Nonprofit Advisory"):

- **Fundraising Advisory Boards:** These boards assist the nonprofit in fundraising through the development and execution of plans and projects. Not all nonprofit organizations possess the resources or capacity to consistently engage in fundraising efforts independently. This board can also be subdivided into committees dedicated to specific fundraising campaigns.

- **Young Professional (YP) Advisory Boards:** The young professionals board's objective is to nurture upcoming board members and stakeholders for an organization, serving as a valuable introduction to the nonprofit and critical part of an organization's board pipeline. Frequently, YP boards brings a dynamic energy and creativity to the organization with new ideas and perspectives.
- **Program or Event Advisory Boards:** These boards are advisory in nature and exist to manage specific nonprofit programs or events and are helpful in providing volunteer labor when staff resources are limited. For example, a nonprofit that hosts an annual educational conference might assemble an advisory board to plan the event and execute event logistics.
- **Regional or Chapter Advisory Boards:** Affiliate nonprofits with multiple regional chapters or branches often have individual boards for each location, advising local operations while adhering to the overall mission. Affiliate organizations have just *one* overall governing board for the organization at the national or international level that is charged with oversight, legal fiduciary responsibility, and decision-making power, but the chapter, branch, or affiliate offices can engage leaders through their own local advisory boards.

The above represent some of the most common types of advisory boards, but this list certainly is not exhaustive. Essentially, nonprofits can create an advisory board of any type to address their individual needs. Fundamentally, regardless of the type or category, the primary objective of all advisory boards is to support the nonprofit organization. It is also important to note that to avoid confusion between the governing board of directors and advisory board of directors, some nonprofits choose to refer to advisory groups as "committees" as opposed to "boards."

Duration of Advisory Boards

An advisory board or committee can be standing or ad hoc. **Standing advisory boards** are typically established for ongoing, major activities that last longer than a year. Young professional advisory boards are typically permanent groups, some even with their own appointment cycles and leadership subgroups, so they are often one example of a type of standing advisory board.

"Ad hoc" is a Latin phrase meaning literally "for this" ("Ad Hoc" 2023), so it stands to reason that **ad hoc advisory boards** are assembled for shorter-term activities or for a special purpose (Carter). If a nonprofit needs to assemble a group for purposes of addressing a short-term issue, such as the need to make a capital investment in a new facility, for example, it may form an ad hoc advisory board to study the issue and make recommendations but disband at the conclusion of the project (Spector 2023). Other forms of organizational teams that can be mechanisms for organizing volunteers are covered in Chapter 9.

LO 7-5: Describe nonprofit board leadership positions, explain their relationship with staff, and discuss how board members are selected.

Board Leadership

Chapter 5 addressed the importance of organizational structure and design, and this applies not just to paid staff roles, but also to boards. Leaders should take care to ensure that their boards are well designed, including job design for board roles and making decisions around departmentalization, hierarchy of authority, delegation, and span of control.

Advisory Board Leadership

A **volunteer chair** is the leader of a designated nonprofit group. While governing board leaders are sometimes given the title of president, it is just as common for them to receive the designation of "chairperson." Lead volunteers of advisory boards, or committees, are also often designated with a "chair" title. Because advisory board members are typically appointed, not elected, the chair may also bear responsibility for recruiting members to his or her board or committee. Advisory boards are not necessarily bound to the same rules and procedural requirements set forth in the bylaws as are governing boards, so advisory board chairs have more autonomy in how they lead.

There can be overall advisory board chairs, which oversee a designated advisory board as a whole, or subgroup chairs that lead a smaller group within an advisory board. The overall chair provides guidance, presides over advisory board meetings, facilitates discussions, and represents the organization to external stakeholders. They play a crucial role in setting the board's agenda, fostering effective governance, and ensuring the organization's mission and goals are upheld.

Some nonprofit advisory boards can be very large and complex, with multiple positions and layers of volunteer authority. In these situations, it is important to be intentional in organizational design to designate those leader chair positions and to develop an organizational chart to visually represent the relationship of positions on the advisory board. This also includes developing and providing clear and detailed job descriptions for each advisory board member position, and for chair roles clarifying the leadership expectations. An example of an organizational chart for a nonprofit advisory board, in this case an event advisory board, is represented in Figure 7.4.

Advisory board chairs frequently have a **dotted line relationship** with a designated staff partner, meaning their hierarchical relationship is less direct and formal than a solid line relationship, which would represent a direct reporting relationship (Lindenfeld Hall 2023). Recall that advisory boards do not have hierarchical authority over paid staff. In a dotted line relationship, there is a link between the parties, but it does not involve direct managerial authority or direct supervision. The dotted line relationship is evident on the sample org chart (Figure 7.5) and is a visual representation of the volunteer/staff partnership, as these two positions work collaboratively to lead various facets of the organization, in this case, a specific event.

The advisory board or committee chair is tasked with working in partnership with their staff partner to lead the assigned volunteer group in executing on their designated program, event, or area of specialty, which includes among other things, setting meetings and agendas. The frequency of these meetings can vary greatly, depending on the purpose of the committee. Leaders can also designate subgroups or subcommittees, which may then branch off and conduct their own separate meetings and activities, and report back to the overall group.

Governing Board Leadership

Organizational design is important for both advisory and governing boards, especially those of larger size. While the hierarchical structure of an advisory

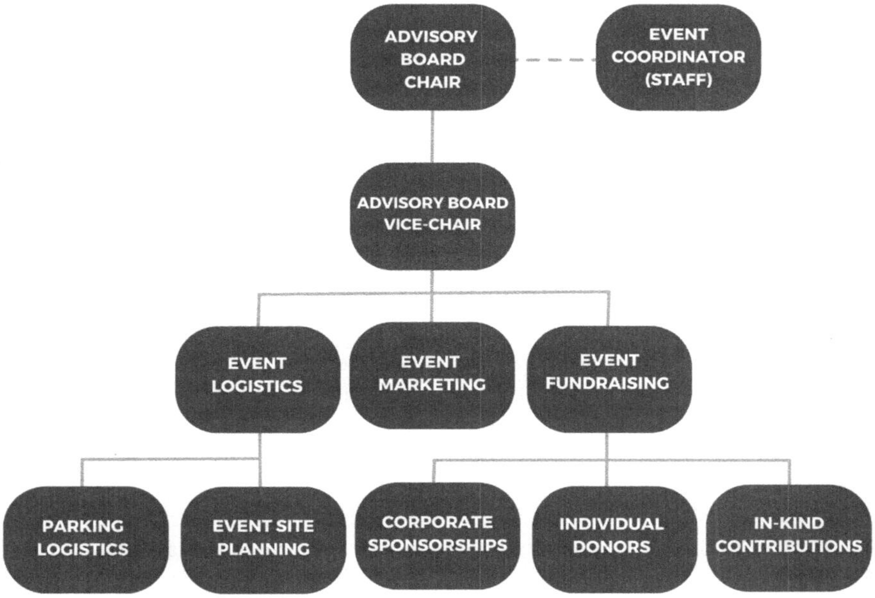

Figure 7.5 Event Planning Advisory Board Organizational Chart

board might vary greatly across programs and organizations, most nonprofit governing boards have a consistent hierarchy. This generally includes an executive committee that leads the board as a whole

A governing board's **executive committee** holds distinct responsibilities and higher authority compared to a general board member position, and its primary role is to streamline decision-making between board meetings, particularly in critical or urgent situations. If permitted by the bylaws, it can make decisions on behalf of the entire board, and it frequently serves as the communication conduit to the CEO/executive director ("Understanding" 2023). Legally, three members are required to serve on a nonprofit board ("How Many"), although many organizations choose to have four executive committee members, which most commonly are: president (or chairperson), vice president (or vice-chairperson), treasurer, and secretary.

A nonprofit **board president** is the individual board member elected to lead and preside over the board of directors. They work in partnership with the executive director to collaboratively lead the organization by providing strategic leadership, guiding board discussions, facilitating decision-making, and representing of the organization to external stakeholders. The **board vice president** is a board member who holds the position of deputy to the board president and who may assume the president's responsibilities in their absence, lead specific initiatives or committees, and provide support in various governance and leadership activities ("Understanding" 2023).

The nonprofit **board treasurer** is a board member responsible for overseeing the financial matters of the organization. They manage financial records, budgets, and financial reporting, provide guidance on financial decisions, and ensure the organization's financial health and accountability. A **board secretary** is a board member responsible for maintaining accurate records of board meetings, including minutes and official documents. They help ensure compliance with legal requirements, handle communication related to board matters, and assist in maintaining the organization's governance documentation.

Some nonprofits have additional positions on their governing board executive committees to include other important leadership positions beyond just the four detailed above, including for example strategic planning chair, nominating chair, communications chair, and others. Executive committee membership, election procedures, roles, and term limits are outlined in the organization's bylaws, and usually, the executive committee meets more frequently than the full board, with the board president presiding over both.

Board Development

A central responsibility of the board president is to work in partnership with the executive director, and sometimes the nominating chair if such a position exists at that nonprofit, to develop the board. **Board development** is the process of systematically enhancing the effectiveness, composition, and performance of a nonprofit organization's governing board of directors. Some nonprofit leaders choose to formalize this as a **board development plan,** which is a strategic tool used to recruit, train, and retain effective board members who can advance their mission (Barlow 2019).

Nominating Process

The **board nominating process** refers to the organized procedure a nonprofit organization follows to identify, evaluate, and select suitable candidates for board of director positions, and these procedures are detailed in the organization's bylaws ("Building" 2022). While the specific process can vary, however, they typically follow a similar series of steps, including the following:

- **Nominations:** Nonprofit leaders solicit nominations of board members from the community, often using a formal online application and required submission of candidates' resumes. In soliciting nominees, leaders should take care to cast a wide net to ensure a diverse candidate pool.
- **Candidate Evaluation:** The individuals charged with the process, often a formal nominating committee, then vets candidates by reviewing their qualifications and skills. This sometimes involves formal interviews with one or more members of the nominating committee (Dean 1998). Some organizations require a background check.
- **Board Approval:** Existing board members typically vote to approve and elect new members. This can occur electronically or during a formal board meeting. Many nonprofits hold the board vote during their annual meeting, which is open to everyone in the community.
- **Orientation:** Once approved, new board members may undergo an orientation process to familiarize themselves with the organization's mission, activities, governance structure, and responsibilities. Some organizations assign a seasoned board member as a mentor to incoming new members ("Board Orientation").

The length of board terms and the roles of board members, including executive committee membership, is defined in the bylaws. **Term limits** refer to the predetermined maximum length of time that individuals can serve on the board of directors before they are required to step down from their positions. Term limits are established to ensure board refreshment, promote diversity, and prevent stagnation by allowing new perspectives and expertise to enter the board. Although the majority of nonprofit boards (87.5%) report having term limits, they are not a legal requirement for nonprofits ("Term Limits" 2022). The specific duration of term limits can vary among organizations, but common terms are typically between two and six years.

Most nonprofits report using three-year terms, renewable for a maximum of two terms (Haddad 2019).
Given the limited terms of board members, to ensure a strong and diverse board, nonprofit leaders should engage in **succession planning**, which is a strategic process that identifies and prepares potential future leaders to assume key roles as they come vacant. It ensures stability and continuity of leadership (Johnson 2022). Succession planning can include development of a **board pipeline**, which refers to the ongoing process of identifying, nurturing, and preparing potential candidates to serve on a nonprofit organization's board of directors in the future (Voudouris 2023). Thinking ahead of talented individuals who can fill upcoming vacancies on the board and/or executive committee can allow leaders to have advance conversations with these prospects and prepare and groom them for the role, making for a more streamlined transition and minimizing the risk of leaving important positions vacant.

Many nonprofits struggle with common board development problems, such as aging boards and lack of diversity. The topic of board diversity is discussed in depth within Chapter 15. Strengthening the board pipeline can help combat these issues and enhance the likelihood of an effective and engaged board. One common source of a nonprofit board pipeline is advisory boards, which can serve as a proving ground for prospective governing board members to demonstrate that they have the skills and attributes in alignment with the nonprofit's needs and expectations.

> LO 7-6: Evaluate how nonprofit boards of directors make decisions.

Board Decision-Making

Nonprofit organizations must hold regular meetings of their governing board to carry out their fiduciary obligations to their organizations, and they are required to keep and distribute **meeting minutes**, which are official written records that capture the key discussions, decisions, actions, and outcomes of board meetings or other organizational gatherings ("Nonprofit Actions" 2022). In the United States, the Internal Revenue Service (IRS) and many states expect nonprofit boards to meet at least once per year, although most meet more frequently such as quarterly or monthly.

As noted at the introduction of this chapter, a key defining characteristic of governing boards is their decision-making authority. How these decisions get made can vary by nonprofit, but are defined in the organizational bylaws, which establish protocols for parliamentary procedure when enacting approval on important decisions. Many nonprofits follow **Robert's Rules of**

Order, which provides a framework that allows groups to have majority rule while allowing minority voices to be heard (Hoy 2023).

Boards vote on resolutions on matters of major import, such as setting strategic plans, hiring or firing key staff members such as the executive director, removing a board member, approving a budget, or implementing a significant new program, but they also vote on more rudimentary measures such as a proposal to change an upcoming meeting date. Parliamentary procedure according to Robert's Rules typically dictates the following steps for making a vote during a board meeting (Hoy 2023):

- **Presentation and Debate:** A motion is presented, and then discussion among the board is opened to deliberate about the topic.
- **Call for the Vote:** The board president asks if there are any further comments or questions before proceeding to the vote. A board member then makes a motion for vote, another board member must "second" that motion.
- **Voting:** Board members cast their votes. The methods can include voice vote, show of hands, or a more formal ballot. The board president tallies the vote and announces the results, indicating whether the motion was carried (approved) or lost (rejected).
- **Recording:** The result of the vote and names of those involved in submitting and approving the motion are recorded in the formal meeting minutes.

Some nonprofit bylaws require that a **quorum** for vote, which refers to the minimum number of eligible members required to be present at a meeting for the meeting to be valid and for decisions to be made. A quorum ensures that decisions are not made by a small or unrepresentative group, promoting broader participation and legitimacy in the decision-making process ("Quorum" 2023). The bylaws will also state the minimum number of votes required to pass a resolution, with many allowing passage by **majority vote,** meaning more than half of the votes cast by persons legally entitled to vote.

An interesting dynamic of nonprofit boards and its decision-making power is the role of the executive director. Nonprofit executive directors sometimes serve on their own boards, but as non-voting members, to avoid any conflicts of interest. Others do not formally include the executive director as a member, but simply invite the executive director to meetings to have a voice, but not a vote (Cullinane 2023).

> LO 7-7: Explain ways nonprofit leaders evaluate board performance and engagement.

Board Engagement

Board development goes beyond just recruitment and selection of board members, however, and includes work toward enhancing board performance and engagement. **Board engagement** refers to the active participation, commitment, and involvement of board members in the fulfillment of their board obligations, contributing their skills and expertise to advance the organization's mission and goals ("Board Engagement"). It is the responsibility of the executive director and board president to measure board effectiveness and engagement and intervene when either is lacking (Banner 2019). While board performance and engagement can certainly be formally assessed for both governing and advisory boards, it is most often done with governing boards.

Measuring performance of nonprofit staff was covered in Chapter 4, and some of these same approaches, such as management by objectives (MBOs) and behaviorally anchored rating scales (BARS), can be implemented to measure board member performance and ensure accountability. Some nonprofit leaders, however, opt to use simpler performance measurement tools for board engagement, such as assessments and scorecards. The frequency of these measures varies by organization, with some assessing annually and others more often, such as at every board meeting (Kersey-Stapleton 2023).

A **board self-assessment (BSA)** is a questionnaire sent to individual board members to gather their input and feedback to measure the collective performance of the board ("Board Self-Assessment" 2023). A **peer-to-peer assessment (P2P)** is a survey that asks board members to evaluate their own performance as well as the performance of their fellow board members, aiming to understand how the overall performance and culture of the entire board are influenced by the individual members' styles and engagement ("Board Evaluations" 2023).

A **board scorecard** is a document that details the expectations of board members and measures that member's performance or contribution to each area. This can include measures such as annual giving expectations, hours of service, meeting attendance, event participation, money raised or solicitations made, and others. The scorecard allows the organization to track key performance indicators and reinforce expectations to board members ("Self Assessments").

It is incumbent upon nonprofit leaders to not just measure performance, but to also act to address performance issues that arise either with the collective board or individual board members. Effective pipeline management and board engagement can help assure performance, but regularly assessing performance, and correcting deviations, is important. Board members who do not perform can be removed from the position prior to the end of their term through a board vote.

Takeaways

LO 7-1: Nonprofit governance involves systems that guide the management of the organization and includes a board of directors, which is a group of individuals elected or appointed to provide oversight and guide the organization toward achieving its mission.

LO 7-2: Nonprofit boards carry three legal and fiduciary responsibilities, duty of care, duty of loyalty, and duty of obedience, as well as other responsibilities that can be summarized into three categories: obligation to lead, obligation to fund, and obligation to advocate.

LO 7-3: There are two main types of nonprofit boards: governing and advisory. A governing board has a legal fiduciary responsibility and authority for overall governance and strategic direction and makes decisions, whereas an advisory board provides expertise, guidance, and recommendations without decision-making authority. All nonprofits are required to have a governing board, and most also utilize one or more advisory boards.

LO 7-4: There are numerous nonprofit advisory boards, but commonly used ones include fundraising, young professionals, programs or events, and regional or chapter advisory boards. Advisory boards are either established on a standing basis for ongoing, major activities that last longer than a year or ad hoc, meaning for a short-term specific purpose.

LO 7-5: Governing boards are required to have at least three leadership positions, although most opt for four: president, vice president, treasurer, and secretary, and the president partners with the executive director to lead the organization, with that position being hired and overseen by the board. There are formal procedures established for the election of governing board members and term limits apply. Advisory boards are often bound by fewer formalized procedures and are led by volunteer "chairs" and these positions, both leadership and non-leadership, are typically appointed, rather than elected. Succession planning can be instrumental for both types of boards.

LO 7-6: Nonprofit governing boards must follow established protocol and procedures set forth in the organization's bylaws when making decisions and voting on resolutions, and many organizations choose to follow Robert's Rules of Order for parliamentary procedure. In voting on decisions, there are considerations such as following proper order, having a quorum, documenting in meeting minutes, and others.

LO 7-7: Nonprofit board performance can be evaluated through general performance evaluation measures such as MBOs and BARS, or instead use a simpler and more board-specific measurement tool such as a board self-assessment (BSA), peer-to-peer assessment (P2P), or a board scorecard.

Bibliography

"5 Critical Board Engagement Survey Questions." *OnBoard*, 26 Jul. 2022, www.onboardmeetings.com/blog/board-engagement-survey-questions/. Accessed 28 Jun. 2023.

"Ad Hoc Definition & Meaning." *Merriam-Webster*, www.merriam-webster.com/dictionary/ad%20hoc. Accessed 18 Apr. 2023.

Banner, Jeb. "A how-to Guide for Nonprofit Board Engagement." *NonProfit Pro* (Online), 2019.

Barlow, Jeremy, et al. "Board Development Best Practices." *BoardEffect*, 4 Jan. 2019, www.boardeffect.com/blog/board-development-best-practices/.

"Board Engagement." *National Council of Nonprofits*, www.councilofnonprofits.org/running-nonprofit/governance-leadership/board-engagement. Accessed 29 Sept. 2023.

"Board Evaluations: The Complete Q&A Guide for Nonprofits." *Boardable*, 20 Sept. 2023, boardable.com/resources/board-evaluations/.

"Board Orientation." *National Council of Nonprofits*, www.councilofnonprofits.org/running-nonprofit/governance-leadership/board-orientation. Accessed 29 Sept. 2023.

"Board Roles and Responsibilities." *National Council of Nonprofits*, www.councilofnonprofits.org/running-nonprofit/governance-leadership/board-roles-and-responsibilities. Accessed 27 Apr. 2023.

"Board Self-Assessment." *BoardSource*, 21 Feb. 2023, boardsource.org/board-support/assessing-performance/board-self-assessment/.

"Building Strong Board Nomination Processes." *Giving Compass*, 19 July 2022, givingcompass.org/article/building-strong-board-nomination-processes.

"Can Board Members Be Paid?" *National Council of Nonprofits*, www.councilofnonprofits.org/running-nonprofit/governance-leadership/can-board-members-be-paid. Accessed 24 Jun. 2023.

Coule, Tracey M. "Nonprofit Governance and Accountability: Broadening the Theoretical Perspective." *Nonprofit and Voluntary Sector Quarterly*, vol. 44, no. 1, 2015, pp. 75–97.

Cullinane, Mollie. "Nonprofit Law Basics: Can the Executive Director Serve on the Board of Directors?" *Cullinane Law Group*, 16 Jan. 2023, cullinanelaw.com/nonprofit-law-basics-can-the-executive-director-serve-on-the-board-of-directors/. Accessed 27 Jun. 2023.

Dean, J.C. "The Nominating Committee." *Fund Raising Management*, vol. 28, no. 12, 1998, pp. 27–31.

"Fiduciary Duty." *Ethics Unwrapped*, 5 Nov. 2022, ethicsunwrapped.utexas.edu/glossary/fiduciary-duty#:~:text=A%20fiduciary%20duty%20is%20the,best%20interest%20of%20their%20clients.

"Good Governance Policies for Nonprofits." *National Council of Nonprofits*, www.councilofnonprofits.org/running-nonprofit/governance-leadership/good-governance-policies-nonprofits. Accessed 20 May 2023.

Haddad, Duke. "Advisory Board versus Governing Board-Is There a Difference?" *NonProfit PRO*, 28 Oct. 2016, www.nonprofitpro.com/post/advisory-board-versus-governing-board-difference/.

Haddad, Duke. "Does Your Nonprofit Board have Term Limits?" *NonProfit Pro* (Online), 2019.

Hoy, Toni. "Robert's Rules of Order Cheat Sheet for Nonprofits." *Boardable*, 9 May 2023, www.boardeffect.com/blog/roberts-rules-of-order-cheat-sheet/. Accessed 22 Jun. 2023.

"How Many Board Members Should My Nonprofit Have?" *Springly*, www.springly.org/en-us/blog/how-many-board-members-should-a-nonprofit-have/. Accessed 28 Jun. 2023.

Johnson, Brian L. "Pass the Torch: Leadership Development and Succession Planning in Nonprofit Organizations." *Journal of Philanthropy and Marketing*, vol. 27, no. 4, 2022, pp. n/a.

Jowdy, Jeff. "To have a Supportive Nonprofit Advisory Board… You must Support it." *NonProfit Pro* (Online), 2018.

Kersey-Stapleton, Joh M., Benjamin Tay, and Fazlin Abdullah. "Developing, Evaluating, and Validating a Nonprofit Board Performance Framework." *Nonprofit Management & Leadership*, vol. 34, no. 1, 2023, pp. 179–193.

Lindenfeld, Hall Sara. "What Is Dotted-Line Reporting?" *RSS*, lattice.com/library/what-is-dotted-line-reporting#:~:text=In%20a%20perfect%20world%2C%20a,resources%20across%20departments%20or%20divisions. Accessed 29 Sept. 2023.

"Nonprofit Actions That Require a Vote." *Church Law Center*, 14 May 2022, www.churchlawcenter.com/nonprofit/5-nonprofit-actions-that-require-a-vote/. Accessed 24 Jun. 2023.

"Nonprofit Advisory Boards: What They Are & Why They Matter." *Boardable*, boardable.com/resources/advisory-boards/. Accessed 22 Jun. 2023.

"Quorum for Nonprofit Board Meeting." *BoardSource*, 27 July 2023, boardsource.org/resources/board-meeting-quorum/.

"Self-Assessments for Nonprofit Boards." *National Council of Nonprofits*, www.councilofnonprofits.org/running-nonprofit/governance-leadership/self-assessments-nonprofit-boards. Accessed 29 Sept. 2023.

Spector, Bren. "Unlocking the Power of Committees: How Nonprofits Can Maximize Impact with Ad Hoc Committees." *Resilia*, 19 May 2023, www.resilia.com/blog/how-nonprofits-can-create-standing-and-ad-hoc-committees-to-maximize-their-impact#:~:text=Ad%20hoc%20committees%20are%20short,once%20their%20task%20is%20completed.

"Term Limits." *BoardSource*, 11 May 2022, boardsource.org/resources/term-limits/.

Trower, Cathy A., and ProQuest (Firm). *The Practitioner's Guide to Governance as Leadership: Building High-Performing Nonprofit Boards*. Jossey-Bass, San Francisco, 2013.

"Understanding Board Committee Structure: Executive Committee." *BoardSource*, 12 Apr. 2023, boardsource.org/resources/executive-committee/. Accessed 24 Jun. 2023.

Voudouris, Elizabeth. *How Strong Is Your Board's Leadership Pipeline?*, bvuvolunteers.org/how-strong-is-your-boards-leadership-pipeline/. Accessed 29 Mar. 2023.

8 Volunteer Engagement

Learning Outcomes

After reading this chapter, you should be able to:

LO 8-1: Describe effective design of volunteer programs, including implementation of volunteer engagement strategies and organizational design approaches.
LO 8-2: Illustrate the elements of effective volunteer-staff relationships and explain the impact and importance specifically of the executive director-board president relationship.
LO 8-3: Categorize the profile of a volunteer, including the general factors that motivate their contributions of time, and explain the framework that describes the attributes of a good volunteer.
LO 8-4: Summarize the steps of the volunteer engagement cycle and define volunteer turnover.
LO 8-5: Describe volunteer exit and factors that contribute to volunteer turnover.
LO 8-6: Justify the implementation and use of volunteer contracts as part of an organization's volunteer program.
LO 8-7: Apply theories of motivation to volunteer management.

> LO 8-1: Describe effective design of volunteer programs, including implementation of volunteer engagement strategies and organizational design approaches.

Volunteer Programs

Approximately 61 million Americans, or 23% of the adult population, volunteer for nonprofit organizations each year ("60.7" 2023) and engaging volunteers and manging those stakeholder relationships is essential for nonprofit leaders. Most nonprofits have a formalized **volunteer program**, which

DOI: 10.4324/9781003380030-11

is a structured and organized initiative within an organization that recruits, supervises, and engages individuals who offer their time, skills, and services willingly and without financial compensation ("Volunteers").

Volunteer Engagement

An outcome of an effective volunteer program is **volunteer engagement**, which is an organizational strategy that encourages collaboration between staff and volunteers to develop meaningful volunteer opportunities that positively impact the organization and the community (Rosenthal 2015). Many nonprofits have formalized volunteer programs within their organizations, and larger agencies may even have one or more paid staff positions dedicated specifically to the purpose of volunteer program oversight. In some agencies, just one or a handful of volunteers may work closely with a designated staff partner to lead a specific initiative, event, or program.

Even for organizations with the resources to fully support a volunteer program, however, the task still does not come easy. There are natural tensions that tend to arise when volunteers and paid staff are working together toward a shared objective. There can be power struggles, particularly when there is ambiguity around the organization's hierarchy of authority. As noted in Chapter 5, effective organizational design is the building block to successful organizations, and this holds true for the volunteer-staff partnership. Here are ways that good organizational design can positively impact these relationships:

Organizational Design in Volunteer Programs

Job Design

Just like paid staff, volunteers are fulfilling important roles in the organization, so good job design is just as essential with volunteer positions as it is with staff positions. This includes conducting a job analysis, being intentional in job design, and then producing a job description, which is then used for the recruitment phase of the volunteer engagement cycle.

By providing clarity and understanding about their roles, responsibilities, and contributions within an organization, the organization can prevent misunderstandings and misaligned expectations between staff and volunteers. An effective job description aids with this by conveying these important elements and is tailored to attract the right candidates. In addition to the job title, it includes, at a minimum, the following (Johnson 2023):

- **Mission:** Provide the name of the organization and state the organizational mission. This helps ensure alignment of the applicants' values with that of the organization.

- **Role and Responsibilities:** Complete a job analysis and then articulate the specific tasks the volunteer is expected to perform, along with their responsibilities. Describe the hierarchy of authority so the applicant knows the reporting structure and how the position fits within it.
- **Time Commitment:** Be transparent in specifying the expected time commitment, including the number of hours per week or month, and whether the role requires a fixed schedule or offers flexibility. This information allows volunteers to assess whether they can accommodate the commitment.
- **Qualifications and Skills:** Detail the preferred or required combination of education, experience, and skills needed for the volunteer who will fill the position.
- **Benefits and Impact:** Highlight the positive impact the volunteer's efforts will have on the organization and the community it serves. This allows volunteers to feel good about contributing their time.
- **Application Information:** Advise interested applicants of how they can apply for the position.

By including these essential elements in a volunteer job description, organizations can attract suitable candidates, set expectations, and ensure a positive and productive experience for both volunteers and the organization. While volunteer job descriptions vary in exactly how the information is presented, Figure 8.1 provides an example of one.

Hierarchy of Authority

A beautifully designed job and well-written job description provides a great start, but does not fully address the question of authority, which can be a common source of volunteer/staff or even volunteer/volunteer tension. So, just as organizational design is applied to structuring staff positions, it is also important for structuring volunteer roles. Organizations must decide who holds what levels of authority, especially around decision-making, and formally communicate this (Ensor 2023).

Establishing a hierarchy of authority for a volunteer program provides structure and clarity, ensuring that roles, responsibilities, and decision-making processes are well-defined, allowing volunteers to understand their positions and contributions. Further, a hierarchy empowers volunteers by defining their authority and the extent of their decision-making, enabling them to contribute effectively. An organizational chart, such as the one presented in Figure 8.2, can help volunteers and staff visualize these reporting relationships. This figure displays how the hypothetical volunteer inventory coordinator position fits within the hierarchy of the fictional Helping Hands of Houston organization. This agency uses functional departmentalization

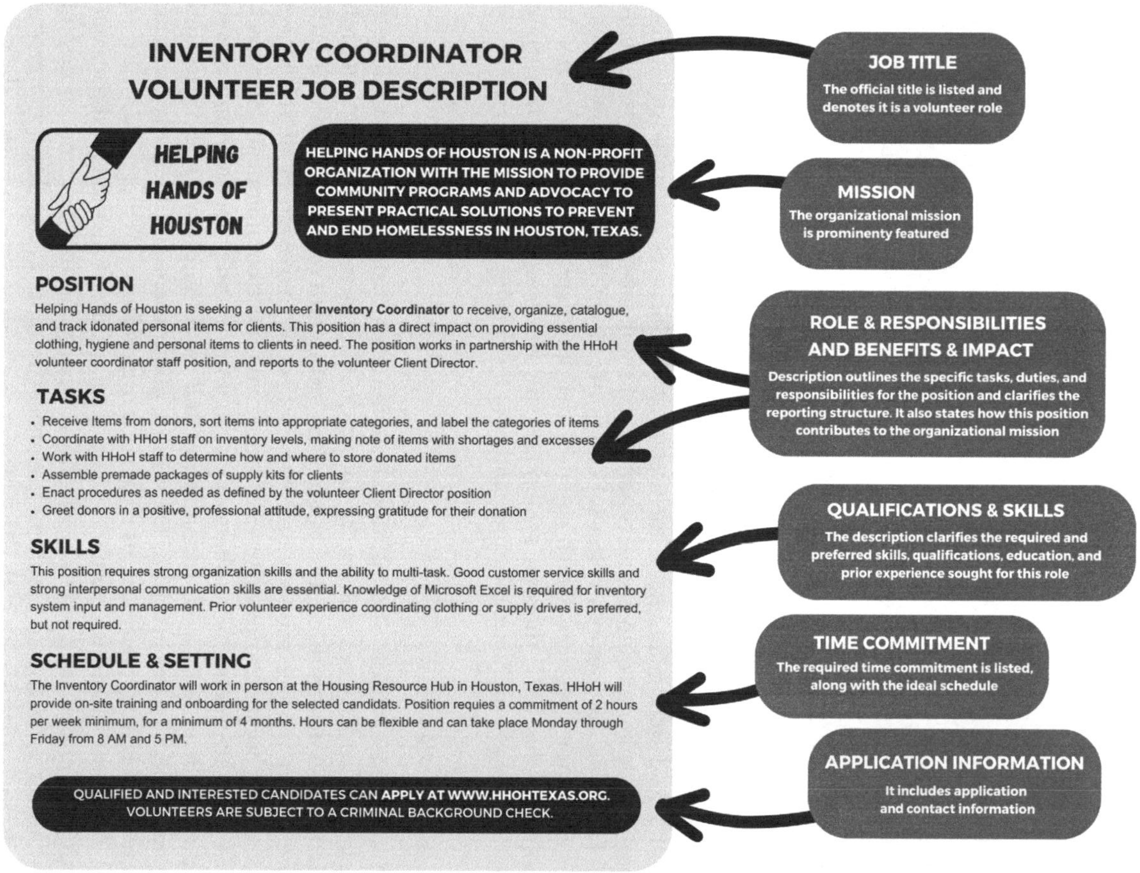

Figure 8.1 Volunteer Job Description

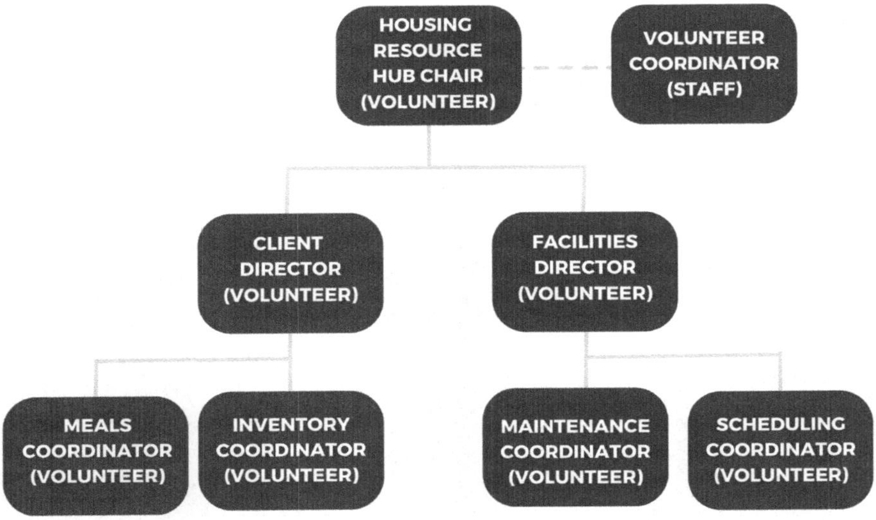

Figure 8.2 Volunteer Committee Organizational Chart

for this particular committee, grouping volunteers based on their job function.

Power struggles can arise not just between volunteers and staff, but also within and among volunteers themselves, and a hierarchy of authority is also useful in defining volunteer-to-volunteer reporting relationships. The org chart in Figure 8.2 represents a volunteer committee charged with program delivery of community services, which is led by the designated community chair. As noted in Chapter 7, the staff position usually holds a dotted-line relationship with the lead volunteer, meaning neither is the other's formal boss.

Communications

Another aspect of organizational design that can facilitate a smooth relationship between volunteers and staff is effective communications. Job design, job descriptions, and established hierarchies of authority are of little use if they are not properly conveyed. Effective management of volunteers as a stakeholder group involves strategic **volunteer communications**, which refers to the practice of reaching out to volunteers and potential volunteers to educate them about your organization and its volunteer work, activate and inspire them to get involved, learn more about them and their experiences, and build lasting relationships with your organization (Waters 2023).

A **communications channel** is a specific medium or method used to transmit information and messages from one party to another, and successful volunteer programs use multiple channels (Colquitt 2021). Most nonprofits typically communicate with their current and prospective volunteers through

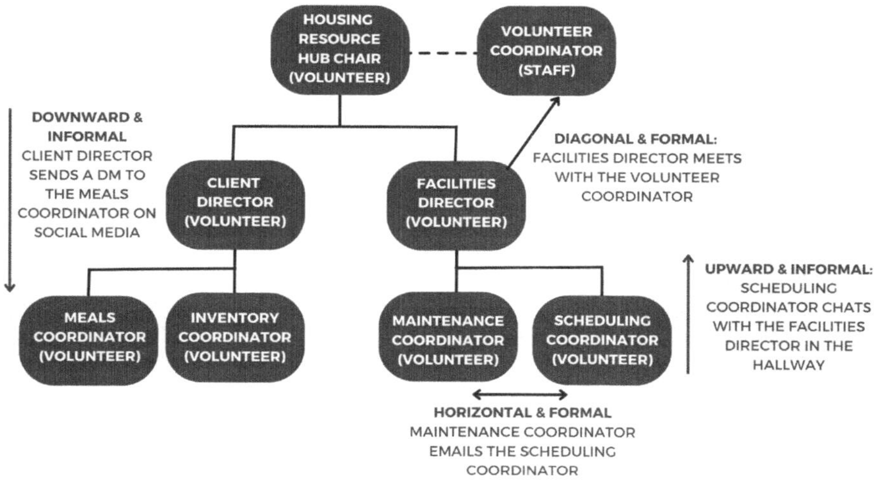

Figure 8.3 Volunteer Communications

in-person meetings, volunteer websites and newsletters, social media, live events, email, and others. Reflecting on what we learned about communications in Chapter 5, Figure 8.3 represents the type (informal or formal) and direction (upward, downward, horizontal, or diagonal) of communications that might occur within our hypothetical volunteer committee of Helping Hands of Houston.

Recall that the silo effect can occur when departments in an organization become isolated and compartmentalized. Silos can occur within any hierarchy, be it staff or volunteer. In the sample organization presented in Figure 8.2, if the client director and facilities director do not coordinate, communicate, and collaborate, the negative impacts of the silo effect can occur. As one example, if the inventory coordinator reports to her direct report, the client coordinator, that Helping Hands of Houston has a massive oversupply of donated items, it is essential that the client director work with the facilities director to determine where to place the inventory and handle the issue. If this communication is not effective, the space in the housing resource hub facility can become overwhelmed, potentially causing overcrowding issues.

Just as effective communication is central to the success of organizations within an among the staff positions, it's just as important within a nonprofit volunteer program. In fact, it's arguably *more* important, given the complexities of the volunteer-staff partnership.

LO 8-2: Illustrate the elements of effective volunteer-staff relationships and explain the impact and importance specifically of the executive director-board president relationship.

Volunteer-Staff Relationships

While nonprofit and for-profit organizations are more similar than dissimilar, perhaps the most notable distinction between the two is the dependence that the former has on unpaid volunteer labor. As such, it is essential that paid staff work well in partnership with volunteers in ensuring that they are aligned on goals and objectives. Except for some administrative positions, most nonprofit staff interact regularly in some way with volunteers, so understanding the importance of the volunteer-staff partnership is important.

The **volunteer-staff partnership** refers to the collaborative relationship between volunteers and paid staff within an organization and involves working together harmoniously to achieve shared goals, utilizing their respective skills, expertise, and resources to enhance the organization's impact and effectiveness (Netting, et al. 2004). In the example provided in Figure 8.2, the staff volunteer coordinator position is the assigned staff partner with the housing resource hub volunteer chair. Their dotted-line relationship indicates that neither is the other's direct supervisor, and they must work together to lead this function of the organization. The goal is to achieve a **balanced partnership**, where there is a relatively equal and equitable exchange of resources, rewards, and costs between two or more individuals.

A **volunteer management platform**, or VMP, is helpful in organizing volunteers logistically. A VMP is a digital tool or software designed to streamline and enhance the process of recruiting, organizing, and coordinating volunteers for nonprofit organizations. It provides a centralized hub for managing various aspects of volunteer engagement (Gunn 2022). Organizing information is just one small piece, however, successful volunteer-staff partnerships are built on strong relationships, and here are some key factors that drive these:

- **Clear Communication:** Open communication between staff and volunteers is important to a positive and effective relationship. This involves information sharing, updates and reports, and reciprocal feedback.
- **Shared Goals and Mission Focus:** Sharing a commitment to the organizational mission, and collaborating on achieving shared goals, can foster a better volunteer-staff relationship.
- **Respect and Recognition:** Both volunteers and staff members should be treated with respect and appreciation for their contributions. Recognizing and acknowledging their efforts fosters a positive atmosphere.
- **Defined Roles and Expectations:** Defining roles, authority, and expectations of both staff and volunteer positions through job descriptions can help prevent misunderstandings and power struggles.
- **Collaboration and Inclusion:** Encouraging collaboration and involving volunteers in decision-making processes helps them feel valued and engaged. Staff members should actively seek input from volunteers and consider their perspectives. Decisions should be made democratically, not autocratically.

Despite the best designed volunteer programs and efforts toward fostering a fruitful volunteer-staff partnership, relationships can still go sour. Organizational conflict and conflict resolution strategies are topics covered in Chapter 9.

The Executive Director-Board President Partnership

Of all the volunteer-staff relationships in a nonprofit agency, arguably the most important one is that of the executive director and board president, as these two pivotal roles work in partnership to provide overall leadership for the organization. Effective nonprofit executive directors use their leadership to empower others through shared and distributed leadership, with an empowered executive team, strong second-in-command, and engaged boards (Crutchfield 2012). Leader effectiveness in a nonprofit also hinges on the strength of the partnership of the executive director and board president as co-leaders of the organization (Jäger 2012). While this partnership is critical, the relationship between chairs and executive directors has unfortunately been largely neglected in research on nonprofit governance (Cornforth 2016).

The executive director-board president partnership can be a complicated one, as there can be conflicts with power dynamics, differing personalities, and leadership styles, communication challenges, and turnover as new board presidents are cycled through every few years due to term limits. As with the volunteer-staff relationship, the objective here is to achieve a balanced partnership.

One situation that can cause tension is a lack of clarity around roles and expectations. **Role ambiguity** arises when various parties hold conflicting expectations regarding an individual's responsibilities (Colquitt 2021). This can lead to friction within the executive director-board president partnership. Engaging in good organizational design practices like clarifying the expectations and responsibilities of both roles through a well-written job description, maintaining transparent and frequent communication, and engaging in succession planning can alleviate some of these tensions.

> LO 8-3: Categorize the profile of a volunteer, including the general factors that motivate their contributions of time, and explain the framework that describes the attributes of a good volunteer.

The Profile of a Volunteer

Part of a successful volunteer-staff partnership is understanding the volunteer, including their motivations for engaging with the organization, and identifying the characteristics of a good volunteer.

Volunteer Motivation

Generally speaking, individuals volunteer for nonprofits out of three general motivating factors. **"Head, heart, halo"** is a concept commonly used in the nonprofit sector to describe these three central motivations that drive individuals to support charitable organizations:

The **head motivation** refers to the logical reasons people use to justify support of a nonprofit. Donors are motivated rationally by facts about the organization, its mission and impact, and awareness of the impact their support will have on the agency's goals. **Heart motivation** is related to the emotional reasons that individuals support an organization and how they connect to the cause on a personal or emotional level. Finally, **halo motivation** represents the social aspect and reputational benefits of supporting a cause. Some individuals are driven to support an organization out of a desire to be perceived as a caring person. The "head, heart, halo" concept can be applied to nonprofit support not just through the approach of soliciting financial support, but also in recruiting prospective volunteers.

In essence, "head, heart, halo" recognizes that people support nonprofits for a combination of rational, emotional, and social reasons. Nonprofits often tailor their communication plans and volunteer engagement strategies to appeal to these different motivations to engage them.

Attributes of Good Volunteers

Just as "head, heart, halo" presents a memorable way to remember the motivations of volunteer support, there's a similarly alliterative way to think of the three primary attributes of a good volunteer. Nonprofits sometimes use the **three D's framework**, representing doers, donors, and door-openers, as a way of categorizing volunteers based on their level of engagement and commitment. These categories help organizations understand how volunteers contribute and how they can be effectively managed. It also easily identifies the three things nonprofits hope to gain from each volunteer.

Doers refer to volunteers who provide hands-on labor in completing tasks; through participation in events, volunteering for programs and services, or completing work needed by the organization. **Donors** primarily contribute by providing direct financial support to the organization. Finally, **door-openers** refer to supporters who are willing to use their personal and professional networks and relationships to "open doors" for the organization to solicit support (Trembacki 2016).

When recruiting volunteers, especially for governing board positions, nonprofit leaders often specifically seek out individuals who have at least two, or preferably all, of the "three D's," which are represented below in Figure 8.4. It is not uncommon for "donors" to also be "doers," as some reports estimate that 76% of volunteers also donate to the organizations for which they volunteer ("2020"). They should also take measures to ensure that their volunteer bases are diverse, a topic addressed in Chapter 15.

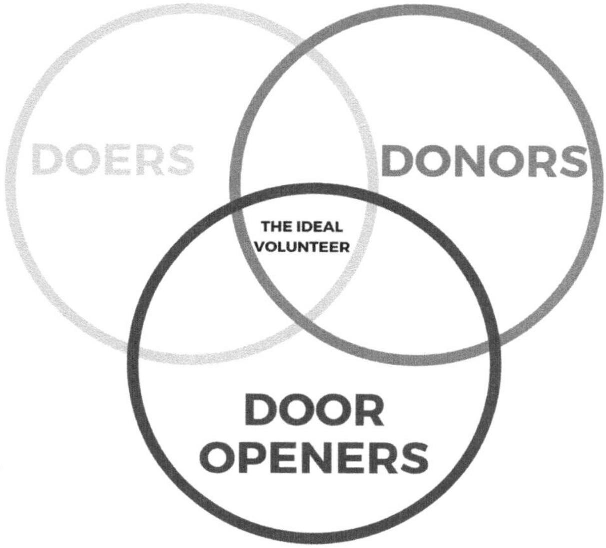

Figure 8.4 Three D's Framework

Another common reference used to describe supporter contributions to nonprofits is the **three T's framework**, representing the concepts of time, talent, and treasure ("The 3 Pillars" 2022). It is like the three D's framework, in that both describe in a memorable and catchy way the diverse means that supporters contribute to nonprofits.

LO 8-4: Summarize the steps of the volunteer engagement cycle and define volunteer turnover.

Volunteer Engagement Cycle

The **volunteer engagement cycle** outlines the stages through which individuals progress when becoming and remaining involved as volunteers in a nonprofit organization. This cycle helps organizations understand and enhance the volunteer experience (Johnson 2021). The stages can be summarized as follows and is represented in Figure 8.5.

- **Recruitment:** Nonprofits recruit volunteers by posting job descriptions and then vetting applicants.
- **Placement:** Just as training and onboarding are critical for new staff positions, the same holds true for volunteer positions, as well. Once

Figure 8.5 Volunteer Engagement Cycle

recruited, volunteers go through an orientation process where they learn about the organization's mission, vision, and goals, and receive training specific to their position.

- **Supervision:** Once volunteers are placed in their roles, the designated staff or volunteer leaders for that position supervise the volunteer, providing guidance and support.
- **Recognition:** This stage of the cycle involves thanking donors for their support, and this appreciation is often expressed verbally or with thank you notes, awards, and recognition at events.

The volunteer engagement cycle is an ongoing process, as churn happens, with existing volunteers exiting the organization and new ones joining. **Volunteer turnover** refers to the rate at which volunteers discontinue their involvement with a nonprofit organization, whether due to completing their assignments, transitioning to other commitments, or other reasons. The average volunteer stays in their position for one to two years ("Volunteer Demographics"). Volunteers are an essential component of successful nonprofits, and leaders should engage volunteers through formalized volunteer programs and strategic implementation of the volunteer engagement cycle.

LO 8-5: Describe volunteer exit and factors that contribute to volunteer turnover.

Volunteer Exit

As noted above, volunteers cycle out of nonprofit organizations for various reasons. It may be as simple as administrative reasons, such as completion of an assignment for an ad hoc advisory board, or reaching a term limit for a board member, or for personal reasons, such as a loss of job, moving, or having a family-life change. Volunteer exits can also occur as a result of volunteer burnout. Like employee burnout, **volunteer burnout** happens when a state of physical or emotional exhaustion is reached and performance deteriorates (Moreno-Jiménez 2010).

Volunteers, on average, spend 50 hours per year donating their time to nonprofits ("40 Volunteer"), although this number can vary widely from person to person, with some volunteers contributing the equivalent of full-time unpaid labor to their organization of choice. Volunteers who contribute high hours of volunteer time are at greater risk of experiencing burnout, and leaders should manage these situations as they would with staff. This includes strategies like job rotation, setting realistic expectations, providing meaningful recognition, fostering a supportive community, and periodically assessing volunteers' workload and well-being.

Not all volunteer exits are voluntary. "You can't fire a volunteer!" is a joking statement heard frequently in nonprofit organizations, but this is patently untrue. While volunteers are not paid employees, their participation in any nonprofit organization is not a right, but a privilege. Just as volunteers are free to exit their involvement with a nonprofit, the leadership of a nonprofit has the freedom to enforce an involuntary volunteer exit when the situation calls for it. This can occur because of a volunteer engaging in unethical behaviors, consistently creating conflict with other volunteers or staff, and badmouthing the organization, as just a few examples (Hawthorne 2022).

Some nonprofit leaders are reticent to remove a volunteer, but for the health of the organization and its culture, it is sometimes a necessary step. In these instances, leaders should take care to approach a removal much as they would when terminating a paid member of the staff. This includes documentation of the behaviors that warrant removal, performance-improvement planning to attempt to change the undesired behaviors, and open communication to ensure consistent messaging and prevent misunderstandings.

While "firing" a volunteer is sometimes necessary, this action should be used as a last resort. Sometimes removal occurs as a result to lack of required participation or follow-through of responsibilities by the volunteer. In these cases, the door can be left open for the volunteer to potentially return in the future if their circumstances change to allow them to dedicate more time to fulfilling their volunteer obligations. Regardless of the cause, however, removal of a volunteer from an organization should be executed with empathy, open communication, and professionalism (McCurley 2023).

LO 8-6: Justify the implementation and use of volunteer contracts as part of an organization's volunteer program.

Volunteer Contracts

Aligning expectations is a critical element to avoid conflict and prevent premature volunteer turnover and firing. **Volunteer contracts**, sometimes referred to as volunteer agreements or volunteer service agreements, are formal but not legally binding written agreements between a nonprofit organization and its volunteers that outline the terms, expectations, and commitments for both parties involved in the volunteer engagement ("Writing" 2021). They typically include much of the same information detailed on the volunteer job description, such as specifications of roles and responsibilities and expected time commitment, as well as the organization's code of conduct and expectations of volunteer behavior. Volunteers may be asked to physically sign a paper copy of their volunteer contract, or e-sign a digital version, to verify their acceptance of the contract and ensure alignment of values and expectations.

Volunteer contracts help avoid misunderstandings by ensuring in written form that both the nonprofit organization and the volunteer have a clear understanding of their respective roles and obligations, fostering a positive and productive volunteer experience. In addition to a volunteer contract, nonprofit leaders should ensure that all volunteers review and sign the organization's conflict of interest policy. This applies not only to new volunteers but should also be an annual procedure for *all* volunteers.

LO 8-7: Apply theories of motivation to volunteer management.

Motivating Volunteers

We understand the three general facets (head, heart, and halo) of what motivates volunteers to contribute their time and support to a nonprofit organization, but we can also apply the previously discussed theories of motivation to volunteer programs.

Volunteers are unpaid, but the concepts of equity theory still apply, as leaders need to take strides to ensure that volunteers perceive that they are treated fairly and equitably. Not all outcomes are pay and can also include things such as rewards and recognition. If a volunteer perceives an imbalance of treatment of how these outcomes are allocated, relative to inputs, they may experience dissatisfaction and motivation may suffer.

Expectancy theory also applies to volunteers, just as it does to staff management. This theory tells us that a volunteer must have confidence in themselves that their efforts will lead to successful performance, and that performance will translate into outcomes they value. And as is the case with equity theory, outcomes aren't always financial in nature. To motivate volunteers, nonprofit leaders can implement volunteer incentive programs that provide outcomes of value in exchange for performance, and place volunteers in the appropriate positions where they have the skills needed to achieve success.

Finally, we know from goal-setting theory that setting specific and challenging goals leads to increased motivation, effort, and performance, as individuals strive to achieve those objectives, aided by clear direction and feedback. This goes not just for paid staff, but volunteers as well. Good volunteer programs are designed with volunteer performance-evaluation protocols and goal-setting strategies. Just as employees are tasked with completing goals that are specific, measurable, achievable (but difficult), realistic, and time-bound, volunteers should also have SMART goals and be held accountable to achieving them.

Regardless of their personal motivations, however, most volunteers are driven at least in part by the "heart" aspect, meaning that they are motivated when they can see that their efforts directly contribute to making a positive impact on the organization's mission or the community it serves. Feeling that their work matters and creates real change can be highly motivating. As such, one of the simplest actions leaders and staff partners can take to motivate volunteers is to regularly communicate, commend, and reinforce this impact to the volunteer.

Takeaways

LO 8-1: A nonprofit volunteer program is a structured initiative to recruit, train, manage, and engage volunteers, and part of this is a volunteer engagement strategy to encourages collaboration between staff and volunteers to develop meaningful volunteer opportunities. Successful volunteer programs include aspects of effective job design.

LO 8-2: The relationship between volunteers and paid staff is a critical element of a nonprofit's success, and no relationship is more important than the one between the organization's executive director and board president. Engaging in good organizational design practices, such as implementations of job descriptions to prevent role ambiguity, can contribute to positive and effective relationships.

LO 8-3: Volunteer motivation is generally referenced as "head, heart, halo," which recognizes that people support nonprofits for a combination of rational, emotional, and social reasons. The ideal volunteer is one that embodies one or more, ideally all, of the attributes of the three D's framework, meaning they are a doer who contributes time to complete tasks, a donor who contributes financial resources, and a door-opener who uses their influence and personal networks to assist in the organization's efforts toward mission achievement.

LO 8-4: The volunteer engagement cycle includes four recurring steps: recruitment, placement, supervision, and recognition, and volunteer turnover refers to the rate at which volunteers leave the organization within a specified period.

LO 8-5: Volunteer exit happens when volunteers leave an organization, and this can occur voluntarily for administrative reasons, such as the conclusion of an ad hoc advisory board's work, or voluntarily for personal reasons, such as life changes or volunteer burnout. Exit can also happen involuntarily when a volunteer is terminated from his or her position.

LO 8-6: Like job descriptions, volunteer contracts clearly define roles, expectations, and responsibilities and are presented in a written form. While not legally binding, volunteers are typically asked to physically sign their volunteer contract as a measure to ensure alignment of values and expectations.

LO 8-7: Leaders can integrate knowledge from the theories of motivation, including equity, expectancy, and goal-setting theory, into volunteer program design. This includes strategies around ensuring equity of volunteer outcomes such as rewards and recognition, defining volunteer expectations, and setting goals that are specific yet difficult.

Bibliography

"2020 Global Trends in Giving Report." *Nonprofit Tech for Good*, 2020, assets-global.website-files.com/5da60733afec9db1fb998273/5f5f8fedbd440fd3e98de74c_2020-Giving-Report-English.pdf. Accessed 19 Jul. 2023.

"40 Volunteer Statistics That Will Blow Your Mind." *Volunteer Hub*, www.volunteerhub.com/blog/40-volunteer-statistics/#:~:text=Volunteers%2C%20on%20average%2C%20spend%2050,time%20to%20the%20greater%20good. Accessed 25 Jul. 2023.

AmeriCorps. *60.7 Million Americans Volunteered in 2021, AmeriCorps Reports*. Targeted News Service, Washington, DC, 2023.

Bussell, H., and D. Forbes. "Understanding the Volunteer Market: The What, Where, Who and Why of Volunteering." *International Journal of Nonprofit and Voluntary Sector Marketing*, vol. 7, no. 3, 2002, pp. 244–257.

Chacón, F., M.L. Vecina, and M.C. Dávila. "Motives and Profiles of Volunteers in Social Organizations." *Social Behavior and Personality: An International Journal*, vol. 35, no. 5, 2007, pp. 647–662.

Clary, E.G., M. Snyder, R.D. Ridge, J. Copeland, A.A. Jr. Stukas, J. Haugen, and P. Miene. "Understanding and Assessing the Motivations of Volunteers: A Functional Approach." *Journal of Personality and Social Psychology*, vol. 74, no. 6, 1998, pp. 1516–1530.

Colquitt, Jason, Jeffery LePine, and Michael Wesson. *Organizational Behavior: Improving Performance and Commitment in the Workplace*. McGraw Hill, 2021. New York, NY.

Cornforth, Chris, and Rob Macmillan. "Evolution in Board Chair–CEO Relationships: A Negotiated Order Perspective." *Nonprofit and Voluntary Sector Quarterly*, vol. 45, no. 5, 2016, pp. 949–970.

Crutchfield, Leslie R., Heather M. Grant, and Inc ebrary. *Forces for Good: The Six Practices of High-Impact Nonprofits*. Jossey-Bass, San Francisco, 2012.

Einolf, C.J. "Understanding Why People Volunteer: An Examination of Motives in a Mega-Sporting Event Context." *Nonprofit and Voluntary Sector Quarterly*, vol. 40, no. 3, 2011, pp. 508–528.

Ensor, Kristine. "Nonprofit Organizational Charts: What Are They and Why Are They Vital?" *Nonprofit Blog*, 30 Aug. 2023, donorbox.org/nonprofit-blog/nonprofit-org-chart.

Gunn, Rochelle, et al. "How to Choose Volunteer Management Software." *Volunteer Management Software*, 21 Dec. 2022, www.rosterfy.com/blog/how-to-choose-volunteer-management-software.

Handy, F., R.A. Cnaan, and L. Hustinx (eds.). *A Cross-National Study of Volunteering in Later Life: Comparing the Experience of Volunteering among Older Adults in the United States*. Johns Hopkins University Press, Japan, 2010.

Hawthorne, Randy. "How and When to Let a Volunteer Go: Nonprofit Blog." *Nonprofit Hub*, 18 Apr. 2022, nonprofithub.org/how-and-when-to-let-a-volunteer-go/.

Jäger, Urs, and F. Rehli. "Cooperative Power Relations between Nonprofit Board Chairs and Executive Directors: Cooperative Power Relations between Board Chairs and Executive Directors." *Nonprofit Management & Leadership*, vol. 23, no. 2, 2012, pp. 219–236.

Johnson, Tobi. "10 Must Have's for a Well-Crafted Volunteer Job Description." *VolunteerPro*, 8 Feb. 2023, volpro.net/right-volunteer-job-description/.

Johnson, Tobi. "The Ultimate Guide to Managing Volunteers." *VoluntePro*, Feb. 2021, https://volunteeringhub.org.au/wp-content/uploads/2021/02/Tobi%20Johnson's%20Ultimate%20Guide%20to%20Managing%20Volunteers.pdf.

McCurley, Steve. "How to Fire a Volunteer and Live to Tell about It." www.volunteerlimerick.ie/resources/volunteer-mangement/32-how-to-fire-a-volunteer. Accessed 29 Sept. 2023.

Moreno-Jiménez, M.P., and M.C.H. Villodres. "Prediction of Burnout in Volunteers." *Journal of Applied Social Psychology*, vol. 40, no. 7, 2010, pp. 1798–1818.

Netting, F.E., et al. "Volunteer and Paid Staff Relationships: Implications for Social Work Administration." *Administration in Social Work*, vol. 28, no. 3–4, 2004, pp. 69–89.

Rosenthal, Robert J., and Ohio Library and Information Network. *Volunteer Engagement 2.0: Ideas and Insights Changing the World*. Wiley, Hoboken, 2015, doi:10.1002/9781119154792.

Smith, D.H., R.A. Stebbins, and M.A. Dover. "A Model of Volunteer Participation: Choice Versus Constraint." *Social Forces*, vol. 84, no. 2, 2006, pp. 1273–1299.

"The 3 Pillars of Giving: Time, Talent & Treasure." *Foundation Source*, 28 Sept. 2022, foundationsource.com/blog/the-3-pillars-of-giving-time-talent-treasure/.

Trembacki, Mark. "First-Time Nonprofit Board Members – Maximize Your Impact!" *LinkedIn*, 11 Nov. 2016, www.linkedin.com/pulse/first-time-nonprofit-board-members-maximize-your-impact-trembacki.

"Volunteers." *National Council of Nonprofits*, www.councilofnonprofits.org/running-nonprofit/employment-hr/volunteers. Accessed 26 Aug. 2023.

"Volunteer Demographics and Statistics in the US." *Zippia*, www.zippia.com/volunteer-jobs/demographics/. Accessed 20 Jul. 2023.
Waters, Addison. "Communicating with Your Volunteers: A Handbook for Volunteer Leader." *Volunteer Management Blog*, 23 Jul. 2023, www.galaxydigital.com/blog/volunteer-communications-handbook. Accessed 25 Jul. 2023.
Wilson, J. "Volunteering." *Annual Review of Sociology*, vol. 26, no. 1, 2000, pp. 215–240.
"Writing a Volunteer Agreement." *NCVO*, 21 Apr. 2021, www.ncvo.org.uk/help-and-guidance/involving-volunteers/recruiting-and-welcoming-volunteers/writing-a-volunteer-agreement/#/.

9 Teams, Conflict, and Personality

Learning Outcomes

After reading this chapter, you should be able to:

LO 9-1: Distinguish between groups and teams.
LO 9-2: Identify the various types of groups commonly used in nonprofits.
LO 9-3: Describe the different types of teams common in nonprofits.
LO 9-4: Apply the traits of high-performing teams using Lencioni's model.
LO 9-5: Explain the types of organizational conflict and describe how conflict can benefit organizations.
LO 9-6: Summarize the five common approaches used to manage conflict.
LO 9-7: Define personality and describe the big five personality traits.

LO 9-1: Distinguish between groups and teams.

Teams

Nonprofits are complex organizations made up of various individuals, groups, and teams comprised of volunteers, staff, and board of director leaders engaging in various roles and tasks, sometimes interrelated and sometimes not, but all in support of the overarching organizational mission. While effective staff hiring and management (Chapter 4), strategic organizational design (Chapter 5), good strategic planning (Chapter 6), successful board development (Chapter 7), and robust volunteer programs (Chapter 8) serve as the foundation of a nonprofit, effective management of these stakeholder groups and their functions is also dependent upon forming and leading strong teams and navigating conflict.

Groups vs. Teams

Groups and teams sound similar but serve distinct purposes within organizations. **Groups** are simpler in nature, referring to the assembly

DOI: 10.4324/9781003380030-12

of individuals who come together for various reasons, either formally or informally, with individual outcomes and accountability. **Teams**, on the other hand, are much more structured and refer to groups of individuals who work collaboratively to achieve shared goals, which requires interdependence and collective accountability (Colquitt, LePine & Wesson 2021). While all teams are groups, not all groups are teams. To rise to the level of a team, a group must meet the characteristics of a team, primarily sharing a collaborative purpose. The distinctions between groups and teams are highlighted in Figure 9.1.

> LO 9-2: Identify the various types of groups common in nonprofits.

Group Types

Groups can be either formal or informal. **Formal groups** are assembled by leaders to perform a specific task for an organization, and an example of a formal group in nonprofits is a workgroup or some forms of volunteer committees. For instance, a leader may assemble a workgroup of nonprofit staff and volunteers to brainstorm ideas for a new fundraising event (Surbhi

	GROUPS	TEAMS
GOALS	INDIVIDUAL	SHARED
ACCOUNTABILITY	INDIVIDUAL	INDIVIDUAL AND SHARED
OUTCOMES	INDIVIDUAL SUCCESS OR FAILURE	COLLECTIVE SUCCESS OR FAILURE
STRUCTURE	LESS FORMAL	MORE FORMAL
ADVANTAGES	EFFICIENT AND ALLOWS FOR INDIVIDUAL GROWTH	COLLABORATIVE AND BETTER FOR PROBLEM-SOLVING
DISADVANTAGES	LACK OF TEAM BUILDING AND NOT AS GOAL-ORIENTED	CAN BE INEFFICIENT AND LIMIT INDIVIDUAL GROWTH

Figure 9.1 Groups vs. Teams *Adapted from ("Group" 2023)*

2018). The group may have a facilitator, but there is no clear leader and no established hierarchy of authority.

Informal groups form organically around common interests, identities, or social goals. A group of nonprofit employees who meet up after work together every Thursday at a local bar for weekly trivia night is an example of an informal group. Regardless of the formality of groups, they differ from teams due to the differences in structure and shared goal-orientation (Surbhi 2018). The accountability, goals, and success or failure of the groups tends to be more individualized, rather than shared as a collective, as they are with teams. The distinctions between the two are highlighted in Figure 9.1.

Groups are efficient and can be formed quickly. They also allow for greater individual growth due to the individualized nature of accountability and responsibility for outcomes. The downside of groups, however, is that this individualized aspect can limit team-building opportunities, and the lack of shared goals may not advance organizational goals.

LO 9-3: Describe the different types of teams common in nonprofits.

Team Types

In organizations, there are various types of teams, and some of the most common ones in the nonprofit sector are departmental teams, functional teams, task forces, and committees. **Departmental** or **functional teams** are composed of individuals who work within the same department or functional area of the organization. These teams are a natural outcome of the departmentalization function of organizational design, discussed in Chapter 5. Other types of teams include **task forces** and **committees**, assembled to address specific issues or make decisions ("Types"). The distinction between the two is that task forces are usually temporary, much like ad hoc boards discussed in Chapter 7, and committees are longer-term. Organizing volunteers into committees, for example, is a common way of forming teams in nonprofits and is a topic covered in depth within Chapter 8.

Teams require more effort to form and do not allow for as much individual growth of members compared to groups, but they have the advantage of serving as a collaborative force, resulting in better brainstorming, problem-solving, and team building. Sometimes groups transition into teams either through intentional effort or changes in dynamics to evolve into greater collaboration, shared accountability, interdependence, and goal-orientation.

Assembling people into groups is relatively easy, but managing stakeholders in a way that generates the shared goals and collaboration of teams is much more challenging. This objective, however, is an essential ingredient for success. As just one example, a growing body of research shows that there is strong evidence that the effectiveness of an organization's governance system relies on an effective board operating well together as a team (Nicholson 2012). Forming a group of volunteers and calling it a board is not good enough; leaders must create the group and manage efforts to elevate that group into a high-functioning team.

> LO 9-4: Apply the traits of high-performing teams using Lencioni's model.

TRAITS OF HIGH-PERFORMING TEAMS

High-performing teams are comprised of members with the skills and attitudes needed to achieve team objectives, and who work together in a culture of collaboration, support, and trust (Dyer 2020). Author and leadership consultant Patrick Lencioni identified five key traits of high-performing teams, presented in a pyramid-like model, illustrated in Figure 9.2, with each trait serving as a foundation for the one above it. **Lencioni's model of high-performing teams** puts forth the idea that high-performing teams prioritize these traits and work to address any dysfunctions that may hinder their effectiveness (Aggarwal 2023). The five traits include trust, conflict, commitment, accountability, and results.

Trust serves as the foundation of high-performing teams, as members must have confidence in each others' intentions, capabilities, and reliability. Trust also involves open and honest communication where members can express their thoughts and concerns without fear of judgment or reprisal.

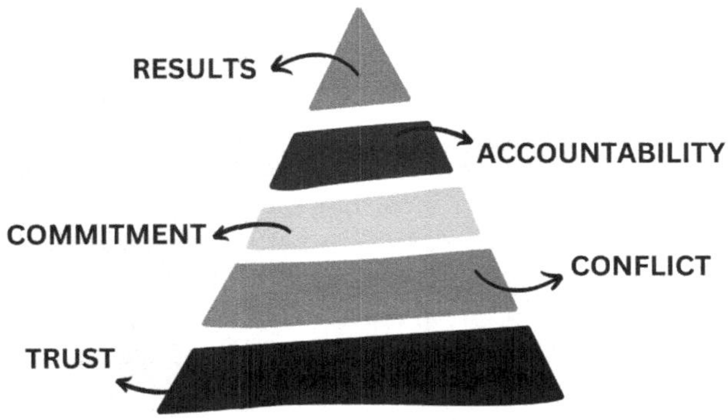

Figure 9.2 Lencioni's Model of High-Performing Teams

The topic of conflict is addressed in the next section, and it may surprise you to learn that not all conflict is bad. In fact, according to Lencioni, *conflict* is the next step in the pyramid. Teams that trust each other are more likely to engage in constructive debates and discussions, and this conflict can be an opportunity to challenge ideas, seek different perspectives, and arrive at the best possible solutions. High-performing teams embrace conflict as a means to make better decisions and avoid artificial harmony.

The next step of the pyramid is *commitment*, meaning that team members are fully committed to the team's goals and are aligned in how the team will work together to achieve them. A hallmark of teams, and factor that sets teams apart from groups, is shared accountability, and this trait is the next step of Lencioni's pyramid. *Accountability* ensures that team members hold one another responsible for their commitments and performance and establishes clear expectations and standards of behavior. The peak of the pyramid is *results*. Ultimately, high-performing teams are focused on achieving measurable and meaningful results, and they prioritize collective success over individual interests.

> LO 9-5: Explain the types of organizational conflict and describe how conflict can benefit organizations.

Conflict

Organizations are comprised of humans, and a natural outcome of human interactions is conflict. But as noted in Lencioni's model, conflict is a central trait of high-performing teams, and properly managed conflict can even lead both personal and organizational benefits (Silverthorne 2005). While some nonprofit leaders may seek to avoid conflict, the most effective ones channel conflict in a positive direction.

Types of Conflict

Conflict is a disagreement or discord arising from differences in interests, opinions, or perspectives among individuals, groups, or teams, and those individuals or groups block or thwart one another's attempts to achieve their objectives (Jones 2013). **Constructive conflict** is disagreement that is directed in a positive and productive manner, leading to positive outcomes. It is beneficial because it allows for diversity of perspectives, which translates to more effective decisions and innovative ideas ("Organizational" 2022).

As Lencioni's model suggests, teams that achieve the base level of trust feel empowered to engage in healthy disagreement, so constructive conflict can serve as an indicator of trust. Further, constructive conflict can also signal engagement, as team members who do not concern themselves with outcomes generally will not bother to contribute to debate. Those who are willing to tread into constructive conflict are often more engaged and committed employees. In summary, well-managed conflict can benefit an organization and even strengthen relationships among team members.

Groupthink can be a problem in organizations, where team members conform to a dominant viewpoint without critical evaluation. Healthy conflict encourages diversity of thought and prevents premature consensus through groupthink (Russell 2015).

While constructive conflict can be positive, **destructive conflict** is not. This is a form of disagreement characterized by hostility and personal attacks that ultimately harms productivity and relationships ("Organizational" 2022). Nonprofit leaders must effectively manage conflict and enact measures to ensure that disagreements are constructive, rather than destructive. This includes measures to foster a culture of trust and open communication and employee conflict resolution training.

> LO 9-6: Summarize the five common approaches used to manage conflict.

Managing Conflict

For conflict to be constructive, it must be effectively managed, so it is important to understand the various approaches or strategies people use to address and resolve conflict, as the approach used to address the discord may largely influence the outcome of the conflict (Canaan 2016). These approaches are referred to as **conflict resolution styles**, and, just as leadership can be situational, so can conflict resolution styles (Wilmot 2000). They can vary in their effectiveness and suitability depending on the circumstances and the personalities of those involved in the conflict (Ejaz 2012), and the five common conflict resolution styles include accommodation, compromise, avoidance, competition, and collaboration.

One commonly used method to explore the diverse approaches individuals use when dealing with conflict is the Thomas-Kilmann Conflict Mode Instrument, which was developed using two key dimensions: one focused on assertiveness and the other on cooperativeness, resulting in a 2×2 matrix. According to the Thomas-Kilmann model, conflict resolution actions can be categorized based on both their level of cooperativeness, ranging from cooperative to uncooperative, and their level of assertiveness, which can be either assertive or unassertive (Jones 1976). This matrix is visualized in Figure 9.3.

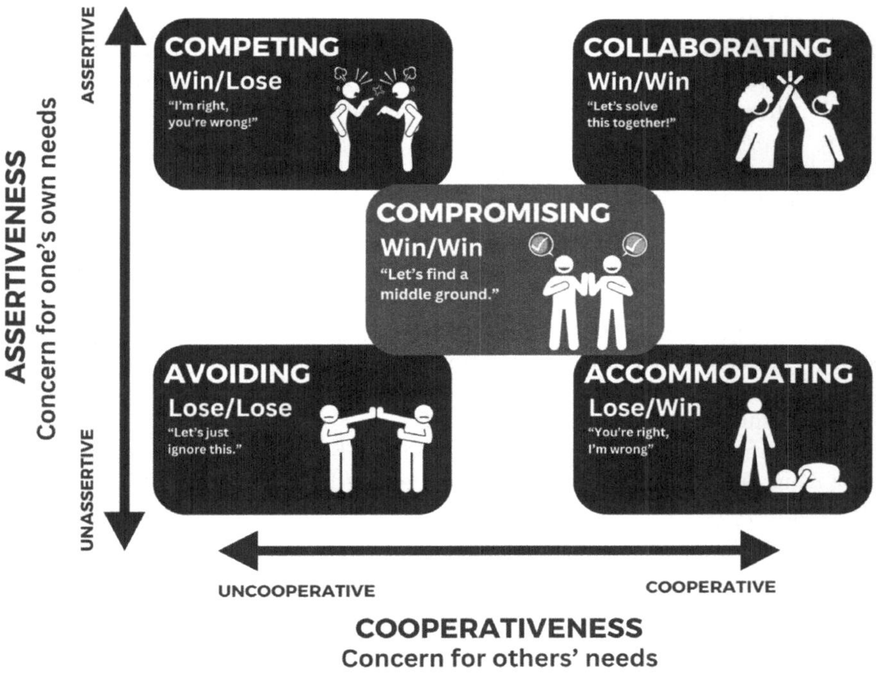

Figure 9.3 Conflict Resolution Styles

The assertive, uncooperative, or "win/lose" approach is competing. The **competing style** is where one party prioritizes their own interests and goals over those of the other party, and that person may use authority, power, or assertiveness to win the conflict. This is sometimes referred to as a dominating style and occurs when quick and decisive action is necessary or when one party's position is significantly stronger than that of the other party (Thomas 2008).

In some situations, people avoid conflict. The unassertive, uncooperative "lose/lose" approach is avoiding. The **avoiding style** is the conflict resolution approach where conflicting parties choose not to address the conflict directly and instead choose to delay dealing with it or ignore it entirely. Avoidance can be an appropriate approach for minor conflicts or when it is not feasible to immediately address an issue.

The cooperative, assertive "win/win" approach is collaborating, which is sometimes referred to as an integrating approach. The **collaborating style** involves working together to find a mutually beneficial solution and requires open communication, active listening, and a willingness to compromise to meet the needs and interests of all parties involved. This approach aims to preserve or improve relationships while resolving the conflict.

The cooperative yet unassertive "lose/win" approach is accommodating. The **accommodating style**, sometimes referred to as an obliging approach, happens when one party yields their own needs to the preferences or needs of the other party. It can be an appropriate approach when maintaining harmony or preserving a relationship is more important than achieving a particular outcome.

The style that fits right in the middle of cooperativeness and assertiveness and, like the collaborating style, is a "win/win" approach to conflict is compromising. While the approaches are similar, the compromising approach is less assertive and less cooperative than the collaborating approach. The **compromising style** seeks a middle ground where both parties make concessions to reach an agreement, involving negotiation and finding solutions that partially satisfy the interests of each party. Compromise aims to provide a fair and equitable resolution to the conflict.

None of these approaches is better than the other, and none are right or wrong, as each has its own advantages and disadvantages. Further, the choice of approach may vary dependent on the circumstances of the conflict and people involved in the disagreement.

> LO 9-7: Define personality and describe the big five personality traits.

Personality

One of the factors that determines how people function within groups and teams and navigate organizational conflict is their individual personality. **Personality** refers to an individual's unique and enduring pattern of thoughts, feelings, behaviors, and characteristics that shape their consistent way of interacting with and responding to the world around them. Many theorists agree on the concept of the five core personality dimensions, commonly known as the "big five" or the "five-factor model," and use these to characterize individuals and their personality traits (Canaan 2016).

These five personality traits can be remembered with the acronym CANOE, representing the qualities of conscientiousness, agreeableness, neuroticism, openness to experience, and extroversion (Goldberg 1993), which is represented in Figure 9.4. People typically possess a *combination* of these five traits, rather than just one dominant one, and their personalities can be described by this mix.

Conscientiousness relates to a person's level of responsibility, organization, self-control, and dependability, and designates that individuals are highly motivated and goal-oriented (Judge 2002) and therefore more likely to attain their objectives (Robbins 2007). Individuals high in conscientiousness are often seen as reliable, organized, disciplined, and detail oriented. They set and achieve goals consistently.

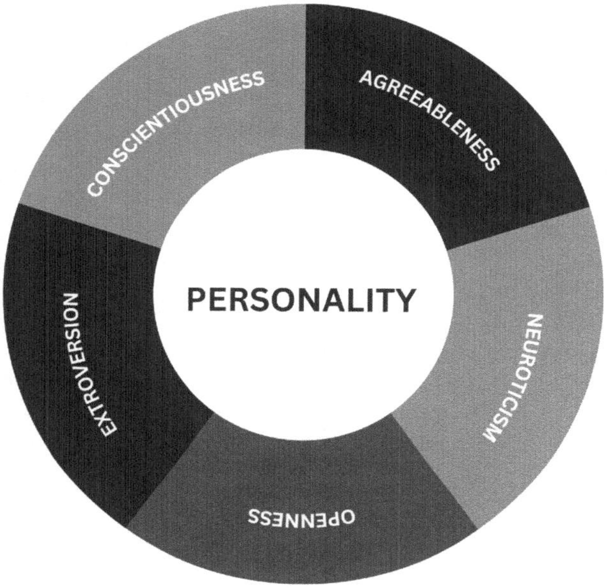

Figure 9.4 Big Five Personality Traits

Agreeableness refers to person's general concern for social harmony and assesses their degree of warmth, kindness, and cooperativeness in interpersonal relationship (Canaan 2016). People high in this trait are pleasant, trusting, kind, and warm, and value getting along with others.

The first two dimensions are associated with positive traits, but the third aspect of the five-factor model, neuroticism, is negative. **Neuroticism**, sometimes reversed and measured instead as emotional stability, measures an individual's emotional reactivity and tendency to experience adverse feelings, such as anger, nervousness, or despair, especially in threatening situations and loss (Lahey 2009). Individuals high in neuroticism tend to be depressed, worried, and anxious (Jeronimus 2014).

The **openness to experience** trait reflects an individual's willingness to be open to new ideas, experiences, and ways of thinking. People high in openness tend to be creative, curious, imaginative, and are drawn to new things (Chamorro 2009).

The final trait, **extroversion**, is associated with a person's ease in navigating external relationships and situations (Laney 2002). People high in extroversion generally enjoy socializing with others and even seek out social experiences. They tend to be more positive, talkative, energetic, friendly, and outgoing (Srivastava, Angelo & Vallereux 2008).

Differences in personality can sometimes serve as a source of conflict, as these individual differences result in different end goals and methods and approaches to achieve them. Further, while conflict resolution approaches can be situational, personality can influence how an individual navigates conflict. For instance, research indicates that people with a greater degree of openness to experience, for instance, tend toward a collaborating style, whereas those high in neuroticism are more likely to take an accommodating approach (Wang 2010).

Personality can also impact individuals' contributions to groups and teams, with those high in agreeableness, for example, tending to be consummate team players, and those who are highly conscientious driving team goal-orientation and achievement (Peeters, et al. 2006). The personality of the designated team leader can also serve as a determining factor for team performance (Fu 2020). Understanding personality differences and how they influence team performance and dynamics can help leaders assemble more effective teams.

Takeaways

LO 9-1: Groups and teams are interrelated concepts, but function differently. Groups are collections of individuals who are assembled without shared accountability and goals, whereas teams are more structured share in goals and outcomes.

LO 9-2: Formal groups, such as workgroups, are generally assembled to perform a specific task for an organization, whereas informal groups typically form organically around common interests of individuals within an organization.

LO 9-3: Examples of nonprofit teams include departmental teams, functional teams, task forces, and committees.

LO 9-4: Lencioni's model of high-performing teams suggests that high-performing teams share five traits: trust, conflict, commitment, accountability, and results.

LO 9-5: Unmanaged conflict can be destructive, harming productivity, relationships, and the overall well-being of the organization, but when channeled positively can be constructive,
leading to positive outcomes such as innovation and avoidance of groupthink.

LO 9-6: The five approaches to conflict resolution include competing, avoiding, collaborating, accommodating, and compromising. These are classified across two dimensions: assertive vs. cooperative and concern for self vs. concern for others.

LO 9-7: Personality refers to an individual's unique pattern of behaviors and characteristics that influence the way they interact with others, and the "big five model" is often used to characterize individuals across five personality traits: conscientiousness, agreeableness, neuroticism, openness, and extroversion.

Bibliography

Aggarwal, Anil. "A Study of Lencioni's Model of Dysfunctional Groups." *International Journal of e-Collaboration*, vol. 19, no. 1, 2023, pp. 1–19.

Canaan, Messarra, Leila Silva Karkoulian, and Abdul-Nasser El-Kassar. "Conflict Resolution Styles and Personality: The Moderating Effect of Generation X and Y in a Non-Western Context." *International Journal of Productivity and Performance Management*, vol. 65, no. 6, 2016, pp. 792–810.

Chamorro-Premuzic, T., S. Reimers, A. Hsu, and G. Ahmetoglu. "Who Art Thou? Personality Predictors of Artistic Preferences in a large UK Sample: The Importance of Openness." *British Journal of Psychology*, vol. 100, no. 1, 2009, pp. 501–516.

Colquitt, Jason, Jeffery LePine, and Michael Wesson. *Organizational Behavior: Improving Performance and Commitment in the Workplace*. McGraw Hill, New York, 2021. Print.

Dyer, W.G., Jr, J.H. Dyer, and Ohio Library and Information Network. *Beyond Team Building: How to Build High Performing Teams and the Culture to Support Them*. Wiley, Hoboken, 2020.

Ejaz, S.S., F. Iqbal, and A. Ara. "Relationship among Personality Traits and Conflict Handling Styles of Call Center Representatives and Appraisal of Existing Service Model." *International Journal of Psychological Studies*, vol. 4 no. 4, 2012, pp. 27–36.

Fu, Jianping, et al. "A Cross Level Analysis of the Influence of a Team Leader's Personality, Gender Diversity and Group Participation on University Students' Academic Performance." *Innovations in Education and Teaching International*, vol. 57, no. 5, 2020, pp. 555–564.

Goldberg, L.R. "The Structure of Phenotypic Personality-Traits." *American Psychologist*, vol. 48, no. 1, 1993, pp. 26–34.

"Group vs. Team: What's the Difference?"*Asana*, 15 Mar. 2023, asana.com/resources/group-vs-team. Accessed 19 Jul. 2023.

Jeronimus, B.F., H. Riese, R. Sanderman and J. Ormel "Mutual Reinforcement between Neuroticism and Life Experiences: A Five-Wave, 16-Year Study to Test Reciprocal Causation." *Journal of Personality and Social Psychology*, vol. 107, no. 4, 2014, pp. 751–764.

Jones, G., J. George, and O. Belkhodja. *Contemporary Management*, McGraw-Hill/Irwin, New York, NY, 2013.

Jones, John E. "Instrumentation." *Group & Organization Studies*, vol. 1, no. 2, 1976, p. 249.

Judge, T.A., and R. Ilies. "Relationship of Personality to Performance Motivation: A Metaanalytic Review." *Journal of Applied Psychology*, vol. 87, no. 1, 2002, pp. 797–807.

Lahey, B.B. "Public Health Significance of Neuroticism." *American Psychologist*, vol. 64, no. 1, 2009, pp. 241–256.

Laney, M.O. *The Introvert Advantage: How quiet people can thrive in an extrovert world*.. Workman Publishing, New York, NY, 2002, pp. 28–35.

Nicholson, Gavin, Cameron Newton, and Myles McGregor-Lowndes. "The Nonprofit Board as a Team: Pilot Results and Initial Insights." *Nonprofit Management & Leadership*, vol. 22, no. 4, 2012, pp. 461–481.

Organizational Conflict: New Insights. Edited by Josiane Fahed-Sreih. IntechOpen, 2022, doi:10.5772/intechopen.78825.

Peeters, G., et al. "Personality and Team Performance: A Meta-Analysis." *European Journal of Personality*, vol. 20, no. 5, 2006, pp. 377–396.

Robbins, S.P., and T.A. Judge. *Organizational Behavior*, 12th ed. Pearson Education Inc., Upper Saddle River, NJ, 2007.

Russell, Jeffrey S., John Hawthorne, and Lara Buchak. "Groupthink." *Philosophical Studies*, vol. 172, no. 5, 2015, pp. 1287–1309.
Silverthorne, C.P. *Organizational Psychology in Cross-Cultural Perspective*. New York University Press, New York, NY, 2005.
Srivastava, S., Angelo, K. M., and Vallereux, S. R. "Extraversion and Positive Affect: A Day Reconstruction Study of Person–Environment Transactions." *Journal of Research in Personality*, vol. 42, no. 6, 2008, pp. 1613–1618.
Srivastava, S., O.P. John, S.D. Gosling, and J. Potter. "Development of Personality in Early and Middle Adulthood: Set Like Plaster or Persistent Change?" *Journal of Personality and Social Psychology*, vol. 84, no. 1, 2003, pp. 1041–1053.
Surbhi, S. "Difference between Formal and Informal Groups (with Comparison Chart)." *Key Differences*, 26 July 2018, keydifferences.com/difference-between-formal-and-informal-groups.html#:~:text=In%20a%20formal%20group%2C%20the%20relationship%20between%20the%20members%20is,problems%2C%20information%20with%20each%20other.
Thomas, Kenneth W. "Thomas-Kilmann Conflict Mode." *TKI Profile and Interpretive Report*, vol. 1, no. 11, pp. 1–11 2008.
"Types of Teams." *Hello Vaia*, www.hellovaia.com/explanations/business-studies/organizational-behavior/types-of-teams/#:~:text=There%20are%20various%20types%20of%20teams%20in%20an%20organization.,system%20(team%20of%20teams). Accessed 29 Sept. 2023.
Wang, X. *The Relationship between the Five-Factor Personality and Conflict Management Styles in a Manufacturing Setting*. University of Phoenix, Phoenix, AZ, 2010, 271pp.
Wilmot, W.H., and J.L. Hocker. *Interpersonal Conflict*, 6th ed. McGraw-Hill, New York, NY, 2000.

Part 4

Donors

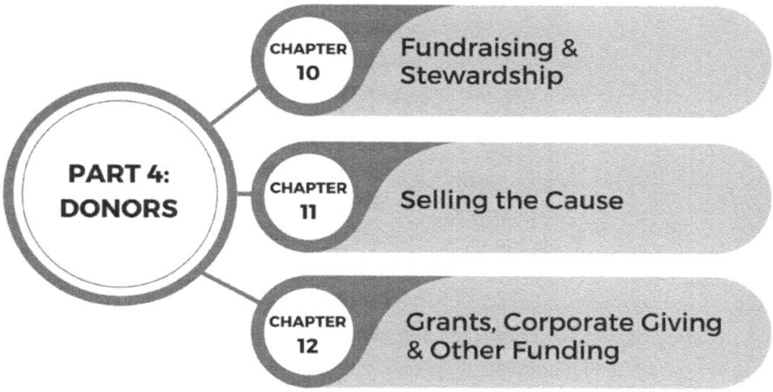

10 Fundraising and Stewardship

Learning Outcomes

After reading this chapter, you should be able to:

LO 10-1: Describe and categorize the various types of nonprofit donors and their donations, including various donation forms, levels of donations, and classifications of frequency and use of donations, and explain how the 80/20 rule applies.
LO 10-2: Articulate the steps of the donor fundraising cycle in nonprofits.
LO 10-3: Explain how fundraisers identify, qualify, and cultivate potential donors, including the primary motivations that drive giving behavior.
LO 10-4: Summarize the process of soliciting and securing gifts as well as strategies around donor stewardship.
LO 10-5: Identify and describe commonly used nonprofit fundraising channels.
LO 10-6: Demonstrate ways to engage volunteers in development work and fundraising.
LO 10-7: Synthesize the steps of the negotiation process in fundraising and explain how these steps relate to the donor fundraising cycle.

> LO 10-1: Describe and categorize the various types of nonprofit donors and their donations, including various donation forms, levels of donations, and classifications of frequency and use of donations, and explain how the 80/20 rule applies.

Donors

Nonprofits rely on a variety of funding sources to support their operations and activities in work toward fulfilling their organizational mission, and a key source comes from fundraising, including contributions from individual

DOI: 10.4324/9781003380030-14

donors and foundations, grants and government funding, and foundations and corporate sponsorships. According to a recent Congressional Research Service report, charitable support from individuals represents the vast majority of nonprofit funding, as represented in Figure 10.1 ("Tax" 2023). A **donor** is an individual or entity that contributes funds, goods, or services to support a nonprofit organization's mission and activities. While the focus of this chapter will be on individual donors and foundations, much of the content presented is relevant to other types of funders as well, such as corporate sponsors, which is discussed in Chapter 12.

Nonprofits receive money from donors through various **fundraising channels**, which can include support from events, email, direct mail, online platforms, social media campaigns, and others ("Multi" 2016). An **individual donor** refers to a person who provides individual and voluntary financial support to a nonprofit organization. This is different than public and private foundations, discussed in Chapter 1, that represent collective financial support for nonprofits from multiple individuals. Donor contributions can also come in other forms, such as matching gifts and peer-to-peer fundraising, which are covered in subsequent chapters.

Fundraising work is traditionally the responsibility of nonprofit development staff, although engaging volunteers in this work is a common approach discussed later in this chapter. Many development staff join the **Association of Fundraising Professionals (AFP)**, a global nonprofit professional association

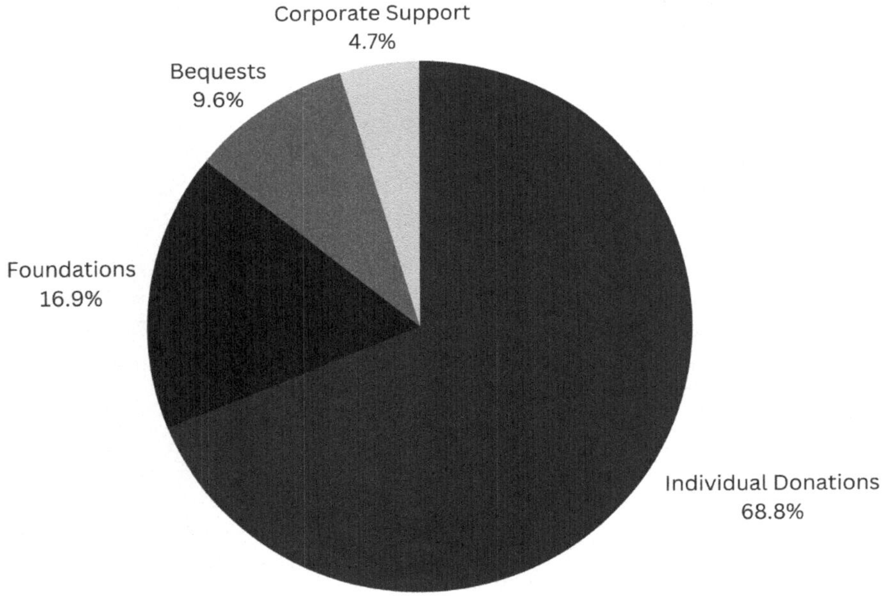

Figure 10.1 Nonprofit Funding Sources
("Tax" 2023)

that supports and promotes ethical and effective fundraising and philanthropy. They do so to access resources, participate in networking opportunities, receive professional development, and learn and share best practices to enhance their fundraising knowledge and skills ("Join" 2023). Another association that provides development staff opportunities for professional development and networking is CFRE International, which also administers the **Certified Fund Raising Executive** (CFRE) credential. Some development professionals opt to pursue the CFRE credential for continuing education and to bolster their professional credibility ("Certification" 2023).

Forms of Donations

Donors make contributions in a range of forms, encompassing various categories. The most direct form of donor giving, and easiest to receive and use are **monetary gifts**, which consist of cash donations, checks, credit card payments, and electronic funds transfers. **In-kind gifts** are non-monetary contributions of goods or services. For example, a grocery store does not donate cash as a monetary gift to a nonprofit for its upcoming 5K charity run, but instead donates 150 cases of bottled water, which saves the nonprofit from having to buy it. **Gifts of securities** refers to the donation of stocks, bonds, or other marketable financial assets to nonprofit organizations. This type of donation allows donors to contribute appreciated securities, often resulting in potential tax benefits, while supporting the nonprofit's mission ("8 Types" 2023).

Some gifts are not immediate, but deferred, including **legacy gifts**. Sometimes referred to as planned gifts or bequests, these are contributions that individuals include in their wills or estate plans to be donated to a nonprofit after their passing. **Tribute or memorial gifts** are contributions made in honor of someone living or in memory of someone who has passed away, often making the donation in recognition of a special occasion or to commemorate a loved one ("8 Types" 2023). There are certainly other types of contributions, but these five, represented in Figure 10.2, are the most common.

Additionally, some nonprofits choose to categorize gifts or donors based on the *amount* or *frequency* of the contribution. Nonprofits categorize and segment donors in these ways to better understand their giving patterns, tailor communication and engagement strategies, and cultivate stronger relationships based on donors' preferences and interests. When categorizing gifts or donors based on size of contribution, most simply use terminology such as low-level, mid-level, and major.

Levels of Donations

The naming of these categories can vary, as can the dollar amounts that a nonprofit uses to designate each level, depending on the agency's size, scope,

Figure 10.2 Forms of Gifts

and funding needs. To illustrate, in the case of a smaller or newer nonprofit, a "major gift" could start at $1,000 or more. However, for organizations that are larger and more established, it might require a donation of at least $50,000 to be considered a major gift ("Nonprofit" 2023). Therefore, a **major gift** in nonprofits refers to a substantial and impactful donation from an individual, organization, or entity that significantly supports the organization's mission and programs ("What Are" 2021). Other terms commonly used to categories a major gift, or subcategories to further define the general major gift category, include principal gift, leadership gift, or transformative gift.

Defining the major gift criterion in terms of minimum contribution then impacts what a nonprofit considers a mid-level gift. A **mid-level gift** in nonprofits refers to a moderately sized donation that falls between smaller, regular contributions and larger, major gifts, often indicating a higher level of donor engagement and support. Mid-level gifts are usually defined as a range and, like major gifts, vary by agency ("What Are" 2021). As one example, if a nonprofit considers a $10,000 or above contribution a major gift, it may set a range of $1,000–$9,999 as a mid-level gift.

An **entry-level gift** in nonprofits refers to the initial or modest donation made by a supporter. Defining donations falling at this level, under the mid-level threshold, can present challenges, as donors might perceive the label "low-level gift" as insensitive. While some nonprofits opt to still utilize this term, it is usually for internal purposes only. Other agencies designate these as "entry-level" contributions, although that is not always an accurate description, such as for a donor who has contributed small gifts for years. Some agencies opt to not establish a formal definition at all, simply referring to these in general terms as gifts or contributions.

Categorizing donors according to their giving levels within nonprofits serves the purpose of determining strategy to request these donations, as well as allocating resources effectively for the solicitation process. Research indicates that, on average, more than 88% of a nonprofit's funding originates from just 12% of its donors, representing a significant part of the agency's income. Given this scenario, it is logical for nonprofits to allocate a significant portion of their resources toward nurturing and cultivating this specific category of donations.

While the exact ratio of major donors to all other donors can vary from agency to agency, and is also dependent upon the ranges used to define each giving level, for most nonprofits, the Pareto principle applies. The Pareto principle, better known as the **80/20 rule**, signifies that roughly 80% of results or contributions stem from around 20% of donors (Nenn 2017). If the top 20% of donors are classified as major donors for an agency, a visual representation of the 80/20 rule might look like the graphic represented in Figure 10.3.

Frequency and Use of Donations

Nonprofits also categorize donors based upon their way of giving or the frequency of the donor's contributions ("8 Types" 2023). **Recurring gifts** are ongoing, scheduled donations made at regular intervals by individuals or

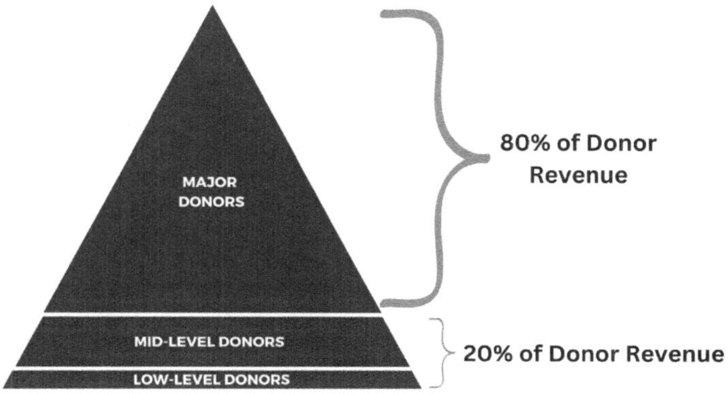

Figure 10.3 80/20 Rule in Nonprofits

organizations to support a cause, institution, or nonprofit ("8 Types" 2023). Common recurring gifts are monthly or annual gifts. **Monthly giving** refers to donors who commit to making regular, recurring donations on a monthly basis, providing a consistent source of funding for the nonprofit. **Annual giving** refers to the practice of individuals or organizations making regular, yearly charitable donations to support a cause, institution, or nonprofit. With recurring gifts, the amounts can stay the same or they may vary. Unlike monthly or annual giving, a **one-time gift** is a singular, non-recurring donation made by individuals or organizations to support a cause, institution, or nonprofit.

Major gifts are often made as one-time gifts, and can be paid all at once, or made as a **pledge**, which is a commitment made by an individual or organization to contribute a specific amount of money to a cause or nonprofit over a specified period ("Nonprofit Accounting"). For instance, instead of writing a check for $100,000, a donor may instead opt to pledge and pay $20,000 over a five-year period. Major gifts are also sometimes made with the intention of being endowed. One-time major gifts are sometimes made as endowed gifts. An **endowment** or endowed gift is a substantial donation that is invested, and the generated income or interest from that gift is used to support the cause while preserving the initial gift intact (Bowman 2012).

On occasions, when providing a donation, a contributor might designate the intended purpose for its use. **Restricted gifts** are donations made with specific conditions or purposes defined by the donor, dictating how the funds should be used, while **unrestricted gifts** give the receiving organization the flexibility to allocate the funds where they are most needed without specific donor-imposed restrictions (Helms 2012).

LO 10-2: Articulate the steps of the donor fundraising cycle in nonprofits.

Donor Fundraising Cycle

Managing relationships with donors involves understanding the **donor fundraising cycle**, which outlines the process nonprofits follow to engage potential donors, starting from identification and qualification, cultivating relationships, moving through solicitation, and ultimately looping back to ongoing stewardship and relationship-building to encourage continued support (Polivy 2014). Some nonprofits refer to the donor fundraising cycle as a "donor pipeline," the cycle as "pipeline development," and the stages as "moves management" (Tempel 2016). The process is reflected in Figure 10.4 and contains five recurring steps: identification, qualification, cultivation, solicitation, and stewardship. While the steps described in the cycle can

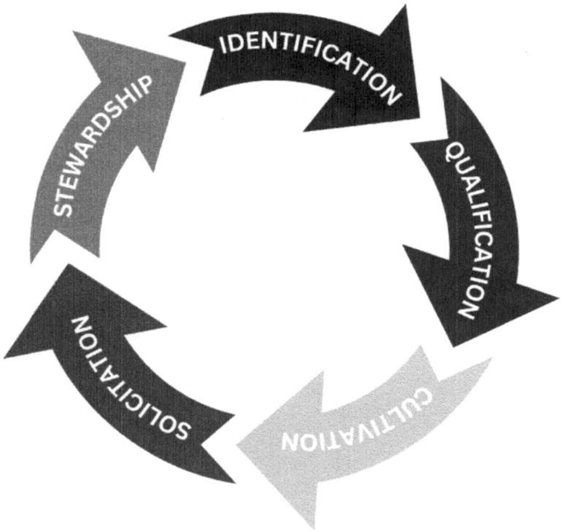

Figure 10.4 Donor Fundraising Cycle

certainly apply to all donors, it is typically formally used to secure major gifts.

> LO 10-3: Explain how fundraisers identify, qualify, and cultivate potential donors, including the primary motivations that drive giving behavior.

Identification

The first step of the donor fundraising cycle is identifying potential donors. Many nonprofits discover prospective donors when they attend events or engage in programs, services, and activities. Or, they may proactively contribute to the organization without a formal solicitation. Many nonprofits utilize donor management systems, or constituent relationship management (CRM) systems. **CRM systems** are designed to help nonprofits track and manage donor information and interactions to better manage the donor fundraising cycle and relationships with supporters. Many CRM systems provide discovery reports, generating lists of high-potential donors for development representatives to pursue.

Identification of a donor prospect can also occur through networking. This includes tapping into the nonprofit's various **spheres of influence**, which is the network of individuals, like board members and volunteers, who are connected to a nonprofit or cause and have the potential to influence others to contribute (Leonard 2022).

Qualification

Once a potential donor is identified, development representatives generally move to the **qualification** step, which involves qualifying a donor prospect in terms of their potential **giving capacity**, which refers to the individual's potential ability to give based on their discoverable financial resources, such as assets, income, and past giving history. Qualification of donors involves **prospect research**, used to determine if prospective donors meet the agency's major gift criteria. Given the 80/20 rule and resource constraints, nonprofit fundraisers will generally prioritize their efforts around prospects who have the capacity to make a major gift at the level designated by the agency.

Cultivation

Once a donor prospect is identified, the organization moves to **cultivation**, which involves forming relationships by providing information, involving them in events and programs, and demonstrating the impact of their potential contributions on the mission of the organization (Polivy 2014). In forming these relationships, development representatives can determine the prospect's motivation for giving which, like with volunteers, can generally be categorized as "head, heart, halo." Instead of these three central motivating factors driving the contribution of *time*, however, in this context it is related to the contribution of financial resources.

The **head motivation** of donors is the prospect's rational assessment of why donating is beneficial; either in terms of impact, or even simple practical reasons such as tax benefits for the donor. **Heart motivation** of donors is a gift made from emotional motivation, such as when there is a personal connection to the cause, or the prospect is passionate about the mission. Finally, **halo motivation** of donors comes from a prospect's desire to be associated with a reputable organization and receive positive social or reputational benefits by contributing to a good cause. Understanding the prospective donor's motivation, which may be a combination of these three, can help the fundraiser in the solicitation stage of the process.

The cultivation stage often involves an assessment of a prospective donor's **propensity to give**, which is their likelihood of donating. This assessment can include consideration of factors such as information gleaned from meetings with the prospect about their interest in donating, past giving history, and other characteristics. Many CRM systems are capable of producing reports indicating donors' propensity to give ("AlumniFinder" 2010). To learn more about prospective donors and their interests and propensity to give, many nonprofits opt to host **cultivation events**, which are events hosted by a nonprofit for the purpose of engaging with current and prospective donors. These events provide opportunities to share information with donors about the agency's mission and impact and build or strengthen relationships among development representatives and potential donors (Schroeder 2019).

LO 10-4: Summarize the process of soliciting and securing gifts as well as strategies around donor stewardship.

Solicitation

Once a donor has been identified, qualified, and properly cultivated, a development representative moves to the next stage of the donor fundraising cycle. **Solicitation** is the formal request for a donation, which is often presented with a compelling case for support and explains how the donor's contribution will make a difference. While some nonprofit supporters will proactively donate without being formally solicited, a *Psychology Today* study indicated that 85% of respondents said the reason they gave to a nonprofit was simply because someone asked them, so it is important to not just engage individuals and wait for them to offer their financial support, but to formally solicit a gift (Konrath 2017).

During this phase, the development representative may either verbally ask for a donation or present a **donation proposal**, which is a written document that outlines the details of the solicitation, including information about the requested donation amount and need and the intended use of the contribution. Donation proposals will also generally outline the terms of the allowed use of the gift, which is generally either for unrestricted use, or restricted in some way such as designated to a **capital campaign**, which is a time-specific effort focused on raising significant funds for a specific project (Woronkowicz 2017).

Stewardship

Stewardship is the next stage of the donor fundraising cycle and involves thanking donors for their support, continuing to nurture the donor relationship. Stewardship activities can include ongoing touchpoints, updates on organizational activities, sharing impact reports, inviting donors to events, sharing success stories, engaging donors as volunteers, and finding ways to connect donors to the cause (Harrison 2018).

One aspect of the stewardship phase is **donor acknowledgment**, which is the process of expressing gratitude and formally recognizing a donor's contribution. This can come in one of many forms, or a combination of them, such as a hand-written thank you note, tax letter, phone call to express appreciation, and others ("Gift"). Some nonprofits host annual donor appreciation events to celebrate and recognize donors, and others have formalized donor acknowledgment activities embedded in their volunteer programs, where board members and volunteers are tasked with thanking donors. Many publish **donor impact reports**, which account for the donations that a nonprofit received over a period of time, describe what was accomplished with these funds, and sometimes list the names of donors ("Key" 2022).

Good stewardship practices can bolster **donor retention**, which is a measure of how many donors continue to donate to the organization, help in the process of converting one-time donors into loyal recurring donors, and aid in increasing the size of a donor's gift, potentially moving a supporter from a mid-level donor, for example, to a major gift (Love 2019).

Sometimes development staff refer to their time spent on the phases of the donor fundraising cycle as "the 4 R's," suggesting that the proportion of time is spent approximately as follows: research (identification and qualification) about 25% of the time; romance (cultivation) about 60% of the time; request (solicitation) about 5% of the time; and recognition (stewardship) about 10% of the time.

LO 10-5: Identify and describe commonly used nonprofit fundraising channels.

Fundraising Channels

While the 80/20 rule tells us that 80% of a nonprofit's contributions come from just 20% of supporters, typically major donors, that does not mean that all fundraising activity should focus exclusively on that population. Not only is the remaining 20% of the fundraising proportion important to sustain operations, but most major donors do not start out as major donors. Many engage first as volunteers, or as casual entry-level supporters, and over time develop into major donors. Nonprofit leaders should ensure that their organizations have multiple fundraising channels to connect with and engage all levels and types of supporters.

As noted at the start of this chapter, fundraising channels are the avenues or methods through which nonprofits seek to collect donations or financial support. These include the following:

Events

Fundraising events are a cornerstone activity of most nonprofits and are covered in depth in Chapter 14. Most of these events raise money not just through ticket sales and corporate sponsorships, but also through some type of donor activity at the event. A black-tie charity gala for example, might have a "fund a need" portion of the event, where attendees are asked to make a donation to the cause. A 5K charity run might have a collection box at the event site, where participants and those there to cheer them on can drop in cash donations. A benefit concert might have a text-to-give portion of the program, where attendees are asked to support the mission by contributing via their smartphone (Mansfield 2014). These are all methods to solicit and receive donations through events.

Direct Mail

Not long ago, direct mail was a central fundraising channel for nonprofits, but its use has fallen in recent years, replaced by more affordable and environmentally friendly options, such as email. Direct mail, however, still has a place as a nonprofit fundraising channel, and has some benefits. Not all donors use email, and in the digital age where physical mail has become less common, a direct mail solicitation may stand out to a donor. The tangible nature of direct mail pieces can create a lasting impression. Supporters can hold, read, and keep the materials, which can increase the likelihood of retention and response.

Online Platforms

Due to its cost effectiveness and ability to track and measure various metrics such as open rate, conversion rate, etc., soliciting donations through email is a common fundraising channel for most nonprofits. Email fundraising can either be direct, where the email is exclusively focused on asking for a contribution and exists for that sole purpose, or indirect, such as embedding a donation ask within a weekly informational newsletter. Incorporating online donation functionalities onto their website is a frequent approach used by nonprofits, as is conducting fundraising campaigns across various social media platforms.

A growing use of online platforms for fundraising is **crowdfunding**, which is a fundraising method where nonprofits raise funds from a large number of individuals online, leveraging the collective contributions of many donors, each giving relatively small amounts, to support the cause (Kim 2022). Many nonprofits rally around **giving days**, which are specified days to promote charitable contributions online during a 24-hour period ("8 Reasons" 2023).

Phone-a-thons

Another opportunity to solicit contributions is through telephone communications. This includes organized phone campaigns where volunteers or staff members call potential donors to request contributions, telethons where the cause is advertised on television and viewers are asked to call to donate, or outsourced telephone campaigns through third-party marketing agencies.

These channels certainly are not an exhaustive list, but instead highlight some of the common methods leveraged by nonprofits to solicit contributions from donors. Using a combination of multiple fundraising channels allows the organization to reach a broader audience, engage supporters through their preferred methods, and reduce dependency on a single source of funding, enhancing financial stability and sustainability.

LO 10-6: Demonstrate ways to engage volunteers in development work and fundraising.

Engaging Volunteers in Fundraising

Many view fundraising as the sole responsibility of development staff, but one could contend that this activity is a shared responsibility of all nonprofit stakeholders, because without donor support, the agency would cease to exist and would fail in achieving their mission. Some volunteers balk at the idea of engaging in fundraising activities, as they find it intimidating, fearing rejection and pressure to achieve. But this viewpoint is held generally because these volunteers tend to view fundraising solely from the solicitation stage, rather than the holistic series of stages of the donor fundraising cycle.

To encourage collective responsibility for fundraising, nonprofit leaders can help volunteers understand the donor fundraising cycle and identify ways these volunteers can contribute to stages other than just the solicitation stage. For example, they can assist with the relationship-building aspects that are ingrained in the other stages of the donor fundraising cycle ("Fundraising?" 2014), detailed below.

Volunteer Fundraising Roles

As noted in Chapter 7, fundraising is an expected task of board members, but it is not just board members who should engage in this task, but other volunteers as well. Some nonprofits choose to establish development advisory boards or fundraising committees to assemble and organize volunteers who are willing to help with fundraising tasks. But aside from formalized and structured groups, here are just a few ways nonprofit leaders can engage volunteers in activities to support fundraising that do not require making solicitations:

- **Networking:** Volunteers can assist with the first step of the donor fundraising cycle, identification, by engaging in networking. This involves bringing new donor prospects to the organization by tapping personal and professional networks and introducing the donor prospect to the organization.

- **Invitations:** Part of the cultivation stage involves engaging donor prospects in cultivation events, and a personalized invitation via email, handwritten note, or phone call can be helpful in assuring their attendance. Making these invitations is a task that can be delegated to volunteers.
- **Event Support:** Hosting donor cultivation and stewardship events requires labor, and some nonprofits lack the staff resources to execute these events, so volunteers can lead the planning and execution of them instead.
- **Donor Appreciation:** Volunteers can lead or support activities to express appreciation of donors and to engage in stewardship, such as writing thank you notes and emails or making personal calls.
- **Administrative Tasks:** Prospect research and other qualification measures can involve administrative tasks that take time, and volunteers can support these development activities through tasks such as data entry.
- **Community Outreach:** One way in which prospective donors sometimes initially engage with a nonprofit is through participation in activities, events, and programs. By representing the organization at these events, and engaging participants in conversation, volunteers can play a helpful role in identifying new potential supporters.
- **Storytelling:** Sharing success stories of individuals positively impacted by the organizational mission is a compelling component of various stages of the donor fundraising cycle. Simply being willing to share their personal stories is an easy way for volunteers to have a big impact on fundraising activities.

LO 10-7: Synthesize the steps of the negotiation process in fundraising and explain how these steps relate to the donor fundraising cycle.

Negotiation

Having strong negotiation skills is an advantage for both fundraisers and nonprofit leaders, as it forms an integral component of the process to secure donations. **Negotiation** is a process in which parties with differing interests engage in discussions and exchanges to reach a mutually acceptable agreement or resolution (Colquitt 2021). The negotiation process involves a series of interactions between parties with differing interests, where they work to find mutually acceptable solutions or agreements by addressing concerns, making compromises, and reaching common ground. While this might look a little different in the nonprofit sector versus a traditional sales setting, it

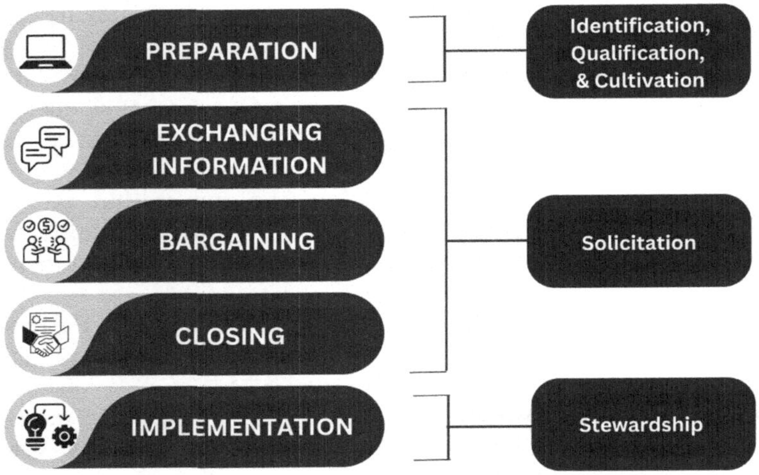

Figure 10.5 Negotiation in Fundraising

essentially follows the same process involving the following steps, illustrated in Figure 10.5.

Preparation

The **preparation phase** is the most important, and occurs when each party identifies their goals, priorities, and potential concessions. In the realm of nonprofit fundraising, this involves the work done by the development representative to identify and qualify the donor, conduct prospect research, and determine the prospect's giving capacity. It also involves cultivating the donor, uncovering their interests and motivations, and gauging their propensity to give. This stage also may involve collaboration with other stakeholders in developing the donor proposal and devising strategies around the approach to making the solicitation.

Exchanging Information

During a negotiation, the **opening** is where parties present their initial positions, outlining what they hope to achieve and setting the tone for the negotiation. In this case, the development representative is seeking a donation, so this is the stage where he or she establishes the purpose of the discussion and opens the conversation around the forthcoming solicitation and donor proposal. In a traditional negotiation, the **exploration** stage is where both sides engage in discussions to understand each other's viewpoints, needs, and concerns. This often involves asking questions and actively listening. Here, the development representative presents and discusses the specifics of the donor proposal and explains the impact that the gift would have on the organization. The discussion can involve exploration of the donor's interests and intentions and determine if the proposal aligns with those.

Bargaining

The donor may not immediately accept the proposal, either the solicited gift amount or terms of the use of the gift, so **bargaining** may ensue, where the parties exchange offers and counteroffers, discussing various terms and potential compromises to bridge the gap between their positions. This is the stage most people imagine when they think of the negotiation process.

The bargaining stage in fundraising is unique, as the nonprofit does not have a tangible product to offer, such as a customer buying a car. As discussed in the next chapter, the nonprofit is "selling hope," or the intangible service of mission work, so the bargaining stage can look a little different in fundraising. Some organizations do have additional things to offer donors, beyond just a promise that the contribution will support the organizational mission, and the specifics of these may be discussed in the bargaining stage. This can include gifts designated to specific projects or purposes or named gifts, such as for facilities and scholarships, as well as the terms and conditions for those.

Closing

Once common ground is reached, the parties finalize the terms of the **agreement**, outlining responsibilities, timelines, and any specific commitments. In the nonprofit world, this is sometimes done through verbal agreement or a more formal approach, the latter applying to major gifts. A **donor agreement** is a formal document in fundraising that outlines the terms, conditions, and expectations related to a donation. It clarifies how the funds will be used, any specific restrictions or conditions attached to the gift, the recognition or naming rights associated with the donation, and the responsibilities of both the donor and the nonprofit. Donor agreements help ensure transparency, alignment of intentions, and proper stewardship of the donated funds. The **closure** stage is reached when the parties review and confirm the agreed-upon terms, addressing any last-minute concerns or clarifications.

Implementation

Negotiation should not just end with closure, however, especially in the nonprofit space where stewardship and sustained relationships are so important. **Implementation** is where agreed-upon terms are put into action, and both parties fulfill their commitments as outlined in the agreement. In fundraising, this means the donor fulfills the financial commitment, and the nonprofit follows through on the commitments made to the donor, which may be as general as a promise to work toward fulfilling the organizational mission. The fundraiser should provide reports to the donor to affirm that the agency is utilizing the donor's contribution as promised, thank the donor for the support, and to report on the contribution's impact on organizational mission.

Takeaways

- LO 10-1: There are many contributors to nonprofits, and one type is the individual donor. Donations can be monetary, in-kind, made in the form of securities, legacy bequests, or tributes or memorial gifts, and can be classified by amount: major, mid-level, and entry-level. The 80/20 rule emphasizes the importance of major gifts, as 80% of a nonprofit's revenues come from the top 20% of its supporters. Gifts can be made on a one-time basis or recurring, with common recurring gift types being monthly or annual gifts. Donations can be given immediately, or pledged over a period, and some major gifts may be endowed. Some donors restrict their contributions for a specific designated use, whereas others make unrestricted gifts.
- LO 10-2: The donor fundraising cycle in nonprofits consists of five steps: identification, qualification, cultivation, solicitation, and stewardship.
- LO 10-3: Fundraisers use CRM systems and other methods such as networking to identify prospective donors and take steps to qualify these prospects by conducting prospect research, which includes determining the prospective donor's giving capacity. Cultivation includes relationship-building and determining donor motivation (head, heart, halo), and some nonprofits host events specifically for the purpose of donor cultivation.
- LO 10-4: A donation proposal is presented when a nonprofit development representative solicits a major gift, and stewardship involves donor acknowledgment and engagement activities.
- LO 10-5: Various fundraising channels are necessary in nonprofits to diversify the means of making solicitations to secure all levels of donors, and include events, direct mail, online platforms, and phone-a-thons, among others.
- LO 10-6: Some volunteers may hesitate to engage in direct solicitation of donations but can play an important role in supporting other activities of the donor fundraising cycle.
- LO 10-7: The negotiation process can generally be applied to most situations where there are parties with differing interests and needs and consists of five steps: preparation, exchanging information, bargaining, closing, and implementation. The preparation stage of negotiation consists of the identification, qualification, and cultivation stages of the donor fundraising cycle; the negotiation stages of exchanging information, bargaining, and closing align with the solicitation stage of the donor fundraising cycle; and the implementation stage of negotiation consists of the stewardship aspect of the donor fundraising cycle.

Bibliography

"8 Reasons to Hold A Nonprofit Giving Day." *Wealth Engine*, 13 Jul. 2023, wealthengine.com/articles/nonprofit-giving-day#:~:text=A%20Giving%20Day%20is%20a,charity%2C%20foundation%2C%20or%20university. Accessed 8 Aug. 2023.

"8 Types of Donations That Nonprofits Accept." *The Giving Block*, 16 Mar. 2023, thegivingblock.com/resources/types-of-donations-nonprofits-accept/.

AlumniFinder, *AlumniFinder Launches WealthScore, a Powerful Tool to Help Development Professionals Identify Donors with the Means and Propensity to Give*. PR Newswire Association LLC, New York, 2010.

"BoardSource." *Fundraising? It's Everyone's Job*, 3 Sept. 2014, blog.boardsource.org/blog/2014/09/03/fundraising-its-everyones-job/. Accessed 8 May 2023.

Bowman, Woods, Howard P. Tuckman, and Dennis R. Young. "Issues in Nonprofit Finance Research: Surplus, Endowment, and Endowment Portfolios." *Nonprofit and Voluntary Sector Quarterly*, vol. 41, no. 4, 2012, pp. 560–579.

"Certification - CFRE International." *CFRE International - Certified Fund Raising Executive*, 30 June 2023, www.cfre.org/certification/.

Colquitt, Jason, Jeffery LePine, and Michael Wesson. *Organizational Behavior: Improving Performance and Commitment in the Workplace*. McGraw Hill, New York, NY, 2021.

"Gift Acknowledgments: Saying "Thank You" to Donors." *National Council of Nonprofits*, www.councilofnonprofits.org/running-nonprofit/fundraising-and-resource-development/gift-acknowledgments-saying-thank-you-donors. Accessed 29 Sept. 2023.

Harrison, Virginia S. "Understanding the Donor Experience: Applying Stewardship Theory to Higher Education Donors." *Public Relations Review*, vol. 44, no. 4, 2018, pp. 533–548.

Helms, Sara E., Brian L. Scott, and Jeremy P. Thornton. "Choosing to Give More: Experimental Evidence on Restricted Gifts and Charitable Behaviour." *Applied Economics Letters*, vol. 19, no. 8, 2012, pp. 745–748.

"Join AFP." *Association of Fundraising Professionals*, 23 May 2023, afpglobal.org/join.

Wiley Periodicals, "Key Components of Donor Impact Reports." *The Major Gifts Report*, vol. 24, no. 5, 2022, pp. 3–3.

Kim, Soobin, Chulhee Kang, and Rafael Engel. "What Convinces Donors? an Analysis of donation-based Crowdfunding Projects from Nonprofit Charities: The Case of South Korea." *Nonprofit Management & Leadership*, vol. 32, no. 4, 2022, pp. 627–649.

Konrath, Sara. "Six Reasons Why People Give Their Money Away, or Not." *Psychology Today*, Sussex Publishers, 26 Nov. 2017, www.psychologytoday.com/us/blog/the-empathy-gap/201711/six-reasons-why-people-give-their-money-away-or-not.

Leonard, Jay. "Understanding Who's in Your Sphere of Influence." 21 Dec. 2022, www.business2community.com/marketing/understanding-whos-sphere-influence-01789074. Accessed 29 Sept. 2023.

Love, Jay. "7 Methods to Improve Donor Retention with Fundraising Tech." *NonProfit Pro* (Online), 2019.

Mansfield, Heather, and Ohio Library and Information Network. *Mobile for Good: A how-to Fundraising Guide for Nonprofits*. McGraw-Hill Education, New York, 2014.

"Multi-Channel Fundraising." *Fundraising for Social Change*, edited by Kim Klein. John Wiley & Sons, Inc, Hoboken, NJ, 2016.

Nenn, Kerry. "Apply the 80/20 Rule to Fund Development." *Successful Fundraising*, vol. 25, no. 7, 2017, pp. 1–1.

"Nonprofit Accounting Academy." nonprofitaccountingacademy.com/wp-content/uploads/2019/09/What-is-a-pledge-3.pdf. Accessed 29 Sept. 2023.
"Nonprofit Glossary: Major Gifts." *Kindful*, kindful.com/nonprofit-glossary/major-gifts/#:~:text=There%20is%20no%20industry%20standard,gift%20of%20%241%2C000%20or%20more. Accessed 8 May 2023.
Polivy, Deborah K., and Ohio Library and Information Network. *Donor Cultivation and the Donor Lifecycle Map: A New Framework for Fundraising*. Wiley, Hoboken, New Jersey, 2014.
Schroeder, Thomas. "Cultivation Events that Strengthen Donor Relationships." *The Major Gifts Report*, vol. 21, no. 11, 2019, pp. 8–8.
"Tax Issues Relating to Charitable Contributions and Organizations." *Congressional Research Service*, 4 Aug. 2020, crsreports.congress.gov/product/pdf/R/R45922. Accessed 8 May 2023.
Tempel, Eugene R., et al. *Achieving Excellence in Fundraising*. Wiley, Hoboken, NJ, 2016.
"What Are Major Gifts? Plus 7 Other Donation Types - Kindful Glossary." *Kindful*, 24 Feb. 2021, kindful.com/nonprofit-glossary/major-gifts/#:~:text=There%20is%20no%20industry%20standard,gift%20of%20%241%2C000%20or%20more.
Woronkowicz, Joanna, and Jill Nicholson-Crotty. "The Effects of Capital Campaigns on Other Nonprofits' Fundraising." *Nonprofit Management & Leadership*, vol. 27, no. 3, 2017, pp. 371–387.

11 Selling the Cause

Learning Outcomes

After reading this chapter, you should be able to:

LO 11-1: Describe the concept of marketing and target markets.LO 11-2: Categorize and describe the "four P's of marketing" and how they apply specifically to the nonprofit sector.
LO 11-3: Illustrate what products are in nonprofits and explain how nonprofits must engage in the activity of "selling hope" in marketing their product.
LO 11-4: Define and identify the aspects of a promotion mix.
LO 11-5: Explain the concept of market segmentation and identify the four general segmentation strategies commonly used.
LO 11-6: Articulate the specific methods nonprofits can deploy as market segmentation strategies based upon the behavioral factors of how stakeholders engage with them.
LO 11-7: Formulate strategies nonprofits can use to leverage storytelling in effective marketing practices.

LO 11-1: Describe the concept of marketing and target markets.

Marketing

While many nonprofits originate as **grassroots organizations**, meaning they are locally based, community-driven initiatives or movements that work to address specific issues from the ground up, many evolve into organizations with broader reach (Khoury 2022). To expand and maximize impact, nonprofits must engage in **marketing**, which is the strategic process of identifying, creating, promoting, and delivering products or services that fulfill customer needs and generate value for both the business and its target audience.

DOI: 10.4324/9781003380030-15

The primary goal of marketing is to create value by identifying and understanding customer needs and preferences, offering products or services that satisfy those needs, promoting them effectively, and ultimately generating sales while achieving the organization's objectives. While it might feel counterintuitive to approach nonprofit work from such a commercial perspective, what works in for-profit enterprise can apply to the nonprofit sector, as well. Strategic use of formal marketing strategies can help nonprofit leaders maximize awareness, fundraising, and reach, ultimately expanding on their ability to impact the communities they serve (Grau 2021).

In marketing, a **target market** is a specific group of potential customers or consumers that an organization aims to reach with its products, services, or marketing efforts (McKinley-Floyd & Shrestha 2008). Understanding the target market helps leaders tailor initiatives and communication to effectively reach and fulfill the needs of the intended beneficiaries or supporters. In the space of a nonprofit organization, a general target market is made up of those impacted by the cause or purpose that the mission aims to address. Depending upon the organization and its mission, this target market can be very broad, underscoring the need to break down the market into smaller segments, described later in this chapter.

Formalized marketing is an area in nonprofits that is often neglected, particularly in smaller or newer agencies, with many organizations choosing to integrate marketing tasks into the job descriptions of development and program delivery staff, rather than investing in specialized marketing staff positions (Stuart 2011). This can create conflicting priorities, taking staff away from the important work of development and program delivery, all while neglecting the important marketing functions needed for a nonprofit organization to succeed. Another problem is that many nonprofits are hesitant to invest not just staff labor, but also financial resources to fund a proper marketing strategy, fearing criticism to minimize any expenses not directly related to mission fulfillment. As such, these agencies unintentionally stifle their growth by not properly selling their mission.

> LO 11-2: Categorize and describe the "four P's of marketing" and how they apply specifically to the nonprofit sector.

The Marketing Mix

Engaging with and serving stakeholders requires effective marketing, and the root of that is the **marketing mix**, which represents the combination of product, price, promotion, and place strategies that organizations use to effectively market their products or services to target audiences (Ferrell 2021). These factors can be easily remembered as "the four P's of marketing," and are just as essential in nonprofits as they are for commercial enterprises, although they may be approached a little differently. The nonprofit marketing mix is represented in Figure 11.1.

LO 11-3: Illustrate what products are in nonprofits and explain how nonprofits must engage in the activity of "selling hope" in marketing their product.

Product

In a marketing mix, the **product** is the most visible of the four P's, and refers to the tangible or intangible goods, services, or offerings that a company provides to fulfill the needs and wants of its target customers ("The Four" 2023).

Figure 11.1 Nonprofit Marketing Mix

Nonprofits, however, are not selling a traditional product. Instead, they are selling a belief that support of the organization will result in achievement of its stated mission; in essence, they are selling *hope*. Instead of physical goods, the *mission* is the product, and the agency provides to customers the intangible service of working toward achieving that mission.

The range of different products or services offered by a company or brand is known as **product mix** ("Product" 2023). Nonprofit revenues come not just from donations, but other revenue streams as well, and those represent various products in the agency's product mix. While it is easy to identify the product mix of any commercial organization, determining the "products" of a nonprofit can prove more challenging, but can be categorized as mission, events, programs, and tangible products (C, Ron 2017). Differentiating between the offerings within an organization's product mix is important, as the marketing tactics and strategies employed will differ for each of them.

The **primary product** for an organization refers to the main or core offering, which serves as the central focus of its operations and provides the primary value or benefit to its customers or stakeholders (Brechan 2016). Not surprisingly, mission is the primary product for nonprofit organizations because, as noted above, this is the driving force behind its existence and stakeholder support. While it is not a traditional product, mission is an intangible service, as the daily operations revolve around work that drives the mission forward. In a sense, "customers" support a nonprofit by being aware of the mission, buying into it, and believing that the organization has what it takes to deliver on its stated mission.

Secondary products are additional offerings or services provided by an organization that complement its primary product or core offerings, and along with the primary product comprise the remainder of the product mix (Brechan 2016). Most nonprofit secondary products can be categorized as events, programs, and tangible products.

Fundraising events, covered in Chapter 14, represent a substantial revenue source for many nonprofits, and can include things such as 5K runs and walks, cocktail parties and black-tie galas, benefit concerts, golf outings, dance-a-thons, and others. Fundraising events can also include events that raise resources other than money, such as food or clothing drives. While most nonprofit programs and services are offered to beneficiaries at a low or no cost, it is important to distinguish this as its own product category, as it is still necessary to engage in marketing strategies to drive participation in them. Examples of programs include participation in support groups; attendance at educational programs; use of sheltering, disaster relief, or food pantry resources by those in need; and others.

Finally, while it is generally a modest revenue source for many nonprofits, some sell traditional tangible products. This can include selling branded merchandise such as apparel that features the nonprofit's logo, or engaging in social enterprise where a nonprofit operates a commercial-like business, but with revenues from product sales being directed back to the cause.

Social Bite's Product Mix

Social Bite is a nonprofit organization in Scotland, with its mission centered around tackling homelessness and providing support to people in need. In addition to providing services to those in need, Social Bite operates social enterprises including a restaurant and coffee shops, selling traditional products to customers to provide an additional revenue stream to support its operations ("Meaningful" 2023). Social Bite's product mix includes not just its mission to end homelessness, but also events such as their annual 100-mile challenge, and their sale of tangible products through their social enterprise activities.

Figure 11.2 characterizes a typical product mix in a nonprofit organization, with the mission serving as the overarching primary product, and events, programs, and tangible products representing secondary products.

Figure 11.2 Nonprofit Product Mix

Place

In a marketing mix, **place** refers to where the target customer can buy the product, or where they discover it ("The Four" 2023). For nonprofits, this includes decisions related to online donation and event registration platforms, warehouses, distribution centers for beneficiary resources, and any other points of sale or interaction with customers. The goal is to ensure convenient access for customers and efficient delivery of products or services.

Mission

The "product" of mission is primarily supported through donations, so nonprofit leaders must make decisions around how, when, and where to accept donations. Most agencies offer donors the option to make donations through online platforms, the organization's website, mobile apps, direct mail, by phone, and even in person at events.

Events

Nonprofit leaders must determine where to host events and how to make ticket sales or registration available to prospective attendees. Not all events require registration, but for those that do, attendees need easy access to register or purchase tickets, including online options. Some nonprofits still offer registration by mail or in person.

Programs

The location where beneficiaries can access program resources is an important factor, as some individuals may not have access to private transportation. For instance, a food pantry should locate in an area that is central and easily accessible to its beneficiaries, and ideally in proximity to public transportation.

Tangible Products

The type of product sold by a nonprofit will impact the decisions around place. If a nonprofit sells a tangible product, leaders must decide where the products will be stored, and how they will be delivered to customers once sold. Some agencies opt to outsource the sale of branded merchandise to a third-party vendor, as to not bear the storage costs nor burden staff or volunteers with the task of fulfilling orders. For nonprofits engaged in social enterprise, their leaders must decide where to locate the businesses.

Price

Price is the cost that a customer pays for the product ("The Four" 2023). Given that the primary product of a nonprofit is not a traditional service or product, the consideration of "price" will differ from that of a for-profit organization. Instead of selling a product for a specified price, nonprofits set pricing around donations and sponsorships.

Mission

While donations may be of any amount and do not have a set "price," some nonprofit organizations choose to establish giving societies. A **giving society**, or donor recognition program, is a structured framework established by nonprofit organizations to acknowledge donors based on different giving levels, with each offering various benefits such as exclusive events, recognition in publications, or special access to the organization's activities (Cabral 2018). Figure 11.3 provides an example of nonprofit giving society levels.

These programs are designed to show appreciation for donors' support and encourage ongoing engagement and giving. Giving societies typically target mid-level and major donors and the levels and names of the levels can vary from nonprofit to nonprofit. Setting the levels – or prices – of these societies is often deliberate and strategic, and established to offer donors distinct choices for engaging with the organization, providing them with a potential path of giving that allows them to visualize contributing at various levels as they progress on their donor journey (Smith 2022).

Events

When it comes to events, some of them are offered at no cost to participants or beneficiaries, but others involve sometimes complex pricing structures for ticket sales and corporate sponsorship levels. Decisions regarding pricing need to be considered even for events that are not focused on fundraising, as the choice between offering free or low-cost admission can influence attendance, with free events often leading to a much higher no-show

Figure 11.3 Giving Society Levels

rate than events with a fee, potentially wasting organizational resources ("Should I" 2023).

Programs

As noted above, the difference between free admission and low-cost admission can impact the no-show rate, and this is a factor that should be considered when establishing program pricing. Some nonprofits offer program delivery at a cost, choosing to subsidize part of it rather than cover it in whole. Habitat for Humanity, for example, does not provide free houses to beneficiaries, but requires the contribution of "sweat equity" investment in building the home, and then offers the home for an affordable price ("Frequently"). Nonprofit leaders must decide how to "price" their programs, as they are not always offered at no cost.

Tangible Products

Determining the price of tangible products sold by a nonprofit requires a similar approach to those used by for-profit organizations, including consideration of market trends, perceived customer value, pricing of competing products, desired net profit, and others. Unlike commercial business, however, some nonprofits may intentionally set prices of branded merchandise at a cost that generates little to no profit in order to receive the benefits of increased awareness that occurs when supporters wear apparel in public that features the organization's name and logo.

> LO 11-4: Define and identify the aspects of a promotion mix.

Promotion

Promotion is what most people imagine when they think of the word "marketing," but promotion is just one part of a marketing mix along with product, place, and price ("The Four" 2023). Organizations use various strategies and tools to communicate and promote their products, services, or offerings to their target audiences, and this is called the **promotion mix**. It includes advertising, public relations, personal selling, sales promotion, and direct marketing.

The **advertising** component of a promotion mix involves using paid media to communicate with prospective customers, and includes ads in channels such as TV, print, radio, online, and social media (Ferrell 2021). Some nonprofits struggle to justify a financial investment in advertising, and instead rely exclusively **public relations**, or PR, which unlike advertising is a nonpaid form of promotion (Altamimi 2022). PR activities include efforts to manage awareness of the organization and the nonprofit's image and reputation through activities such as media coverage, events, and press releases (Ferrell 2021).

Personal selling refers to the one-on-one interactions between sales representatives and potential customers, and in the nonprofit setting could relate to the fundraising work done by development professionals as they progress through the donor fundraising cycle. **Sales promotion** involves short-term incentives like discounts, coupons, contests, and giveaways aimed at encouraging immediate purchases or increasing customer loyalty (Dergano 2020). In the nonprofit setting, this could include strategies such as offering a giveaway of a free branded T-shirt to the first 50 registrants for an upcoming event, used as a strategy to encourage participation and generate excitement around the event. Finally, **direct marketing** involves direct communication with targeted individuals through methods like email marketing, direct mail, telemarketing, and online advertising ("What Is").

Mission

Promotion of mission involves building general awareness of the cause and driving donations to the organization. Some nonprofits invest in paid advertising, whereas others choose to focus more on public relations or grassroots efforts. Depending upon the cause and their target consumer, the promotion strategy will vary.

The American Cancer Society (ACS), for instance, might invest in significant advertising, as the mission of the organization relates to those impacted by all forms of cancer, which in the United States represents a significant number, with an estimated 1.9 million new cancer cases diagnosed annually ("Cancer" 2022). The Wilms Cancer Foundation (WCF), which is a charitable organization that supports those impacted specifically by the childhood kidney cancer nephroblastoma commonly known as "Wilms," likely would not find advertising a prudent investment, as there are only an estimated 500–600 new cases diagnosed each year in the US ("Childhood"). Instead of advertising to a general audience, the WCF may invest in a more cost-effective method of communication and promotion of their cause, such as direct marketing to identify Wilms patients and survivors and reach out them directly.

Leaders must make strategic decisions around the ideal promotion mix to support the "sale" of their primary product, which is receiving donations in support of the mission. Further, they must decide how to best promote awareness and participation in their events, programs, and products.

Events

The promotion mix for events is designed to enhance awareness of the event, generate excitement, and attract attendees. The first step of determining the best mix for events is to understand the target market for the event, and tailor the promotion mix to reach the individuals in that market. Many nonprofits use direct marketing to invite prospective attendees and implement paid advertising and unpaid public relations strategies to enhance awareness of the event among the general community.

Programs

The goal of promoting programs is like that for events, where nonprofits strive to grow awareness, create excitement, and drive participation in these programs. As such, an effective promotion mix may include direct marketing, paid advertising, and public relations. Given that many programs are designed to provide free or low-cost programs or services to the community, news agencies are generally willing to provide free publicity.

Products

Commercial organizations use a diverse promotion mix of all elements, depending on the nature of the product and its target market. The promotion of nonprofit products is no different, so the promotion mix for tangible products or social enterprise efforts can consist of any mix of advertising, public relations, personal selling, sales promotion, and direct marketing.

> LO 11-5: Explain the concept of market segmentation and identify the four general segmentation strategies commonly used.

Market Segmentation

While a nonprofit might have a general target market, which is typically individuals impacted by the mission that the agency seeks to achieve, there are many subgroups, as well. A **market segment** is a distinct subgroup of individuals within a larger market who share one or more common characteristics, lumped together for marketing purposes (McKinley-Floyd & Shrestha 2008).

General Market Segmentation Approaches

When engaging in the "promotion" aspect of a marketing mix, segmentation is of particular importance, as the approach used to sell a product to prospective customers should be tailored to the needs and interests of that particular segment. Common approaches to segmenting markets include demographic, geographic, behavioral, and psychographic (Ferrell 2021).

Demographic segmentation divides a market based on demographic factors such as age, gender, income, education, and other factors. **Geographic segmentation** divides people into groups based upon their geographic location. **Behavioral segmentation** divides people into segments based on their actions, such as purchasing behavior, usage patterns, and others. Finally, **psychographic segmentation** divides individuals based on psychological variables such as lifestyle, attitudes, and values.

LO 11-6: Articulate the specific methods nonprofits can deploy as market segmentation strategies based upon the behavioral factors of how stakeholders engage with them.

Nonprofit Behavioral Segments

It would be unproductive for nonprofits to attempt to engage in marketing to a general target market of individuals affected by the cause of the agency's mission, so a more effective method is to target specific groups based upon behavioral market segmentation. **Nonprofit behavioral segments** are distinct subgroups within the larger target market who share common behaviors in terms of how they engage with the nonprofit and its products, and these include donors, service recipients, event attendees, and volunteers, depicted in Figure 11.4.

Donors

One segment of a nonprofit market is those who engage with the nonprofit by contributing financially, and the donor segment is often subcategorized

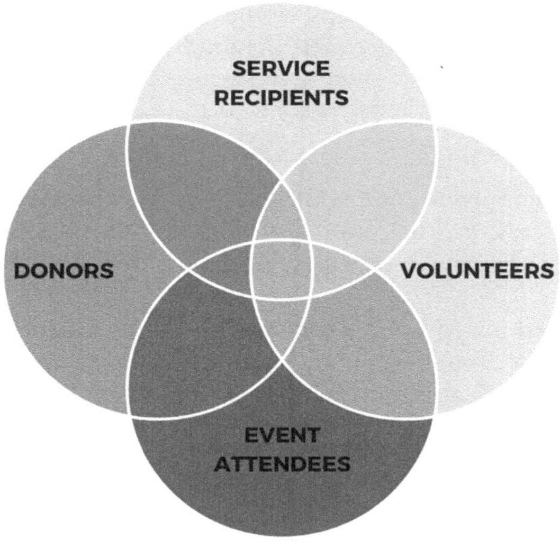

Figure 11.4 Nonprofit Behavioral Segments

further into smaller segments. Chapter 10 identified various types of donors based upon their giving activity, and some nonprofits use these categories to segment donors in tailoring their marketing approach depending upon giving level, frequency, and type.

Another common donor segmentation approach is to identify current vs. lapsed donors, with the former referring to an individual who has made a donation to a nonprofit within the most recent giving period, which could be a year or another defined timeframe. The acronyms LYBUNT and SYBUNT are often used to further segment lapsed donors. **LYBUNT**, pronounced "lie-bunt," stands for "Last Year But Unfortunately Not This" and refers to donors who gave in the previous year or giving period, but have not given in the current year. **SYBUNT**, pronounced "sigh-bunt," references "Some Year But Unfortunately Not This" and represents donors who have given in some previous year or years, but not in the current or most recent year or giving period ("What Are" 2021).

Market segmentation has many benefits, and one of them is improved efficiency. Lapsed donors are significantly more likely than those who have never donated to contribute, for example, so prioritizing limited promotion dollars to target lapsed donors is one way to maximize returns including the cost-per-dollar-raised metric.

Service Recipients

Some individuals in a nonprofit's target market engage with the agency as beneficiaries who receive services provided by the organization, and these service recipients can be segmented based upon the services they use or may potentially use. An elder care agency, for instance, may offer healthcare, companionship programs, family support groups, and at-home meal delivery services. The promotion of family support groups would target a different audience, the families of those who receive elder care, than individuals receiving direct elder care services.

Volunteers

Volunteers are the backbone of nonprofits, and while Chapter 8 discussed in depth the recruitment of volunteers, it is helpful to consider volunteers as a specific market segment, as individuals who engage with the organization by contributing their time.

Nonprofits tailor communications to volunteers based on subsegments, including their skills and expertise, availability, and interests. For instance, a nonprofit might have a need for a significant number of volunteers for an upcoming marathon fundraising event. The volunteer coordinator can pull a list of potential volunteers from the agency's volunteer management platform, and segment based on individuals who have expressed an interest in volunteering at events, not wasting time soliciting potential volunteers from a pool of individuals who have specifically indicated that they are not interested in event volunteerism.

Event Attendees

Some supporters engage with a nonprofit by attending events, and these events can be very diverse, requiring differing marketing strategies to communicate them. For example, an organization with the mission to reduce the number of young people in foster care hosts both an annual $500-per-person black-tie gala and ongoing recruitment events designed to attract new prospective foster families. The agency's marketing strategy to sell gala tickets will differ greatly from the methods used to drive attendance at the recruitment events. The former target audience would likely consist of current and prospect major and mid-level donors with either an established giving history or capacity to give, with the use of direct marketing to make invitations to this segment. The nonprofit would likely use a very different approach, however, to promote their foster family recruitment events, such as advertising and public relations to promote their recruitment events to the general community.

Individuals engage with nonprofits in many ways, and these four categories, donors, volunteers, service recipients, and event attendees, represent four of the main segments. As depicted in Figure 11.3, these segments can be overlapping. Some stakeholders engage solely as donors, for instance, making financial contributions but never volunteering, attending events, or receiving services. Others may partake in all four activities.

> LO 11-7: Formulate strategies nonprofits can use to leverage storytelling in effective marketing practices.

Storytelling

An effective method of selling hope, inspiring people, and fostering belief in a nonprofit's mission is through **storytelling**, which is an approach nonprofits use to connect emotionally with their current and prospective supporters by conveying personal stories and narratives of those positively impacted by the organization and its mission (Keel 2023).

For-profit organizations selling a tangible product or even an intangible service can sell the product by conveying its features and benefits to the targeted customer. Nonprofits, however, cannot exactly make use of this traditional method, as the primary product is the mission. To "sell" this product, nonprofit leaders must convince supporters of the value of the mission and belief that, with their support, the organization can achieve that mission. One way to demonstrate this is through storytelling. Volunteers are typically those tasked with representing the organization in storytelling activities, which can be presented in the following ways (Ibrisevic 2023):

- **Testimonials:** Feature personal testimonials from individuals who have benefited from the work of the organization. These are especially helpful when engaging in public relations activities because they communicate the impact of the cause to the broader community.
- **Impact Reports:** Include in annual and donor impact reports the stories, data, and visuals that illustrate the organization's achievements and the positive changes brought about because of donor contributions.
- **Campaigns:** Develop storytelling campaigns around specific initiatives and fundraising appeals, using narratives to raise awareness and funds. Universities often use this strategy around scholarship fundraising campaigns, in sharing compelling stories about students who would otherwise not be able to pursue a college degree without donor support.
- **Online Platforms:** Share photos, videos, and narratives on the organization's website and other online social media channels to engage the target audience and demonstrate the organizational impact.
- **Newsletters:** Many nonprofits communicate with stakeholders through regular newsletters, which are generally sent in email form. Integrating stories in the newsletter that share good news about individuals positively impacted by the organization, versus solely promoting events and asking for donations, can be an effective approach.
- **Events:** Taking a moment during events to pause the stage programming to share a "mission moment" with stories of impact can help nonprofits better connect with event attendees.

Integrating storytelling as a component of the overall marketing strategy can help nonprofit organizations humanize their work, share the importance of their mission, and make a compelling case for support.

Takeaways

LO 11-1: Marketing is the strategic process of delivering products or services that fulfill customer needs and generate value for both the business and its target audience. A target market is a specific group of potential customers that an organization aims to reach.

LO 11-2: The "four P's of marketing" consist of product, place, price, and promotion. In nonprofits, the primary product is mission; place is where supporters can donate; price corresponds to various giving and sponsorship levels; and promotion refers to how nonprofits communicate about and "sell" their products.

LO 11-3: Given that nonprofits do not have a traditional tangible product or intangible service to sell to consumers, their primary product is the mission and, as such, they must communicate with and convince stakeholders that the organization can achieve its stated mission, as well as inspire hope in the worthiness of the cause and the need to achieve the mission.

LO 11-4: The promotion mix consists of strategies organizations use to communicate about their products to target audiences, and includes advertising, public relations, personal selling, sales promotion, and direct marketing.

LO 11-5: A market segment is a distinct subgroup of individuals within a larger market who share one or more common characteristics, lumped together for marketing purposes, and the four general segmentation bases include demographic, geographic, behavioral, and psychographic.

LO 11-6: Nonprofits tend to divide their general market into segments based upon behavioral aspect in terms of how individuals engage with the nonprofit, including donors, service recipients, event attendees, and volunteers.

LO 11-7: Storytelling is an approach nonprofits use to connect emotionally with their current and prospective supporters by conveying personal stories and narratives of those positively impacted by the organization and its mission. Storytelling can occur through testimonials, impact reports, mission moments at events, and others.

Bibliography

Altamimi, Hala. "Nonprofits May Need to Spend a Third of Their Budget on Overhead To." 22 Sept. 2022, www.philanthropy.com/article/nonprofits-may-need-to-spend-a-third-of-their-budget-on-overhead-to-thrive-contradicting-a-donor-rule-of-thumb.

Brechan, Inge. "The Different Effect of Primary and Secondary Product Attributes on Customer Satisfaction." *Journal of Economic Psychology*, vol. 27, no. 3, 2006, pp. 441–458.

Cabral, Robin. "14 Tips on Developing a Giving Society." *NonProfit PRO*, 9 May 2018, www.nonprofitpro.com/post/14-tips-developing-giving-society-nonprofit-fundraising-program/.

"Cancer Facts & Figures 2022." *American Cancer Society*, www.cancer.org/research/cancer-facts-statistics/all-cancer-facts-figures/cancer-facts-figures-2022.html#:~:text=The%20Facts%20%26%20Figures%20annual%20report,incidence%2C%20mortality%2C%20and%20survival%20statistics. Accessed 29 Sept. 2023.

"Childhood Kidney Cancer." *Wilms Foundation*, www.wilmsfoundation.org/. Accessed 29 Sept. 2023.

Dergano, Francesco. "Marketing Guide -Personal Selling and Sales Promotion (12)." *Medium*, 14 July 2020, raccomandino.medium.com/marketing-guide-personal-selling-and-sales-promotion-12-474a6ac271fc.

Ferrell, O.C.M. *Business*. McGraw-Hill Education, New York, NY 2021.

"Frequently Asked Questions." *Habitat for Humanity*, www.habitat.org/about/faq#:~:text=Habitat%20for%20Humanity%20works%20in,their%20own%20homes%20and%20neighborhoods. Accessed 29 Sept. 2023.

Grau, Stacy L., and Ohio Library and Information Network. *Marketing for Nonprofit Organizations: Insights and Innovations*. Oxford University Press, New York, NY, 2021, doi:10.1093/oso/9780190090807.001.0001.

Ibrisevic, Ilma. "The Ultimate Guide to Nonprofit Storytelling (30+ Tips)." *Nonprofit Blog*, 3 Aug. 2023, donorbox.org/nonprofit-blog/nonprofit-storytelling-guide.
Keel, Astrid L., and A.T.K. Tran. "Increasing Small Nonprofits' Influence through Strategic Storytelling." *Business Horizons*, vol. 66, no. 3, 2023, pp. 359–370.
Khoury, Theodore A., Yuliya Shymko, and Jacob Vermeire. "Simulating the Cause: How Grassroots Organizations Advance their Credibility through the Dramaturgical Curation of Events." *Organization Science (Providence, R.I.)*, vol. 33, no. 4, 2022, pp. 1470–1500.
McKinley-Floyd, Lydia, and Nanda Shrestha. "Segmentation Strategies for Non-Profits: Mining the Emerging Market of 'Black Gold'." *The Journal of Business & Industrial Marketing*, vol. 23, no. 6, 2008, pp. 416–428.
"Meaningful Eats at Vesta Bar and Kitchen." *Social Bite*, www.social-bite.co.uk/what-we-do/vesta-restaurant/. Accessed 8 Aug. 2023.
"Product Mix." *Corporate Finance Institute*, 20 Apr. 2023, corporatefinanceinstitute.com/resources/management/product-mix/.
Ron, C. "Product Marketing Mix for Non-Profit Businesses." *Medium*, Medium, 31 Mar. 2017, ironc.medium.com/product-marketing-mix-for-non-profit-businesses-2be14cdede5c.
"Should I Charge for My Event?" *Localist*, 9 Mar. 2021, www.localist.com/post/should-i-charge-for-my-event. Accessed 8 Aug. 2023.
Smith, Ally. "How to Create Donor Recognition Levels for Your Nonprofit." *Fundraising KIT*, 11 Mar. 2022, fundraisingkit.com/blog/donor-recognition-levels/. Accessed 8 Aug. 2023.
Stuart, John. "Marketing Is an Investment – Even for Non-Profits." *The Guardian, Guardian News and Media*, 27 June 2011, www.theguardian.com/voluntary-sector-network/2011/jun/27/marketing-investment-non-profits.
"The Four PS of Marketing." *American Marketing Association*, 31 May 2023, www.ama.org/marketing-news/the-four-ps-of-marketing/.
"What Are Lybunt & Sybunt Reports? - Nonprofit Glossary." *Kindful*, 24 Mar. 2021, kindful.com/nonprofit-glossary/lybunt-sybunt-reports/.
"What Is Direct Marketing." *DMASA*, dmasa.org/page/what-direct-marketing#:~:text=Direct%20marketing%20is%20a%20form,distribution%2C%20promotional%20letters%20and%20targeted. Accessed 29 Sept. 2023.

12 Grants, Corporate Giving, and Other Funding

Learning Outcomes

After reading this chapter, you should be able to:

LO 12-1: Illustrate the ways that grants serve as an important funding source for nonprofit organizations and how they differ from general donations.
LO 12-2: Identify the primary grant funding sources for nonprofits.
LO 12-3: Describe nonprofit-corporate partnerships and summarize the importance of networking and establishing a value proposition in developing these relationships.
LO 12-4: Identify ways nonprofits can leverage the corporate sponsorship model as a revenue source while balancing various risks.
LO 12-5: Classify and distinguish between the various employee giving programs within nonprofit-corporate partnerships.
LO 12-6: Explain how companies can provide pro bono and cause marketing services as part of a nonprofit-corporate partnership, and identify various approaches to cause marketing.
LO 12-7: Summarize the additional nonprofit funding sources beyond the primary revenue sources of donations, grants, and corporate support.

> LO 12-1: Illustrate the ways that grants serve as an important funding source for nonprofit organizations and how they differ from general donations.

Grant Funding

Some nonprofits are funded in part or entirely by grants. **Grants** are financial awards provided to nonprofit organizations by various entities, such as government agencies, private or public foundations, or other organizations ("What Is" 2022). These entities are often referred to as **grantmakers**, and grants are typically non-repayable funds intended to support either a specific project or general operations of the nonprofit ("Grantmaking"). While grants

DOI: 10.4324/9781003380030-16

are like donations in that both represent forms of financial support provided to nonprofit organizations, they differ in their nature, purpose, and the way they are typically awarded.

Grant Process

The steps of the nonprofit grant process are highlighted in Figure 12.1 and might look familiar, as it is similar to the donor cultivation cycle, although there are some distinctions. The first step of the grant process is to *identify opportunities*. Nonprofits seeking grants must typically meet certain eligibility criteria set by the grantmaker, including alignment with the grant's purpose, nonprofit status, geographic location, and financial stability. Sometimes, the activities of a nonprofit are already nicely aligned with the stated purpose of a grant, but other times, an agency can build new programs or services around a grant opportunity and execute on the new initiative if the grant is awarded.

The next step is to *cultivate relationships* with the grantmaking organization, which involves getting to know the decision-makers in the organization and better understanding their priorities. This will help ensure alignment of interests and goals in the next step of the process, which is to *develop and submit the grant proposal.*

Figure 12.1 The Nonprofit Grant Process

Whereas donations are often the outcome of the donor fundraising cycle, the process for receiving grants looks quite a bit different. Organizations typically apply for grants by submitting detailed **grant proposals** or applications that include information about the project's goals, budget, timeline, and expected outcomes (Rothstein 2019). These applications then undergo a competitive review process, where grantmakers assess the proposals based on their alignment with the funder's priorities and criteria. After receiving a grant, recipients must *manage and administer the award*, which involves ensuring effective and compliant use of the awarded funds for the purpose for which it was designated.

Most grants require an accounting of how the funds were used, so the final step of the grant process is *progress reporting and stewardship*. Grantee organizations assess the outcomes and impact of the grant-funded project, often through program evaluations and impact assessments, and include this information in reports to demonstrate the effectiveness of the project and its alignment with grant goals (Rothstein 2019). At the conclusion of the grant period, the grantee may also submit financial statements and return unspent funds to the grantor ("Grant"). Recall from Chapter 10 that stewardship involves expressing gratitude to donors for their contributions and continuing to nurture the relationship, keeping the donor informed about the organization's activities and making them feel connected to the cause (O'Neal & Carlson 2013). This step is just as important in the grant process as it is in the donor fundraising cycle, especially as some grants are renewable.

Unlike donations, grants are typically more project-focused, involve a competitive application process, and come with specific reporting and accountability requirements. Working for grant awards can be just as labor-intensive as soliciting donor dollars, and in some instances more so. Writing a single federal grant application, for example, takes a nonprofit an estimated average of between 80 and 200 hours (Stombaugh 2019), and that does not account for the time needed for grant administration and follow up.

Because of the process and time required to prepare and present grant proposals and administer and account for grant funding to grantmakers, some nonprofits choose to assign grant writing task roles into specific paid staff positions. Larger nonprofits, or those more dependent on grant funding, may even dedicate an entire position or department to this function, or outsource grant writing work to a contractor.

LO 12-2: Identify the primary grant funding sources for nonprofits.

Grant Funding Sources

Grant funds for nonprofit organizations can come from a variety of sources, and these grantmakers can broadly be categorized as government grants, foundation grants, corporate grants, and individual grants. While grants are, by design, typically specified for use for a specific project or initiative, some grants are **unrestricted grants**, providing nonprofits with the flexibility to allocate funds where they are most needed.

Government Grants

Government grants are financial awards provided by government agencies at the federal, state, or local levels to support various programs or projects that serve the public interest. **Federal grants** are awarded by various federal agencies to support specific functions such as healthcare, education, environmental conservation, and social services, and the most well-known federal grantmakers include the Department of Health and Human Services (HHS), the National Institutes of Health (NIH), and the Environmental Protection Agency (EPA). **State grants** and **local grants** are awarded by state and local governments also for nonprofit projects that address regional needs and priorities. These grants can include funding for community development, education, and public health initiatives, among others ("Federal").

Foundation Grants

Rather than making an unrestricted general donation, some foundations utilize the grantmaking model to allocate charitable contributions. **Private foundations**, such as the Bill and Melinda Gates Foundation and the Rockefeller Foundation, offer grants to nonprofits that align with the foundation's established areas of interest, which generally cover a wide range of social, environmental, and cultural issues ("Private"). **Community foundations** are regional or local organizations that provide grants to nonprofits within a specific geographic area, and often focus on addressing community needs and improving the quality of life in that region ("Foundation" 2022).

Corporate Grants

Corporate giving is covered in the forthcoming section, and one method of their support is through **corporate grants**, where companies establish their own foundations to manage their charitable giving (Israel 2023). These grantmakers operate independently and may have their own grantmaking priorities.

Individual Grants

Another potential source of grant funding is through **individual grants**, provided by high-net-worth individuals, philanthropists, and donors who choose to direct their personal giving through grant programs in support of specific causes or organizations. Often, nonprofit fundraising representatives approach individual grants the same way as soliciting a major gift, although the grant structure of the gift may require a specific grant proposal, rather than a general donation proposal.

Other Grantmakers

International **non-governmental organizations** (NGOs) like Oxfam, Save the Children, or the United Nations are grantmakers that fund grants for nonprofits focused on global issues, and **multilateral agencies** such as the United Nations, World Bank, and regional development banks consist of member states that provide grant funds to nonprofits for projects that align with their global development goals. The role of NGOs is covered in depth in Chapter 15.

Finally, there are other, more niche grantmakers which focus on specific areas of interest, such as faith-based organizations and nonprofits that may offer grants to other nonprofits that share their faith-based missions and objectives. Other organizations offer grants for specialized areas such as arts and culture, environmental conservation, healthcare research, education, and others. As with managing all constituent relationships, partnering with grantmaking organizations requires transparency, accountability, and ongoing stewardship for long-term sustainability and successful grant-seeking efforts.

Grant Success

Overall, most grant applications will not yield success, so those in nonprofits charged with the task of managing grants often submit multiple grant applications as an ongoing process. While data vary, and there is no standardized grant success scoring entity, most sources indicate that nationally, grant writing success rates range from 10–30% industry-wide ("6 Reasons" 2023). Of the various grantmaking sources, most nonprofits yield greater success from private foundations as a percentage of "won" grants ("6 Reasons" 2023).

> LO 12-3: Describe nonprofit-corporate partnerships and summarize the importance of networking and establishing a value proposition in developing these relationships.

Corporate Giving

The financial support extended by corporate partners can serve as a substantial income stream for nonprofit organizations, collectively totaling approximately $450 billion in the United States and representing 2.1% of the gross domestic product, according to a recent Congressional Research Service report ("Tax"

2023). There is a growing movement toward **corporate social responsibility**, or CSR, which refers to a company's commitment to conducting its business in an ethical and socially responsible manner. It involves efforts to contribute positively to society and the environment beyond its profit-making activities and includes initiatives related to sustainability, community engagement, and philanthropy. The prioritization of CSR is what drives many commercial organizations to support nonprofit agencies.

The way nonprofit fundraisers approach corporate giving generally shares similarities with the processes of soliciting and obtaining donations from donors, but the management of these corporate stakeholder relationships may present some distinct characteristics.

Nonprofit-Corporate Partnerships

A **nonprofit-corporate partnership** is a mutually beneficial relationship between a nonprofit organization and a for-profit entity, where both parties commit resources to work together toward a common objective (Alvarez-González 2017, Chow). Corporate support can come in the form of **direct corporate donations**, which support the nonprofit's operations, or indirect forms of giving such as corporate sponsorships, employee giving programs, pro bono work, and cause marketing ("Guide").

Networking

Soliciting donations from donors often involves tapping into the personal tie that the individual may have with the cause. An alumna from a university, for example, may feel compelled to donate to her alma mater out of loyalty and affinity built on her good experience and years of attending that institution. Corporate giving, however, often requires a different approach, and fundraising representatives must often make a more compelling value proposition. A **value proposition** describes the benefits and value that a product, service, or offer provides to its target customers and answers the question of "what's in it for me?". Packaging corporate sponsorship offerings that provide a strong value proposition is one method many nonprofits employ.

Corporate giving is often driven by one or a few key decision-makers within that organization, so building relationships with those individuals is a vital component to corporate giving. As is the case with fundraising from donors, the identification and cultivation phases are necessary in corporate giving. Nonprofit fundraising representatives engage in **networking**, which is the action or process of interacting with others to exchange information and develop professional or social contacts. Attending networking and social events, joining professional organizations, and asking for introductions are just a few ways nonprofit networking happens (Eatough 2023).

While many nonprofit-corporate partnerships are often initially forged due to relationships built between a nonprofit fundraising representative and corporate decision-maker, the best and most long-lasting partnerships are those that are mutually beneficial with advantages for both the nonprofit organization and the corporate business. This is in part because decision-makers may exit the organizations and no longer hold influence with that corporation, and sustaining the support beyond the relationship relies on the nonprofit providing that value to the corporate sponsor. One way to articulate the value proposition of the nonprofit-corporate partnership is through a corporate sponsorship model.

> LO 12-4: Identify ways nonprofits can leverage the corporate sponsorship model as a revenue source while balancing various risks.

Corporate Sponsorships

With a **corporate sponsorship model**, companies sponsor specific programs or events of the nonprofit, offsetting the costs of the event and receiving advertising and other benefits in return ("Guide"). When establishing these sponsorships, leaders should assess their needs of funding or volunteer support sought from corporate partners and decide what reciprocal benefits to offer in return as part of the value proposition. Many nonprofits choose to set structured pricing, but others remain flexible to adapt an offering to the needs of both the nonprofit and corporate partner to assure that mutually beneficial relationship.

Just as a nonprofit fundraising representative would present a proposal to a prospective major donor, a corporate sponsorship ask is presented to a prospective corporate sponsor that outlines the financial commitment requested, as well as the benefits or assurances offered by the nonprofit agency in exchange for the contribution. Figure 12.2 represents a sample corporate sponsor offering for an animal services agency's annual black-tie fundraising gala event. Unlike most other forms of donations, corporate sponsorships are not always completely or even partially tax-deductible, dependent upon the fair market value of the benefits received by the business, in exchange for their sponsorship.

The corporate sponsor offering listing benefits and levels of sponsorship is just one part, however, of a corporate solicitation. While the value proposition is generally more central to corporate sponsor solicitation than those of donors, nonprofit representatives must "sell the cause" and ensure that the corporate stakeholders believe in the organizational mission. Corporate sponsor offerings can be designed not just for fundraising events, but also programs and services. As one example, a regional Cancer Support Community (CSC) affiliate might partner with a local hospital system to

Wofford County Humane Society **FUR BALL SPONSORSHIP LEVELS**

	PLATINUM SPONSOR	GOLD SPONSOR	SILVER SPONSOR
SEATING AT EVENT	TWO TABLES OF 10 SEATS	ONE TABLE WITH 10 SEATS	5 INDIVIDUAL TICKETS
RECOGNITION IN EVENT PROGRAM	FULL PAGE AD IN PROGRAM	HALF PAGE AD IN PROGRAM	LOGO LISTED IN PROGRAM
VIP PERKS	VALET, VIP GIFT, 2 BOTTLES OF WINE FOR TABLES	VIP GIFT, 1 BOTTLE OF WINE FOR TABLE	VIP GIFT
SOCIAL MEDIA RECOGNITION	PRE AND POST-EVENT POSTS ON SOCIAL MEDIA	POST-EVENT POSTS ON SOCIAL MEDIA	LISTING IN MONTHLY NEWSLETTER
COST	**$10,000**	**$5,000**	**$2,500**

Figure 12.2 Nonprofit-Corporate Sponsor Offering Example

financially support and underwrite the cost of their monthly cancer family support groups in exchange for recognition as the "CSC Support Group Sponsor."

The way that corporations determine which causes to support and what levels varies by company. Some organizations have moved to a grantmaking model, requiring nonprofits to go through a process like submitting for grants, with a proposal, competitive selection process, and required reporting. Some larger corporations have established dedicated community relations staff positions, or even entire community relations departments, dedicated to managing the company's interactions with the communities in which they operate, including financial support of nonprofits. Other companies designate this decision-making authority to executive leadership or the board of directors, while others rely on designated philanthropy committees.

Risks

While corporate funding can present a lucrative revenue source, agencies should be intentional when entering into nonprofit-corporate partnerships to ensure alignment of organizational mission and values. Incompatible partnerships can result in conflict and controversy and damage the nonprofit agency's work toward mission.

Consider, for example, a health-focused nonprofit that partners with a fast-food chain. While the financial support is helpful in executing the agency's various events and programs, critics might consider this type of alliance hypocritical because of concerns about unhealthy diets and obesity perpetuated by the fast-food industry. Similar to how donor contributions can be regarded as problematic, or "tainted," corporate backing can also bring about potential repercussions that ultimately outweigh the financial advantages, rendering the partnership less advantageous for the nonprofit (Ferrand 2018).

> LO 12-5: Classify and distinguish between the various employee giving programs within nonprofit-corporate partnerships.

Employee Giving Programs

Corporate support sometimes comes in the form of support from employees of the company, as opposed to the corporation itself, through **employee giving programs**. One approach to employee giving is through **workplace giving campaigns**, which are charitable giving programs facilitated by employers in which employees can donate a portion of their salary or wages through payroll deduction directly to a nonprofit organization of their choice ("Workplace" 2021). Workplace giving programs are voluntary and designed to encourage employees to support charitable causes conveniently through the ease of payroll deductions.

Matching gifts are a component of some employee giving programs, and these provide an employer-provided match for employee contributions, enhancing the impact of employee donations and providing an incentive for them to contribute (Nenn 2018). Workplace giving programs are often contained as a component of a company's broader CSR initiatives and can benefit both employees and the charitable organizations they choose to support.

In some instances, an employee at an organization may take initiative to lead fundraising activities with the support of their employer. **Employee-driven fundraising initiatives** are activities organized and led by employees within a company to raise funds for nonprofit causes through voluntary participation from their coworkers. This can include organized participation in nonprofit fundraising events like walks, runs, or bike rides where the employees participate together; workplace bake sales or fundraisers to raise funds for a selected nonprofit; "jeans days" where employees donate to a cause in exchange for the opportunity to wear casual attire at work; donation drives to collect items such as school supplies, food, toiletries, etc.; and others.

Workplace giving initiatives also sometimes include a "time" and "talent" component of giving, in addition to contributions of "treasure." This is accomplished through **employee volunteer programs**, where companies encourage their employees to volunteer for nonprofits during work hours or provide paid time off for volunteering ("Volunteer" 2021). They may also even organize structured group volunteer activities for their staff.

> LO 12-6: Explain how companies can provide pro bono and cause marketing services as part of a nonprofit-corporate partnership, and identify various approaches to cause marketing.

Pro Bono Work

Another nonprofit-corporate partnership is pro bono work. **Pro bono** is a Latin term that means "for the public good" and refers to the voluntary provision of services or expertise by professionals to individuals or organizations in need, typically without charging a fee ("Pro Bono"). Some corporations offer pro bono services to nonprofit organizations as a form of in-kind contribution and form of volunteerism that leverages professional skills and knowledge for the benefit of the nonprofit agency and, ultimately, to the public. Common pro bono services include legal advice, IT support, marketing services, graphic design, medical services, or other specialized skills.

Cause Marketing

Another form of corporate social responsibility is **cause marketing**, where a company's promotional campaign has the dual purpose of increasing profitability while bettering society ("Cause" 2023), usually by benefiting a nonprofit organization. This approach aims to create a positive image for the company while simultaneously supporting a nonprofit and can take one of several forms, with common ones including donation, awareness, and point-of-sale campaigns.

A **donation campaign** is a type of cause marketing where companies commit to donating a portion of their sales, profits, or a fixed amount for each product sold to a designated nonprofit or cause. Sometimes this is accomplished through a "**get one, give one**" strategy, where a company pledges to donate or provide a product or service to a person in need for each product or service sold or acquired (Daily 2020). Sock company Bombas is an example of a company that uses this approach, promising that for every pair of socks sold by the company, they will donate a pair to someone in need.

Awareness campaigns happen when companies use their marketing channels to raise awareness, rather than funds, for a particular nonprofit or cause (Sebastian 2023). Companies may produce their products in the color pink, for instance, during the month of October in support of Breast Cancer Awareness Month. **Point-of-sale campaigns** solicit donations from customers for a specific nonprofit upon checkout. This can occur through a cashier

Photo 12.1 **ACS Fundraiser** The Buffalo Wild Wings restaurant chain participates in a donation campaign selling bottle koozies to customers for $5, with proceeds benefiting the American Cancer Society. Photo by author.

asking for a contribution, cash collection via an on-site donation drop box, prompt on a credit card PIN pad machine at checkout, or an online check box to designate a contribution for e-commerce transactions.

B Corp Certification

The extent to which organizations engage in corporate social responsibility activities varies, and many use these activities as a marketing tool. Companies that demonstrate high standards of CSR behavior can receive B Corp certification. The term “B Corp” may seem confusing, but this is *not* a legal or tax designation. Instead, a **B Corp certification** is a “designation that a business is meeting high standards of verified performance, accountability, and transparency on factors from employee benefits and charitable giving to supply chain practices and input materials” (“About” 2023).

Photo 12.2 **Certified B Corp** A product that prominently displays the "Certified B Corporation" logo. Many organizations leverage their B Corp certification as a marketing tool to convey to consumers their commitment to social responsibility and ethics. Photo by author.

B Lab is the organization that certifies B Corps, and it is itself a nonprofit organization with the mission to redefine success in business by promoting and fostering a global movement of companies that prioritize social and environmental responsibility alongside profitability. The organization established the B Corp certification as a way for a company to measure their entire social and environmental impact and verify that they meet high standards of performance. Companies that complete the certification process often leverage this in their marketing strategy to demonstrate to customers their care and concern for the communities and stakeholders they serve.

LO 12-7: Summarize the additional nonprofit funding sources beyond the primary revenue sources of donations, grants, and corporate support.

Other Funding Sources

Donations, grants, and corporate support comprise the bulk of funding for most nonprofits, but many benefit from other revenue sources, which can include the following:

- **Endowments:** As noted in Chapter 10, some donations are used to establish or contribute to an endowment, and nonprofits can generate revenue from the interest and dividends generated from these endowments to support their operations. Endowments tend to provide a sustainable, long-term source of income and can become sizable over time. Harvard University, for example, has one of the largest and most well-known university endowments globally, valued at over $50 billion. By and large, however, few nonprofits have endowments, with 50% having less than one month of cash reserves ("Nonprofit" 2023).
- **Events, Programs and Tangible Products:** Chapter 11 highlighted the ways that nonprofits "sell" their various "products," and these include fundraising events, programs, and tangible products through social enterprise, which also represent additional revenue streams for nonprofits.
- **Earned Income:** Nonprofits can earn income from the sale of goods and services (social enterprise), admission fees, membership dues, ticket sales for events, and others.
- **Fee-for-Service Contracts:** Nonprofits can offer specialized services to other organizations or government entities and charge fees for those services, such as providing social services, healthcare, or education programs. Fee-for-service programs can either require mandatory fees or voluntary donations ("Understanding"), and are common in education, healthcare, and national and state parks, among others. Public universities, for instance, are nonprofit institutions that generate revenue through mandatory student tuition and fees.
- **Licensing and Royalties:** Nonprofits that own intellectual property, such as educational materials or content, can generate income by licensing or selling rights to use their assets. The American Society for Prevention of Cruelty for Animals (ASPCA), for example, generates revenue by partnering with for-profit companies that produce and sell pet toys. The for-profit organization benefits from the goodwill and credibility of their association with ASPCA, and the ASPCA benefits by receiving funding for licensing the use of their intellectual property ("Is Your" 2018).
- **Impact Investing:** Some philanthropic individuals and organizations engage in impact investing, which is an approach to investing that focuses on using money to make a positive social impact based on the values of the investors and donors ("Nonprofit Impact" 2023. Nonprofits may receive equity, interest, or dividends from impact-focused ventures as an additional revenue source.

Effective fundraising often involves a mix of these funding sources, tailored to the organization's mission, size, and goals. When approaching diversified revenue streams, however, nonprofit leaders should be mindful of the time and skills required of staff and volunteers and assure that they have sufficient capacity to engage in various revenue-generating activities.

Takeaways

LO 12-1: Grants are financial awards provided to nonprofit organizations by grantmakers and differ from general donations in their structure, purpose, use, and the way they are typically awarded. Grants are generally non-repayable funds intended to support a specific project, program, or the general operations of the nonprofit.

LO 12-2: Grantmakers are the organizations that issue financial awards in the form of grants to nonprofits, and include government agencies, private foundations, corporations, individuals, or other nonprofit organizations.

LO 12-3: A nonprofit-corporate partnership is a mutually beneficial relationship where a nonprofit and a corporate partner both commit resources to work together toward a common goal. Cultivating relationships through networking and presenting a value proposition to prospective partners are both keys to success.

LO 12-4: Nonprofits can leverage the corporate sponsorship model to drive revenue through direct corporate donations or indirect forms of giving such as sponsorships, employee giving programs, pro bono work, and cause marketing. When engaging in these partnerships, nonprofits should ensure alignment of values to avoid potentially controversial relationships.

LO 12-5: Employee giving programs are a form of corporate support where employees are encouraged by the company to support a nonprofit, versus the corporation making a financial contribution directly. This includes workplace giving, matching gifts, employee-driven fundraising initiatives, and employee volunteer programs.

LO 12-6: One way that companies can provide indirect corporate support to nonprofit organizations as part of a nonprofit-corporate partnership is by providing pro bono services, such as legal, marketing, or accounting services, at no cost to the beneficiary organization. Another indirect corporate giving mechanism is cause marketing, where a company's promotional campaign has the dual purpose of increasing profitability while bettering society, usually by benefiting a nonprofit organization. Cause marketing activities can include donation, "get one, give one," awareness, and point-of-sale campaigns.

LO 12-7: Other nonprofit funding sources include endowment or impact investment dividends; revenue from events, programs, and sale of tangible products; earned income; fees from fee-for-service contracts; and licensing revenue and royalties.

Bibliography

"6 Reasons You Shouldn't Ask For A Grant Writer's Success Rate." *Grant News*, 20 Jul. 2022, www.justwritegrants.com/post/successrate. Accessed 20 Aug. 2023.

"About B Corp Certification: Measuring a Company's Entire Social and Environmental Impact." *B Corp*, www.bcorporation.net/en-us/certification/. Accessed 18 Aug. 2023.

Álvarez-González, Luis I., et al. "Business-Nonprofit Partnerships as a Driver of Internal Marketing in Nonprofit Organizations. Consequences for Nonprofit Performance and Moderators." *Brq-Business Research Quarterly*, vol. 20, no. 2, 2017, pp. 112–123.

"Cause Marketing — Definition." *CauseMarketing.Com*, causemarketing.com/research/cause-marketing-definition/. Accessed 18 Aug. 2023.

Chow, Gia. "Nonprofit-Corporate Partnerships: Why They're Important and How to Find Them." *CauseVox*, www.causevox.com/blog/nonprofit-partnerships/#:~:text=A%20nonprofit%2Dcorporate%20partnership%20is,expand%20the%20reach%20of%20programs. Accessed 18 Aug. 2023.

Daily, Laura. "Gifts That Keep on Giving: These Retailers Offer One-for-One Deals or Make Financial Donations." *The Washington Post, WP Company*, 1 Dec. 2020, www.washingtonpost.com/lifestyle/home/gifts-donations-one-for-one/2020/11/27/4b54a840-2de4-11eb-96c2-aac3f162215d_story.html.

Eatough, Erin. "What Is Networking and Why Is It So Important? (Plus Tips)." *BetterUp*, 15 May 2023, www.betterup.com/blog/networking.

"Federal Grants to State and Local Governments." *U.S. GAO*, www.gao.gov/federal-grants-state-and-local-governments. Accessed 29 Sept. 2023.

Ferrand, Michelle. "How Nonprofit Organizations Use Reputational Risk Management." *World Risk Management*, 9 May 2018, wrmllc.com/how-nonprofit-organizations-use-reputational-risk-management/.

"Foundation Basics." *Council on Foundations*, 31 May 2022, cof.org/content/foundation-basics.

"Grant Lifecycle." *Grants.gov*, www.grants.gov/learn-grants/grants-101/grant-lifecycle.html. Accessed 29 Sept. 2023.

"Grantmaking." *Probably Good*, probablygood.org/career-profiles/grantmaking/. Accessed 29 Sept. 2023.

"Guide To Corporate Partnerships For Nonprofits." *Volgistics*, www.volgistics.com/blog/nonprofit-corporate-partnerships/. Accessed 20 Aug. 2023.

"How to Increase Your Chances of Being Awarded a Grant." *Grant News*, 3 Apr. 2023, www.grantwatch.com/grantnews/how-to-increase-your-chances-of-being-awarded-a-grant/. Accessed 20 Aug. 2023.

"How to Write a Value Proposition (+ 6 Modern Examples) - Help Scout." *Help Scout: Shared Inbox, Help Center, & Live Chat Software*, 20 Nov. 2022, www.helpscout.com/blog/value-proposition-examples/.

"Is Your Nonprofit Ready for Product Licensing?" *Selfish Giving*, 7 Jan. 2018, www.selfishgiving.com/blog/cause-marketing-product-licensing. Accessed 20 Aug. 2023.

Israel, Queen. "Exploring the World of Corporate Grants." *LinkedIn*, 31 July 2023, www.linkedin.com/pulse/exploring-world-corporate-grants-queen-israel.

Nenn, Kerry. "Double Your Dollars with Employer Matching Gifts." *Successful Fundraising*, vol. 26, no. 4, 2018, pp. 3–3.

"No Strings Attached: A Guide to Giving Unrestricted Funds." *Submittable Blog*, 1 Feb. 2023, blog.submittable.com/unrestricted-funds/.

"Nonprofit Impact Matters: How America's Charitable Nonprofits Strengthen Communities and Improve Lives." *National Council of Nonprofits*, 2019, www

.nonprofitimpactmatters.org/site/assets/files/1/nonprofit-impact-matters-sept-2019-1.pdf. Accessed 20 Aug. 2023.

O'Neal-McElrath, Tori, Carlson, Mim, and Ohio Library and Information Network. *Winning Grants Step by Step: The Complete Workbook for Planning, Developing, and Writing Successful Proposals*. Jossey-Bass, A Wiley Brand, San Francisco, CA, 2013.

"Pro Bono." *What Is Pro Bono?*, www.law.georgetown.edu/experiential-learning/pro-bono-community-service/what-is-pro-bono/#:~:text=The%20term%20%22pro%20bono%2C%22,those%20in%20the%20legal%20profession. Accessed 29 Sept. 2023.

"Private Foundations." *Internal Revenue Service*, www.irs.gov/charities-non-profits/charitable-organizations/private-foundations. Accessed 2 May 2023.

Rothstein, Anne L., and ProQuest (Firm). *Creating Winning Grant Proposals: A Step-by-Step Guide*. The Guilford Press, New York, 2019.

Sebastian, Sarah. "Nonprofit Awareness Campaigns: Three Strategies for Success." *GrantStation.com*, 27 July 2023, grantstation.com/gs-insights/Nonprofit-Awareness-Campaigns-Three-Strategies-for-Success.

Stombaugh, Heather. "Important Steps to Finding Government Grants for Nonprofits." *LiveAbout.Com*, 20 Nov. 2019, www.liveabout.com/government-grants-for-nonprofits-2502170. Accessed 20 Aug. 2023.

"Tax Issues Relating to Charitable Contributions and Organizations." *Congressional Research Service*, 4 Aug. 2020, crsreports.congress.gov/product/pdf/R/R45922. Accessed 18 Aug. 2023.

"Understanding Fee-for-Service Models." *Strengthening Nonprofits: A Capacity Builder's Resource Library*, d3n8a8pro7vhmx.cloudfront.net/nnaac/pages/129/attachments/original/1405455392/understanding-fe-for-service-models.pdf?1405455392. Accessed 18 Aug. 2023.

"Volunteer Programs That Employees Can Get Excited About." *Harvard Business Review*, 21 Jan. 2021, hbr.org/2021/01/volunteer-programs-that-employees-can-get-excited-about.

"What Is a Nonprofit Grant? - Nonprofit Glossary." *Kindful*, 30 Nov. 2022, kindful.com/nonprofit-glossary/nonprofit-grant/#:~:text=Grant%20organizations%2C%20also%20known%20as,their%20gift%20should%20be%20distributed.

"Why Impact Investing Is Better for Social Good." *Nonprofit Pro*, www.nonprofitpro.com/post/why-impact-investing-is-better-for-social-good/. Accessed 20 Aug. 2023.

"Workplace Giving." *America's Charities*, 3 Aug. 2021, www.charities.org/what-is-workplace-giving-campaign#:~:text=Workplace%20giving%20campaigns%20can%20take,deduction%20and%20other%20payment%20methods.

Part 5

Community

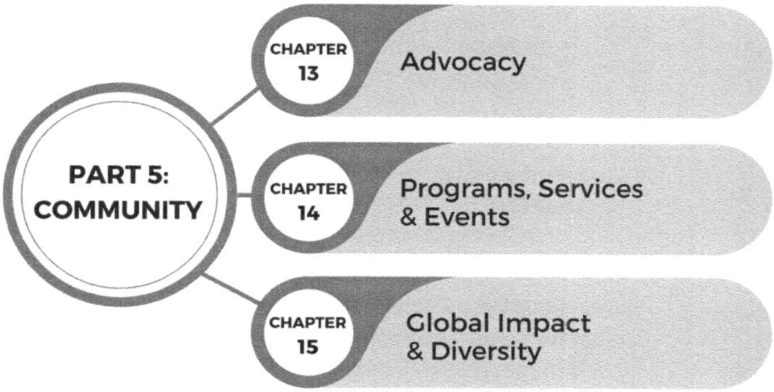

13 Advocacy

Learning Outcomes

After reading this chapter, you should be able to:

LO 13-1: Define nonprofit advocacy and identify its two primary categories.
LO 13-2: Summarize the various public awareness campaigns used by nonprofits to advocate for issues and actions.
LO 13-3: Explain lobbying activity in nonprofits and differentiate between direct lobbying and grassroots lobbying.
LO 13-4: Specify strategies of both direct and grassroots lobbying that are frequently used by nonprofits.
LO 13-5: Justify the need for policy research as a tool for nonprofit advocacy.
LO 13-6: Differentiate between political campaign activity and lobbying and discuss nonprofit limitations on advocacy.
LO 13-7: Examine approaches and strategies to mobilize nonprofit advocates.

> LO 13-1: Define nonprofit advocacy and identify its two primary categories.

Advocacy

Nonprofits advance their mission through building community and awareness of the cause, and legislative action can both advance these mission efforts and generate additional funding. **Nonprofit advocacy** refers to efforts undertaken by nonprofit organizations to influence public policies, laws, regulations, and public opinion in support of their mission (Almog-Bar & Schmid 2014). Advocacy can take many forms, but most can be placed into one of two categories: public awareness campaigns and lobbying. Nonprofit **advocates** are members of the community who volunteer to work on behalf of the

DOI: 10.4324/9781003380030-18

nonprofit to engage in advocacy efforts to influence decisions that advance the cause (Rees 1999).

Some use the terms "advocacy" and "lobbying" interchangeably, but they have distinctions. Advocacy encompasses efforts around not just influencing policy, but also building awareness and providing education, whereas lobbying involves specific, direct communication with government officials to influence legislation. Lobbying is a *form* of advocacy, specifically policy advocacy, but not all advocacy is lobbying, as it also encompasses other activities (Ross 2022). Simply put, advocacy ensures that a nonprofit's mission will be heard, and Figure 13.1 demonstrates the various advocacy activities pursued by nonprofits to make that happen.

Although advocacy work can be meaningful in advancing the organizational mission, surprisingly, research indicates that most nonprofits hold mixed feelings toward advocacy. It is estimated that only about one-quarter of nonprofits engage in some form of advocacy (Child 2007). Most nonprofits abstain from advocacy altogether or dabble in it, although it is not their primary focus or mission. These trends, however, vary systematically based on the *type* of nonprofit organization (Child 2007). Recall from Chapter 1 that nonprofits can be either direct service agencies, providing programs in local communities, or advocacy organizations that raise public awareness and push for policy reform. The latter category prioritizes advocacy work, as it is their main purpose. Not surprisingly, nonprofit organizations with larger budgets and a greater workforce tend to engage in more extensive and intensive advocacy efforts (Almog-Bar & Schmid 2014).

A comprehensive study found that high-impact nonprofits do not solely engage in just direct services or advocacy, but they engage in *both* activities. In other words, they both advocate *and* serve (Crutchfield 2008). Figure 13.2 provides an overview of how nonprofits can be categorized based upon the nature of their work in these areas.

Some direct service nonprofit leaders are reluctant to engage in advocacy work either because they lack confidence in their advocacy skills, preferring instead to prioritize work in delivering direct services and programs, or out of a concern of potential loss of corporate or donor support if the organization becomes "too political" (Crutchfield 2008).

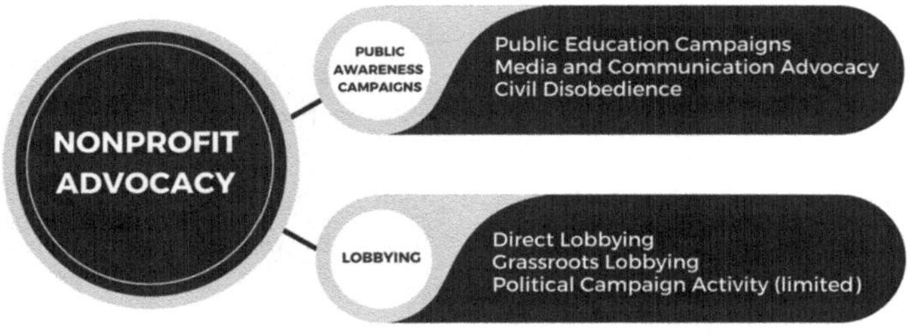

Figure 13.1 Nonprofit Advocacy Activities

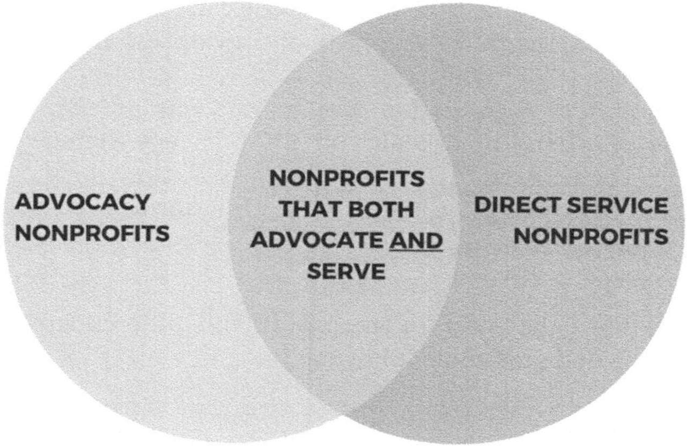

Figure 13.2 Advocacy vs. Service

LO 13-2: Summarize the various public awareness campaigns used by nonprofits to advocate for issues and actions.

Public Awareness Campaigns

Nonprofit **public awareness campaigns** in nonprofit advocacy refer to strategic initiatives to inform, educate, and raise awareness among stakeholders about the nonprofit and its mission and work and are designed to inspire action and mobilize resources to advance the organizational mission (Gauss 2022). These campaigns are typically integrated within the public relations component of a nonprofit's promotion mix as part of its overall marketing strategy, a concept discussed in Chapter 11.

Public education campaigns are public awareness campaigns that have a broader educational objective, aiming to provide the audience with detailed information, knowledge, and understanding of a particular issue. Many nonprofits engage in public education campaigns, often rallying around a certain designated time period such as an "awareness day" or month. No-Shave November, for example, is a web-based public education initiative that encourages participants to stop shaving for the month of November to raise awareness about cancer, educate about the importance of early detection, and support several cancer nonprofits ("No-Shave").

Chapter 11 covered the general premise of public relations, and PR can be leveraged for advocacy initiatives. **Media and communication advocacy** occurs when nonprofits use various media channels to communicate their messages and engage with the public. This can involve writing op-eds, issuing press releases, conducting interviews with journalists, and other activities.

Some nonprofits may even coordinate **civil disobedience** activities, such as sit-ins or other nonviolent actions, as a form of public awareness advocacy to draw attention to an issue of significant importance. Greenpeace is a global environmental nonprofit organization that has successfully engaged in civil disobedience as a means of drawing attention to environmental issues, including their "Save the Arctic" protest in the early 2010s, where the agency's activists attempted to scale a Russian drilling platform to protest Arctic oil production (Fallon 2012.

LO 13-3: Explain lobbying activity in nonprofits and differentiate between direct lobbying and grassroots lobbying.

Lobbying

Public awareness campaigns center on educating and raising awareness, but another form of advocacy – lobbying – has a more specific and action-oriented purpose. **Lobbying** refers to activities undertaken by nonprofit organizations to influence policies, laws, regulations, and decisions (Chand 2017). Public awareness campaigns can be leveraged as a strategic tool to aid lobbying efforts by putting public pressure on legislators and decision-makers.

Lobbying allows nonprofits to engage in the democratic process and advocate for issues aligned with their missions, allowing them to advance their causes, promote changes in public policy, and create a positive impact on the communities they serve. Nonprofit lobbying activities can be placed into one of two categories: direct lobbying and grassroots lobbying. The former refers to actions conducted by nonprofit leaders and the latter to a mobilized base of volunteers acting on behalf of the nonprofit.

LO 13-4: Specify strategies of both direct and grassroots lobbying that are frequently used by nonprofits.

Direct Lobbying

Direct Lobbying refers to efforts to influence lawmakers or government officials through direct communication such as meetings, emails, letters, or phone calls. Nonprofits are permitted to engage in direct lobbying, but should be aware of some legal restrictions and reporting requirements that may apply depending on their tax-exempt status and the laws of their jurisdiction ("Direct").

In addition to nonprofit leaders sending emails, letters, and making calls, an effective form of direct lobbying involves meeting with lawmakers.

Advocacy meetings are facilitated by nonprofits to meet with legislators to lobby for their cause and may include the constituents they serve in addition to representatives from the nonprofit organization, often staff or advocacy volunteers. These meetings include discussion of a particular piece of legislation and a specific ask around it, either in support or opposition. Some nonprofits use these visits as an opportunity to "sell hope" and make an inspirational appeal to the decision-maker by including in the meeting individuals who may be personally affected by the cause to engage in storytelling to share the ways in which the nonprofit has positively impact their life.

Another form of direct lobbying is **public testimony**, which is like storytelling, addressed in Chapter 11. This involves individuals testifying at public hearings or legislative sessions, representing the nonprofit, and sharing their personal stories of how the organization has positively impacted their lives. This testimony is designed to educate lawmakers and influence their decision-making ("How To").

Grassroots Lobbying

An indirect form of lobbying involves mobilizing volunteers and constituents to advocate on behalf of a cause. **Grassroots Lobbying** happens when nonprofits encourage their supporters and the public to contact elected officials on their behalf to express their views on specific legislation or policies ("Direct"). This form of lobbying is a common way for nonprofits to engage their constituencies in advocacy efforts. To inspire and rally their supporters around specific or more urgent policy issues, nonprofits sometimes organize advocacy campaigns called **calls to action**, which are compelling prompts that encourage supporters to take immediate and meaningful action in support of a nonprofit's specific advocacy efforts (Wilkinson 2016).

Nonprofits also sometimes bolster their lobbying power and influence by leveraging strength in numbers through **coalitions**, which involves collaborating with other organizations, advocacy groups, and stakeholders to form coalitions to amplify their efforts (Chin 2018). The Alliance for Gun Responsibility, for example, is a nonprofit coalition with the mission to advocate for gun safety measures, responsible gun ownership, and the reduction of gun violence. The coalition includes dozens of nonprofit organizations that have partnered with the organization on events and projects and/or have endorsed their initiatives ("Partners" 2023). Many nonprofit leaders view the formation of coalitions as the most potent means of shaping policy (Hoefer 2000).

Advocacy Campaigns

Advocacy campaigns include activities such as calling campaigns, online advocacy, petitions, rallies, litigation, and other actions designed to facilitate grassroots lobbying (Vaughn 2021).

Calling campaigns occur when nonprofits urge their supporters in a coordinated and organized fashion to contact their legislators by phone to express their views on a specific policy issue or piece of legislation of concern to the nonprofit organization. These campaigns are designed to influence the legislative process by directly engaging constituents and conveying their concerns or support for specific actions or policy changes.

Online advocacy, or "e-advocacy," takes a similar approach, but instead of supporters contacting legislators by phone, they are encouraged to send emails, tag legislators on social media platforms, write blogs, or contact their representatives via online web forms (Bhagat 2005). To organize a coordinated message, nonprofit leaders will often craft specific talking points or entire messages as templates for supporters to use or simply copy-and-paste in these communications.

Some nonprofits organize **petitions** as a formal appeal to legislators, urging them to act in alignment with the nonprofit's mission. By gathering signatures from supporters, it amplifies the impact of the request by demonstrating support of many people, strengthening the voice for a specific action. Some petitions are circulated in person, but many are facilitated online with electronic distribution and collection of digital signatures.

Rallies are highly visible, public gatherings for stakeholders to convene around a shared issue to express their views to raise awareness around that cause, mobilize public support, and advocate for action. Finally, in some cases, advocacy nonprofits may engage in **litigation** to enact change. This involves filing lawsuits or other legal actions to challenge existing laws or policies that run counter to the organization's mission.

Litigating for Change

In Spring 2023, Tennessee became the first state in America to pass legislation to place strict limits on drag shows (Kruesi 2023). Just months after the passage of the new law, The American Civil Liberties Union (ACLU) affiliate in the state filed a lawsuit to challenge the ban. Founded in 1920, the ACLU founded in 1920, the agency refers to itself as "the nation's guardian of liberty." As an advocacy organization, the ACLU works in the courts, legislatures, and communities to defend and preserve the individual rights and liberties guaranteed to all people in America ("ACLU"). The ACLU filed its lawsuit on behalf of drag performer Flamy Grant, who was hired to perform at the Blount County Pride Festival, asking the federal court of eastern Tennessee to block enforcement of the law, declaring it illegal and unconstitutional. The federal judge ultimately ruled in favor of the ACLU, pride organizers, and Grant, directing that Tennessee law officials could not interfere with the festival (Kruesi 2023). Another federal judge, ruling on a separate case in Tennessee, similarly ruled that the drag show ban is "unconstitutionally vague and substantially overbroad," calling enforcement of the law "discriminatory" (Mattise 2023). This is just one example of the ACLU using litigation to enact change in advancement of its mission to protect civil liberties of American citizens.

The specific advocacy priorities of a nonprofit organization vary, contingent upon its organizational mission. Figure 13.3 showcases some well-known nonprofit organizations and the issues they champion. Advocacy issues may center on advancing a social cause related to the mission, or it may be used to influence decisions. Nonprofits that rely on government funding, for example, may advocate to safeguard critical funding sources to guarantee ongoing financial stability (Mosley 2011). Nonprofit advocacy efforts tend to be successful, with one survey of nearly 400 US-based nonprofit organizations indicating that more three-quarters of responding organizations reported having enacted, stopped, or modified policy (Buffardi 2017).

Figure 13.3 Nonprofit Advocacy Issues

LO 13-5: Justify the need for policy research as a tool for nonprofit advocacy.

Policy Research

When seeking to persuade lawmakers and decision-makers to undertake specific actions, it is advantageous for nonprofit leaders to construct a compelling business argument that rationalizes the advantages of such actions. **Policy research** is the systematic process of conducting studies, analyses, and investigations to gather information, data, and evidence relevant to specific policy issues, often with the goal of informing public policy discussions and decisions.

Policy research provides nonprofits and their advocates with evidence-based information and data to support their advocacy efforts. It equips organizations with credible arguments and facts to effectively communicate their positions and influence policymakers. Facts and figures are often integrated into templates nonprofits provide to advocates when engaging in advocacy campaigns to strengthen the case for a specific action. Instead of simply saying, "Please support our cause!" policy research allows nonprofits to appeal to the rational side of legislators by saying instead, "Please support our cause because research demonstrates it is in the best interest of your constituents and will result in an annual government cost savings of $xx,xxx."

Good policy research also benefits nonprofits by giving them credibility as experts in their fields, which in turn enhances their influence with policymakers and stakeholders. Policy research also allows for data-driven decision-making for nonprofit leaders to inform their own strategic priorities in how to best fulfill their mission and support community needs.

LO 13-6: Differentiate between political campaign activity and lobbying and discuss nonprofit limitations on advocacy.

Advocacy Limitations

While lobbying is allowed for nonprofits, leaders should be cautious when engaging in these activities as to not inadvertently run afoul of Internal Revenue Service (IRS) requirements and face penalties or even jeopardize their tax-exempt status. The IRS allows 501(c)(3) nonprofit organizations, for instance, to engage in lobbying only if it is not a "substantial part" of their activities, although this guideline is vague. Additionally, federal grant funds may not be spent on lobbying, and there are limitations in general on the percentage of nonprofit's annual expenditures that can be devoted to lobbying activities.

One type of lobbying that is limited is **political campaign activity**, which includes organized efforts and actions undertaken to support or oppose political candidates running for public office during an election or campaign season. Under the IRS code, "all section 501(c)(3) organizations are absolutely prohibited from directly or indirectly participating in, or intervening in, any political campaign on behalf of (or in opposition to) any candidate for elective public office" ("The Restriction").

Because nonprofits are supposed to serve a public purpose and represent constituents in an unbiased manner, they should remain **nonpartisan**, which refers to the need to remain impartial and not aligned with any political party or group. Nonpartisan behavior signifies a neutral and unbiased stance, where decisions or actions are made without favoring any specific party, ideology, or affiliation. While political campaign activity to support or oppose political candidates is prohibited, the IRS does allow for some voter-based activities including certain voter education activities, such as publishing voter education guides, and facilitating get-out-the-vote drives, so long as these actions are conducted in a nonpartisan manner ("The Restriction").

While 501(c)(3) nonprofits face some of the most stringent restrictions on political campaign activity, what is permitted varies depending upon the various nonprofit classifications. Social welfare organizations with 501(c)(4) tax-exempt status, for instance, have more latitude to engage in political campaign activity compared to 501(c)(3) nonprofits.

> LO 13-7: Examine approaches and strategies to mobilize nonprofit advocates.

Mobilizing Advocates

Chapter 8 explained why volunteers are motivated to contribute their time and talent to nonprofit organizations. Motivating supporters to engage in advocacy, however, sometimes requires additional efforts to **mobilize**, meaning not just to place volunteers in various roles to complete tasks, but to actively engage them to make a meaningful impact on the organization's mission and activities. Mobilization is closely tied to **community organizing**, which focuses on building grassroots support and networks within communities to effect change. Community organizers then work to mobilize these supporters around the issues and encourage collective action (Oster 2022).

Not all volunteers feel comfortable participating in advocacy activities, but here are some approaches to mobilize this stakeholder group, which is also represented in Figure 13.4 ("7 Ways").

People will not feel inspired to contribute their valuable time if the need for action is not clearly articulated, so the first step of mobilization is to

Figure 13.4 Advocacy Mobilization

specify the need and articulate why advocacy is needed to fulfill that need. Nonprofit leaders must also *present solutions*. Supporters are inspired by solutions, not problems, so presenting clear and feasible solutions to solve the need can help mobilize the advocacy power needed to enact change. The next step is to *tell compelling stories*, because as discussed in Chapter 11, nonprofits must "sell hope," and putting faces and names to the cause and the needs of the organization is a great way to inspire action.

All these actions are not effective, however, if they are not adequately shared, so the next step is to *communicate the message*. Nonprofit leaders can employ the strategies covered in Chapter 11 to communicate the needs, solutions, and stories to get the message out to the targeted audience or even the public in general. Finally, advocates need to have a specific *call to action*. Successful advocacy is dependent upon strength in numbers, and to mobilize large numbers of people to act, nonprofit leaders must direct individuals to a specific desired action.

Many nonprofits engage in recruitment efforts to attract advocates, sometimes alongside their regular volunteer recruitment initiatives, but other times as its own separate activity. These advocates are typically coded and tracked within nonprofit volunteer management platforms, so the nonprofit organization can quickly and easily push out a call to action, when needed, to communicate directly to those who are likely to act on it.

Takeaways

LO 13-1: Nonprofit advocacy refers to public awareness campaigns and lobbying undertaken by nonprofit organizations to influence public policy in support of their mission.

LO 13-2: Public awareness campaigns are designed to inspire action and mobilize resources to advance a nonprofit's mission, and include public education campaigns, media and communications advocacy, and civil disobedience.
LO 13-3: Lobbying refers to attempts by a nonprofit to influence policies and laws and can be categorized as direct or grassroots. Direct lobbying involves direct communication, whereas grassroots lobbying is an indirect form that involves mobilizing supporters to advocate on behalf of an organization.
LO 13-4: Direct lobbying strategies include advocacy meetings and public testimony, and grassroots lobbying includes calls to action, coalitions, and advocacy campaigns.
LO 13-5: Policy research is the systematic process of conducting research to gather evidence relevant to specific policy issues and is used to construct a compelling business argument to decision-makers that rationalizes the advantages of such actions.
LO 13-6: Nonprofits are permitted to engage in lobbying, with certain IRS-imposed limitations, including the requirement that agencies can engage in lobbying only if it is not a "substantial part" of their activities. Additionally, most nonprofits are prohibited from engaging in political campaign activity to support or oppose political candidates.
LO 13-7: Mobilizing advocates requires engaging them in making a meaningful impact through nonprofit advocacy and can be accomplished by a five-step process.

Bibliography

"7 Ways to Mobilize the Masses Around Your Mission." *Fifty and Fifty*, fiftyandfifty.org/7-crucial-ingredients-to-mobilize-the-masses-around-your-mission/. Accessed 20 Aug. 2023.

"ACLU." *American Civil Liberties Union*, 29 Sept. 2023, www.aclu.org/.

Almog-Bar, Michal, and Hillel Schmid. "Advocacy Activities of Nonprofit Human Service Organizations: A Critical Review." *Nonprofit and Voluntary Sector Quarterly*, vol. 43, no. 1, 2014, pp. 11–35.

Bhagat, V. "Online Advocacy: How the Internet is Transforming the Way Nonprofits Reach, Motivate, and Retain Supporters." *Nonprofit Internet Strategies*, edited by T. Hart, J. Greenfield, and M. Johnston. John Wiley, Hoboken, NJ, 2005, pp. 119–134.

Buffardi, A.L., R.J. Pekkanen, and S.R. Smith. "Proactive or Protective? Dimensions of and Advocacy Activities Associated with Reported Policy Change by Nonprofit Organizations." *VOLUNTAS: International Journal of Voluntary and Nonprofit Organizations*, vol. 28, no. 3, 2017, pp. 1226–1248.

Chand, Daniel E. "Lobbying and Nonprofits: Money and Membership Matter—But Not for all." *Social Science Quarterly*, vol. 98, no. 5, 2017, pp. 1296–1312.

Child, Curtis D., and Kirsten A. Grønbjerg. "Nonprofit Advocacy Organizations: Their Characteristics and Activities." *Social Science Quarterly*, vol. 88, no. 1, 2007, pp. 259–281.

Chin, John J. "Service-Providing Nonprofits Working in Coalition to Advocate for Policy Change." *Nonprofit and Voluntary Sector Quarterly*, vol. 47, no. 1, 2018, pp. 27–48.
Crutchfield, Leslie R., Heather M. Grant, and Fuqua School of Business (Duke University). "Center for the Advancement of Social Entrepreneurship." *Forces for Good: The Six Practices of High-Impact Nonprofits*. Jossey-Bass, John Wiley & Sons, San Francisco, 2008.
"'Direct' and 'Grass Roots' Lobbying Defined." *Internal Revenue Service*, www.irs.gov/charities-non-profits/direct-and-grass-roots-lobbying-defined. Accessed 29 June 2023.
Fallon, Myriam. "Save the Arctic Campaign Sets Eyes on Russia." *Greenpeace USA - We Fight for a Greener, More PeacefulWorld*, 20 Aug 2012, www.greenpeace.org/usa/save-the-arctic-campaign-sets-eyes-on-russia/.
Gauss, A. "A Beginner's Guide to Scaling an Awareness Campaign." *Classy*, 22 June 2022, www.classy.org/blog/a-beginners-guide-to-scaling-an-awareness-campaign/.
Hoefer, R. "Making a Difference: Human Service Interest Group Influence on Social Welfare Program Regulations." *Journal of Sociology and Social Welfare*, vol. 27, no. 3, 2000, pp. 21–38.
"How to Write and Deliver Testimony at a Public Hearing." *Conservationvoters. Org*, conservationvoters.org/activist-toolkit/how-to-write-and-deliver-testimony-at-a-public-hearing. Accessed 29 Aug. 2023.
Jeter, Alex. "Nonprofit Advocacy: 5 Successful Strategies and Examples." *Salsa*, 4 Oct. 2019, www.salsalabs.com/blog/nonprofit-advocacy-examples. Accessed 22 Aug. 2023.
Kruesi, Kimberlee. "ACLU Sues Tennessee District Attorney Who Promises to Enforce the State's New Anti-Drag Show Ban." *AP News*, 31 Aug. 2023, apnews.com/article/drag-ban-tennessee-pride-87430f9fa31d3106961943edf55ba588.
Mattise, Jonathan. "Officials Can't Interfere with Local Tennessee Pride Festival under Anti-Drag Law, Judge Rules." *AP News*, 1 Sept. 2023, apnews.com/article/drag-ban-tennessee-pride-8cb18a834869b08176e158c504b11dc0.
Mosley, J.E. "Institutionalization, Privatization, and Political Opportunity: What Tactical Choices Reveal about the Policy Advocacy of Human Service Nonprofits." *Nonprofit & Voluntary Sector Quarterly*, vol. 40, 2011, pp. 435–457. Crossref. ISI.
"No-Shave November." *No-Shave November*, no-shave.org/. Accessed 22 Aug. 2023.
Oster, Russ. "Nonprofit Advocacy: How to Mobilize Supporters for Change." *Nonprofit Courses*, 26 Sept. 2022, www.nonprofit.courses/blog/nonprofit-advocacy/.
"Partners." *Alliance for Gun Responsibility*, gunresponsibility.org/partners/. Accessed 22 Aug. 2023.
Rees, Susan. "Strategic Choices for Nonprofit Advocates." *Nonprofit and Voluntary Sector Quarterly*, vol. 28, no. 1, 1999, pp. 65–73.
Ross, Brennah. "Advocacy vs. Lobbying: What's the Difference? Understanding Regulations for Researchers & Nonprofits." *Research to Policy Collaboration*, 15 Aug. 2022, research2policy.org/advocacyvlobbying/.
"The Restriction of Political Campaign Intervention by Section 501(C)(3) Tax-Exempt Organizations." *US IRS*, www.irs.gov/charities-non-profits/charitable-organizations/the-restriction-of-political-campaign-intervention-by-section-501c3-tax-exempt-organizations. Accessed 22 Aug. 2023.
Vaughn, Corey, and Cleo Dan. "5 Advocacy Examples to Inspire Action and Motivate Change." *Grassroots Advocacy Software*, 29 June 2021, www.muster.com/blog/advocacy-examples.
Wilkinson, Jay. "40 Nonprofit Call to Action Examples That Drive Engagement." *Firespring*, 1 July 2016, firespring.com/solutions-for-nonprofits/40-call-to-action-examples-that-drive-engagement/.

14 Programs, Services, and Events

Learning Outcomes

After reading this chapter, you should be able to:

LO 14-1: Describe how nonprofit programs and services are interrelated, but different.
LO 14-2: Identify the most common forms of nonprofit programs.
LO 14-3: Highlight the elements nonprofit leaders should consider in program design.
LO 14-4: Explain how nonprofit event planners should consider mission moment and guest experience when designing events.
LO 14-5: Distinguish between the most common nonprofit fundraising events.
LO 14-6: Summarize the various categories of nonprofit non-revenue events.

> LO 14-1: Describe how nonprofit programs and services are interrelated, but different.

Programs and Services

A central way that nonprofits serve their communities and work toward mission achievement is through delivery of programs, services, and events. Programs and services might seem similar, but they bear some distinctions. Nonprofit programs are structured initiatives aimed at achieving broader mission-driven goals, while services are specific, immediate offerings designed to directly address individual or community needs. In contrast, nonprofit events are organized gatherings to support mission and are held for purposes such as fundraising, community engagement, education, advocacy, and others. Figure 14.1 illustrates the relationship between programs, which are overarching initiatives that services support.

DOI: 10.4324/9781003380030-19

Figure 14.1 Nonprofit Programs and Services

As discussed in Chapter 1, nonprofits can be broadly categorized as either advocacy organizations or direct service organizations. While the former is primarily focused on advocacy efforts, they can still engage in the delivery of programs, events, and services, although these functions are generally not their primary concerns unless they serve to support advocacy work (Beaton, MacIndoe & Wang 2021). Direct service agencies can engage in advocacy efforts, although we know from Chapter 13 that most do not, but their central focus is on delivery of programs and hosting events.

Recall from Chapter 4 that nonprofit staff positions are organized into four general categories: management, administrative, development, and program delivery. Not surprisingly, it is program delivery staff who tend to manage and execute nonprofit programs and services.

LO 14-2: Identify the most common forms of nonprofit programs.

Programs

Nonprofit programs are broad, structured initiatives designed to achieve specific objectives aligned with the nonprofit's mission and strategic plan. They can encompass a wide range of activities and may involve multiple services or interventions working together toward a common outcome (Rogers 2022).

Given their broad scope, programs tend to be outcome-oriented, with the goal to create lasting change in an area through delivery of various services.

Nonprofit organizations operate an expansive range of programs and services to address diverse social, environmental, and community needs, so these can vary widely, depending on the nonprofit's mission and focus. Further, some nonprofits focus on just one type of program, whereas others engage in multiple types of programs ("How Do" 2023). Here are some common ones:

- **Educational Programs** include initiatives such as tutoring, scholarship programs, after-school programs, financial literacy classes, language classes, and vocational training to enhance learning and skill development.
- **Healthcare Programs** involve the delivery of medical and healthcare services, such as clinics, health screenings, vaccination campaigns, healthy lifestyle initiatives, mental health, and public health outreach programs.
- **Youth and Family Programs** may encompass parenting support, foster care, youth advocacy, mentoring, family counseling, childcare, and other initiatives to strengthen family and child well-being.
- **Resource Programs** address community needs around social issues such as homelessness and housing assistance, food and nutrition, transportation, meal delivery, recovery and addiction, and legal aid.
- **Employment Programs** provide job training, employment placement services, and vocational programs to help people acquire the skills needed for gainful employment.
- **Disaster Relief Programs** provide recovery assistance after disasters, such as floods or hurricanes, and include services such as shelter and food for affected communities.
- **Advocacy Programs** involve coordinated advocacy initiatives around a specific social aspect, such as environmental conservation, arts and culture, or human rights.

Nonprofit programs should address the needs, challenges, or issues the organization aims to address in the mission and deliver appropriate services to beneficiary stakeholders to meet those needs.

Services

While programs are broader in scope, **nonprofit services** are specific activities or offerings to meet immediate needs of the agency's constituency or deliver direct assistance to individuals or communities (Leonard 2019). Services tend to be focused and practical, targeted at providing essential support or resources around particular issues or challenges. While programs are typically built based on a longer-term strategy, services have a more immediate impact.

Figure 14.2 provides an example of how a fictional nonprofit with the mission to serve underprivileged youth might structure its programs and services.

Figure 14.2 Organizational Structure with Product Departmentalization

You may note that this figure looks familiar, like an organizational chart. It is no coincidence that nonprofits that opt to organize based on product departmentalization do so by grouping people together based upon "product"; in this case with the programs serving as the "product mix."

LO 14-3: Highlight the elements nonprofit leaders should consider in program design.

Program Design

When nonprofit leaders design programs, they should primarily be mindful of how the services offered within a nonprofit program are aligned with the program's overall objectives and overarching organizational mission. Decisions also must be made around **resource allocation,** which relates to the distribution of resources, including staff, volunteers, funding, and materials, to deliver the services within the program (Sarikaya 2021). Not all programs will, or should, receive equal distribution of resources, so leaders need to set priorities and disperse resources accordingly. In some instances, collaboration with other nonprofits, government agencies, or community groups can allow nonprofits to deliver programs and services more efficiently by pooling resources and expertise.

While beneficiaries receive services at no or a low cost, that does not mean that the nonprofits delivering them do not have an obligation to provide quality. **Quality assurance** refers to measures taken by nonprofits to ensure that the programs and services provided to beneficiaries meet certain quality standards and adhere to ethical guidelines. These standards are set and monitored by nonprofit leaders, and methods to enhance quality include training staff and volunteers, following best practices, and seeking accreditation or certifications where applicable (Grobman 2014).

Another step to assuring quality is **program evaluation and monitoring**, which involves assessment of the impact and effectiveness of nonprofit programs or services through measuring outcomes, collecting data, and seeking feedback from beneficiaries (Hoefer 2000).

Delivering services is an important part of nonprofit programs, as these are the activities that directly address the needs of the communities that the nonprofit exists to serve. Effective program design ensures that these services are delivered in an efficient and quality manner that aligns with the agency's overarching mission (McNamara 2022).

> LO 14-4: Explain how nonprofit event planners should consider mission moment and guest experience when designing events.

Events

Nonprofit events are organized activities to gather people for various purposes in support of the organizational mission and objectives. Events can center on activities such as fundraising, community engagement, networking, and advocacy, among others. Unlike programs, events do not generally deliver services, but rather serve to raise funds for the organization or engage stakeholders. Nonprofit events can be designed for fundraising or not, and those that can vary from modest fundraisers to events that generate significant funds (Rees 2023).

Fundraising Events

While program delivery staff are responsible for executing nonprofit programs and services, fundraising events typically fall under the purview of development staff. Delivering quality fundraising events requires not just organizational acumen to coordinate event logistics, but also fundraising skill, as the primary purpose of fundraising events is to generate revenue for the nonprofit organization.

Designing fundraising events can vary depending upon the type and nature of the event, but the central priority for all is to prioritize the organization's mission to maintain attendee engagement and ensure a positive experience ("Nonprofits" 2018). In designing fundraising events, nonprofit leaders need to ensure that attendees understand the impact they can make on the cause through a contribution and educate them on the mission of the organization. This is often accomplished through a **mission moment**, which is a dedicated portion of a nonprofit event where the organization stops the festivities, or includes in its stage programming an opportunity to educate guests on the organizational mission and importance of their support. This is often accomplished through speeches and/or videos featuring an individual or family positively impacted by the mission and work of the organization (Jacobwith 2014).

Less of a priority, but still a factor in fundraising event planning to ensure a positive donor experience and attendance retention for future events, is the concept of **guest experience**. This refers to the overall impression that individuals have when attending nonprofit events, encompassing aspects such as engagement, satisfaction with the experience, meaningful interactions, and connectedness to the organization's mission and goals (Axelrad 2022). While mission moments and concern for guest experience are often at the forefront

Photo 14.1 **A Mission Moment** *A beneficiary of the Forever Kings nonprofit addresses guests at the nonprofit's annual black-tie "Building Strong Men" gala to share his personal story of the positive impact that the organization and its mission has had on his life. Photo by author.*

of fundraising events, they should be considered by event planners when designing non-revenue events, as well.

Guest experience at events can positively impact **donor experience**, which is the sum of all touchpoints a donor encounters as they engage with your organization (Locksin 2021). Positive overall donor experiences lead to greater donor satisfaction, higher contributions, and stronger donor retention, with 63% of donors in one study reporting that they would donate to a nonprofit after a positive encounter (Elsey 2020).

LO 14-5: Distinguish between the most common nonprofit fundraising events.

There are no limitations on the type of event that can be leveraged as a nonprofit fundraising opportunity, and there are hundreds of examples of creative approaches to fundraising events. While nonprofit fundraising events are varied, however, there are five common ones that are widely used across the sector, including galas, cocktail parties, endurance events, golf outings, and benefit performances, illustrated in Figure 14.3.

Galas

Galas are typically formal events where guests wear black-tie attire and purchase tickets or sponsor tables in order to attend and enjoy a plated dinner and entertainment. Galas are typically hosted on an annual basis and tend to draw a nonprofit's major donors and top corporate sponsors. Galas primarily generate revenue through ticket sales, table sponsorships, auctions, and fund-a-need campaigns.

Nonprofit auctions are fundraising activities in which items, experiences, or services are auctioned off to the highest bidders, with the proceeds going to support a nonprofit organization. These auctions can be conducted in various formats, such as **live auctions** with an auctioneer; **silent auctions** with written bids, online, or mobile bidding; or **online auctions** conducted over the internet. Auctions can be incorporated into other nonprofit fundraising events, or even as their own standalone fundraising endeavors, but are a well-known and traditional component of charity galas (Meyer 2023).

Fund a need is another fundraising mechanism frequently deployed at gala fundraising events, and functions as a live auction for supporters to "bid" on the mission, rather than an item, experience, or service, as they would in a traditional live auction. Typically, a gala auctioneer will call out various giving levels, and gala attendees can raise their bid cards at their desired level to publicly designate their support of the nonprofit and its mission, receiving nothing in return ("Ignite" 2015).

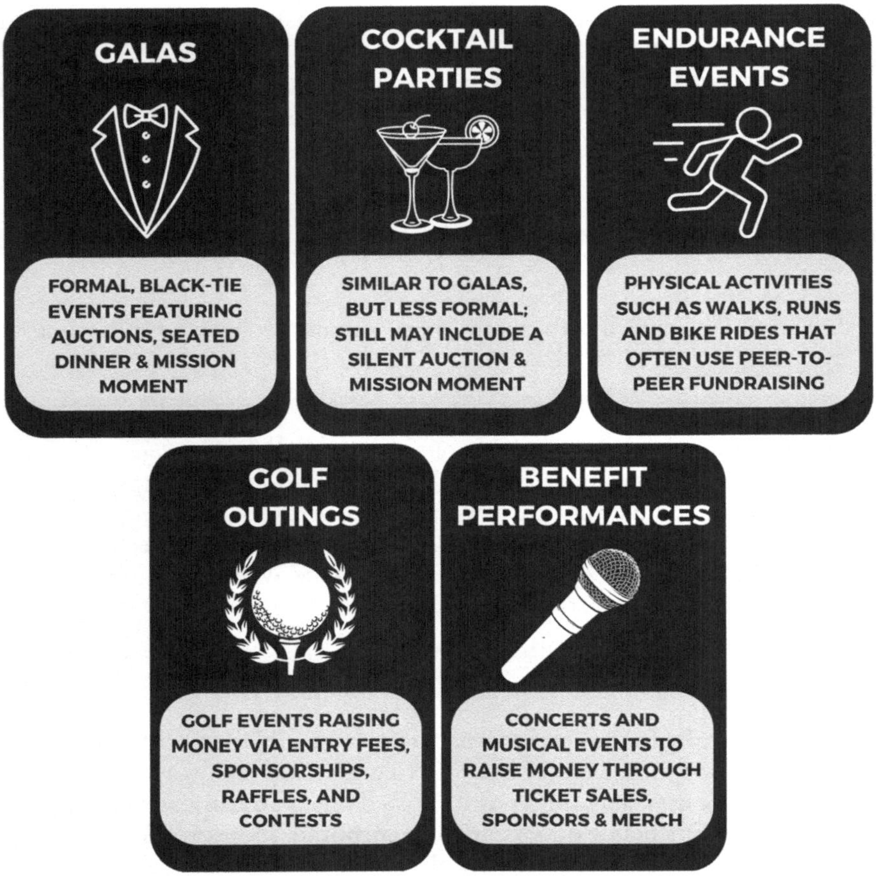

Figure 14.3 Nonprofit Fundraising Events

Cocktail Parties

Fundraising galas can prove lucrative to nonprofits as fundraising events and can serve as a mechanism to engage an organization's top donors and corporate supporters, but they tend to be resource intensive, both in cost and labor, to execute. As such, many nonprofits opt to host smaller scale events like **cocktail parties**, which are fundraising events that are generally less formal than galas but follow a similar format (Rees 2023).

Like galas, many fundraising cocktail parties include food, entertainment, auctions, and a mission moment. Cocktail party auctions may, however, just consist of a silent or mobile bidding auction as opposed to a live auction with an auctioneer. They also generally involve less-formal food choices, such as hors d'oeuvres or food stations, rather than a plated meal served to guests while they are seated. They also require less formal dress from guests, calling for cocktail attire rather than black-tie.

Cocktail parties may also consist of more of a "meet and mingle" networking format instead of the more formal structure of assigned tables with an on-stage program with an emcee and multiple presenters. While cocktail parties are less formal, incorporating the mission moment is still a critical component. Cocktail party fundraisers may generate less revenue than galas but can be executed much more efficiently. A nonprofit fundraising mechanism similar to cocktail parties, but typically less formal and hosted during the day on weekdays, are fundraising luncheons.

Endurance Events

The cost of admission to a gala or even a less formal cocktail party can serve as a **barrier to entry** for prospective attendees, meaning that they are unable to attend due to not having the money required to purchase an expensive admission ticket or to sponsor a table. Or, individuals may have the financial means to attend a gala or cocktail party, but prefer not to, as they generally do not like the structure of those events. Because of the varying needs of donors, many nonprofits choose to diversify their array of fundraising events, to offer different options to their supporters.

Endurance events involve events where participants raise money by engaging in some sort of physical activity such as walking, running, climbing, or biking. These activities can be physically strenuous, such as running a marathon or biking 100 miles, or they can be less so with a shorter "fun run" or easy walk route (Panepento 2018).

Many endurance events are structured as **peer-to-peer fundraisers**, meaning that attendees use their participation in the activity to solicit sponsorships from friends, family, and corporate connections to enhance their individual impact. This approach leverages the personal connections and passion of supporters to drive donations. Some participants may choose to also contribute personally, and these events are often structured in a way that tracks, publicizes, and acknowledges participants based on their overall amount of fundraising. Some nonprofits allow and encourage participants to form teams and recruit other participants to engage with them in the endurance event, with competition between teams to see which can raise the most money for the nonprofit organization (Panepento 2018).

Golf Outings

Another common event is **golf outings**, where sponsors and participants pay to play golf, either as part of a tournament or a less formal golf outing, with proceeds benefiting a nonprofit organization. In addition to entry fees and sponsorships, these events typically include other fundraising components such as contests, raffles, and awards (Ensor 2023).

Golf outings are beneficial, as they may draw from a different donor population who may not be interested in galas, cocktail parties, or endurance events, or who are golf enthusiasts, and they can serve as a draw to corporate sponsors. The primary downside of golf outings, however, is the capacity limitation, as the structure of these outings can only accommodate a certain number of participants. As such, golf outings tend to be more modest fundraising events, relative to other fundraising event types.

Benefit Performances

Nonprofit benefit performances include concerts, performances, or musical events organized by nonprofits to raise funds for their cause and in support of their mission, primarily through the sale of admission tickets (Rees 2023). Additional fundraising mechanisms include corporate sponsorships, merchandise sales, and auctions. Benefit performances both raise funds for the organization, and also raise awareness of the mission of the organization.

Fundraising events are a great way to raise additional funds and also engage existing donors. In a survey of 7,000 donors in the United States and Canada, 44% of respondents said they attend fundraising events such as galas and luncheons and 15% participate in endurance fundraising events ("Global" 2023). While galas, cocktail parties, endurance events, golf outings, and benefit performances are among the most common nonprofit fundraising event types, nonprofit organizations often innovate and tailor their events to fit their unique missions and engage their specific donor base effectively.

> LO 14-6: Summarize the various categories of nonprofit non-revenue events.

Non-Revenue Events

Not all nonprofit events are designed with the primary purpose of raising money, nor are they centered on the delivery of programs and services. Instead, nonprofits sometimes host **non-revenue events** with the intended purpose of building awareness, engaging supporters in advocacy, recognizing supporters, cultivating donors, or educating their constituent base on a certain issue or topic. These event categories are summarized in Figure 14.4. Depending upon the nature and intended purpose of the event, these events may be led by program delivery staff, development staff, or a combination of the two.

Awareness and Networking Events

Some nonprofits host events like community picnics, potlucks, or networking mixers to foster connections among supporters and provide fun, engaging

Figure 14.4 Nonprofit Non-Revenue Events

experiences for stakeholders. Others host these awareness and networking events around their mission. For example, arts and culture organizations may use cultural and arts exhibitions such as art shows, music performances, and cultural festivals to celebrate diversity, showcase local talent, and expand awareness of their cause. Nonprofit community forums are structured events where stakeholders convene to discuss various issues and collaborate on solutions related to the nonprofit's mission.

Advocacy Events

Nonprofits may organize events that support advocacy efforts such as marches or lobbying days to advocate for policy changes, social justice, or specific causes related to their mission (Forbes 2023). As noted in Chapter 13, rallies can also serve as a powerful nonprofit advocacy campaign tool to mobilize public support around critical issues.

Supporter Recognition Events

Recognizing supporters can be an effective donor and volunteer stewardship tool, and many nonprofits achieve this by hosting supporter recognition events. This can include ceremonies with recognition for major donors or events designed to recognize an agency's volunteers (Sumrak 2023).

Donor Cultivation Events

As discussed in Chapter 10, many nonprofits choose to host cultivation events to foster and strengthen relationships with donors. While these events are one part of the donor fundraising cycle, they are not fundraising by nature as standalone events. Instead of soliciting financial contributions from attendees, donor cultivation events instead provide a measure of donor appreciation and opportunity for development staff and nonprofit leadership to engage with donors and share information about the nonprofit's mission and impact (Durbin 2023).

Educational Events

Educational events, such as conferences or symposia, are designed to convene experts, researchers, and stakeholders for discussions, idea sharing, and collaborative efforts related to their mission or field of interest. Other educational events include those designed to inform supporters of the nonprofit's progress toward mission; workshops and seminars to educate the community on specific topics related to mission; events to unveil research findings and share reports and data; and training sessions, among others.

Hosting events requires a diverse skill set that involves not just attention to detail in coordinating event planning and logistics, but also event marketing, guest experience, and, of course, fundraising. Designing events requires a strategic focus that allows the nonprofit to accomplish its objectives, whether it is to educate stakeholders or raise money for mission. Due to resource constraints, it also often requires that event planning staff and volunteers execute these events in an efficient manner.

Regardless of the event, however, all of them, whether fundraising or not, help nonprofits fulfill their missions, engage their target audiences, and create positive impact. They are essential tools for building community, engaging supporters, raising awareness and funds, and ultimately advancing the cause.

Takeaways

LO 14-1: Programs and services are related concepts, but they bear some distinctions. Nonprofit programs are broader, more structured initiatives aimed at achieving more general mission-driven goals, whereas services are a component of programs and are more specific, immediate offerings designed to directly address individual or community needs.

LO 14-2: While there are numerous forms of nonprofit programs, most of them can generally be categorized as educational, healthcare, youth and family, resource, employment, disaster relief, or advocacy programs.

LO 14-3: Nonprofit program design should include alignment of the programs and their objectives with the organization's overarching mission, and consider factors such as resource allocation, quality assurance, and program evaluation and monitoring.

LO 14-4: Whether nonprofit events are fundraising by nature or not, event planners should design events that provide a good guest experience and deliver on a mission moment, which is a dedicated portion of a nonprofit event where the organization educates guests on the organizational mission and importance of their support.

LO 14-5: There are numerous forms of nonprofit events designed to raise money for the cause, but the most common are galas, cocktail parties, endurance events, golf outings, and benefit performances.

LO 14-6: Nonprofits host several types of events that are neither focused on fundraising nor deliver programs or services, and common event categories include awareness and networking; advocacy; supporter recognition; donor cultivation; and education.

Bibliography

Axelrad, Claire. "How to Create Extraordinary Nonprofit Special Event Experiences." *Bloomerang*, 18 Aug. 2022, bloomerang.co/blog/how-to-create-extraordinary-nonprofit-special-event-experiences/.

Beaton, Erynn, Heather MacIndoe, and Tian Wang. "Combining Nonprofit Service and Advocacy: Organizational Structures and Hybridity." *Nonprofit and Voluntary Sector Quarterly*, vol. 50, no. 2, 2021, pp. 372–396.

Durbin, Hannah. "10 Ways to Host the Ultimate Donor Appreciation Event." *Classy*, 31 Aug. 2023, www.classy.org/blog/8-ways-to-host-the-ultimate-donor-appreciation-event/.

Elsey, Wayne. "Home in on Your Nonprofit's Donor Experience." *NonProfit Pro*, vol. 18, no. 3, 2020, pp. 14–8.

Ensor, Kristine. "How to Organize a Golf Tournament Fundraiser [Steps + Ideas]." *Nonprofit Blog*, 12 July 2023, donorbox.org/nonprofit-blog/golf-tournament-fundraisers.

Forbes, Tim. "Planning a Nonprofit Advocacy Event: 4 TIPS for Success: Soapbox Engage: Online Fundraising Platform for Nonprofits." *Soapbox Engage*, 20 Mar. 2023, www.soapboxengage.com/blog/2352-planning-a-nonprofit-advocacy-event-4-tips-for-success.

"Global Trends in Giving Report." *Nonprofit Tech for Good*, journals-sagepub-com.uc.idm.oclc.org/doi/epub/10.1177/0899764020959477. Accessed 22 Aug. 2023.

Grobman, Gary. "Improving Quality and Performance in Your Non-Profit Organization--Chapter 2." *SocialWorker.Com*, 13 Apr. 2014, www.socialworker.com/nonprofit/management/improving-quality-chapter-2/.

Hoefer, Richard. "Accountability in Action: Program Evaluation in Nonprofit Human Service Agencies." *Nonprofit Management & Leadership*, vol. 11, no. 2, 2000, pp. 167–177.

"How Do Nonprofit Organizations Help the Community?" *Instrumentl*, 12 July 2023, www.instrumentl.com/blog/how-nonprofits-help-communities.

"Ignite Generosity with Fund-a-Need Special Appeals." *A Higher Bid*, edited by Kathy Kingston. John Wiley & Sons, Inc, Hoboken, NJ, 2015.

Jacobwith, Lori. "Mission Moments." *Ignited Fundraising*, 3 Dec. 2014, ignitedfundraising.com/mission-moments/#:~:text=Mission%20moments%20are%20short%2C%20inspirational,they%20are%20not%20too%20long.

Leonard, Valerie F. "What's the Difference between Programs and Services?" *Medium*, 8 Oct. 2019, valeriefleonard.medium.com/whats-the-difference-between-programs-and-services-28a01e0f4693.

Locksin, Vanessa. "Level up Your Nonprofit's Donor Experience." *The Best Nonprofit Fundraising Solution*, 6 Sept. 2021, www.funraise.org/blog/level-up-your-nonprofits-donor-experience.

McNamara, Carter. "Overview of Non-Profit Program Planning." 13 Apr. 2022, literacy.kent.edu/Oasis/grants/overviewprogplan.html.

Meyer, Joshua. "Charity Auctions: The Complete Guide for Nonprofits." *OneCause*, 29 June 2023, www.onecause.com/blog/charity-auction/.

Wiley Online Library, "Nonprofits Mostly Hitting the Spot with Fundraising Events." *Nonprofit Business Advisor*, vol. 2018, no. 348, 2018, pp. 1–3.

Panepento, Peter. "Despite Challenges, Endurance Fundraising Has Staying Power - Peer-to-Peer Professional Forum." *Peer*, 14 Nov. 2018, www.peertopeerforum.com/despite-challenges-endurance-fundraising-has-staying-power-for-charities/.

Rees, Sandy. "Which Fundraising Events Bring in the Most Money for Nonprofits?" *Get Fully Funded*, 7 Mar. 2023, getfullyfunded.com/which-fundraising-events-bring-in-the-most-money/.

Rogers, Sierra. "The Nonprofit Program Development Process in 5 Steps." *Capterra*, 3 July 2022, www.capterra.com/resources/a-guide-to-nonprofit-program-development/.

Sarikaya, Serkan, and Hans U. Buhl. "The Challenge of Resource Allocation in the Nonprofit Sector: Determining the Right Amount of Fundraising Expenses." *Journal of Nonprofit & Public Sector Marketing*, vol. 33, no. 1, 2021, pp. 1–28.

Sumrak, Jesse. "How to Demonstrate Volunteer Appreciation as a Nonprofit: 19 Ideas." *Classy*, 11 Jan. 2023, www.classy.org/blog/volunteer-appreciation/.

15 Global Impact and Diversity

Learning Outcomes

After reading this chapter, you should be able to:

LO 15-1: Define NGOs and IGOs and explain their role in the nonprofit sector.
LO 15-2: Identify some of the global issues international nonprofits address.
LO 15-3: Summarize the predominant classification system for NGOs.
LO 15-4: Examine the diversity problems within the nonprofit workforce.
LO 15-5: Explain challenges and opportunities nonprofits face around board diversity.
LO 15-6: Distinguish between diversity, equity, and inclusion.
LO 15-7: Describe DE&I programs and how they are applied to nonprofits.

> LO 15-1: Define NGOs and IGOs and explain their role in the nonprofit sector.

Global Impact

Some nonprofits function primarily as grassroots organizations that serve local communities but, in an increasingly interconnected world, are not isolated from global issues and therefore face local challenges that are influenced by or have an impact on global trends, such as climate change and economic globalization. Nonprofits often work on issues that have both local and global dimensions, making global stakeholders relevant to their mission. Further, not all nonprofits are grassroots by nature, but are instead intended to have broader reach, including globally.

Non-Governmental Organizations (NGOs)

In the introduction of this text, it was noted that nonprofits are called by many names, most of them used interchangeably. One of the terms that

DOI: 10.4324/9781003380030-20

warrants specific analysis in the discussion of nonprofit global impact is the NGO. According to the United Nations, a **non-governmental organization (NGO)** is a nonprofit, voluntary citizen's group that is organized on a local, national, or international level to address issues in support of the public good ("The UN" 2023). An NGO is a type of nonprofit that may engage in political advocacy on issues such as foreign policy, elections, the environment, healthcare, human rights, and others; may lead humanitarian efforts; and may develop new approaches to social and economic problems that governments cannot address alone ("Non-Governmental" 2023).

Data reflecting the number of NGOs worldwide are incomplete (Leverty 2023), so it is difficult to accurately estimate how many nonprofits in general exist worldwide due to both the lack of reliable data and differences in how nonprofits are classified in each country. Estimates, however, suggest that there are more than 10 million nonprofits worldwide, with India leading the world with 2 million, followed by the United States with 1.8 million, and France with 1.3 million ("26" 2023).

In the US, NGOs are a type of nonprofit, but all nonprofits are NGOs. The definition of NGO might sound very similar to the definition of a nonprofit, but NGOs are traditionally considered distinct in the aspect of their global reach and association with international issues. They tend to have a broader focus and wider operational reach. A listing of the five biggest NGOs in the world is provided in Figure 15.1 ("The 15" 2021).

NGOs often collaborate with IGOs to address global issues. An **intergovernmental organization (IGO)** refers to an entity created by treaty, involving two or more nations, to work in good faith, on issues of common interest ("Intergovernmental" 2023). Perhaps the most well-known IGO is the United Nations, or UN, which is a nonprofit organization with the mission of promoting peace, security, cooperation, and development among its 193 member states. The UN works on a wide range of global issues and serves as a system of consultation and collaboration for NGOs. Other IGOs include the European Union (EU), Organization of Petroleum Exporting Countries (OPEC), African Development Bank (ADB), and the World Trade Organization (WTO) ("Intergovernmental" 2023).

LO 15-2: Identify some of the global issues international nonprofits address.

Global Issues

While nonprofit organizations tackle a broad array of issues impacting both communities and individuals worldwide, there are some shared global concerns, including poverty reduction, education, healthcare, human rights, environmental conservation, and world hunger ("Non-Governmental" 2023).

1 **SAVE THE CHILDREN**
Year Founded: 1919
Based in: England
Global Reach: 120 Countries

2 **OXFAM INTERNATIONAL**
Year Founded: 1942
Based in: Kenya
Global Reach: 90+ Countries

3 **DOCTORS WITHOUT BORDERS**
Year Founded: 1971
Based in: France
Global Reach: 70+ Countries

4 **BRAC**
Year Founded: 1972
Based in: Bangladesh
Global Reach: 11 Countries

5 **WORLD VISION**
Year Founded: 1950
Based in: United States
Global Reach: 100+ Countries

Figure 15.1 Biggest NGOs

Many NGOs exist to address global *poverty reduction* by providing access to necessities and emphasizing economic empowerment to help individuals and communities become self-sufficient. Another common cause for NGOs is providing access to quality *education*, particularly for marginalized and underserved populations. This is addressed through building schools, providing scholarship programs, and delivering educational services.

Healthcare is a widespread topic addressed by NGOs and can apply to any health-related global issue such as HIV/AIDS, vaccination campaigns, disease prevention, access to healthcare, maternal and child healthcare, and mental health resources, among others. Many NGOs advocate for *human rights*, such as gender equality and LGBTQ+ rights, prevention of discrimination and violence, support of marginalized and vulnerable groups such as immigrants and refugees, and liberties such as freedom of speech.

Some NGOs emphasize *environmental conservation* by engaging in efforts to protect natural ecosystems, fight climate change, promote renewable energy, and advocate for sustainable practices and issues like clean water. Eradicating *world hunger* is the objective of several NGOs, which aim to ensure food security by providing aid, supporting sustainable agriculture practices, and addressing food supply chain issues.

These are just a few examples of issues NGOs seek to solve, and others include child welfare, peacebuilding, disaster relief, animal welfare, and more. Another trait of NGOs is that they often work in collaboration with other nonprofit organizations, governments, and international organizations to address these complex challenges and make a positive impact on a global scale.

Apart from NGOs that are often explicitly established to tackle global concerns, numerous other nonprofit entities have expanded their influence internationally, even if their initial mission was geared toward local or regional engagement. Just as it is difficult to pinpoint specific data globally on the number of nonprofit organizations, it is equally as challenging to classify them, especially given the diversity of the issues these organizations address.

LO 15-3: Summarize the predominant classification system for NGOs.

The **International Classification of Nonprofit Organizations (ICNPO)** is one widely used framework to categorize and classify nonprofit organizations

Group 1: Culture and Recreation
Group 2: Education and Research
Group 3: Health
Group 4: Social Services
Group 5: Environment
Group 6: Development and Housing
Group 7: Law, Advocacy & Politics
Group 8: Philanthropic Intermediaries and Voluntarism Promotion
Group 9: International Activities
Group 10: Religion
Group 11: Business and Professional Associations, Unions
Group 12: Not Elsewhere Classified

Figure 15.2 International Classification of Nonprofit Organizations
(Source: "Biggest NGOs")

worldwide based on their primary activities and purposes. The ICNPO currently lists 12 different categories, called major activity groups, of nonprofit organizations globally that comprise the "nonprofit sector" (Salamon & Anheier 1992). The ICNPO major nonprofit activity groups are detailed in Figure 15.2.

Nonprofits play an important role in global affairs by addressing critical challenges by bridging gaps left by governments. They provide direct services, programs, and resources and advocate to advance social issues, ultimately working to achieve their missions and improve the well-being of communities worldwide.

> LO 15-4: Examine the diversity problems within the nonprofit workforce.

Diversity

Considering that nonprofits have a fundamental purpose of enhancing the well-being of individuals in their communities and influencing global change, it might be anticipated that the sector would exemplify diversity in the people working and volunteering within those organizations and leading them. However, this is not always the reality. Why does this matter? Not only is ensuring that individuals have equal opportunities the "right" thing to do, but there is a business case for diversity, with a growing body of research suggesting that diversity enhances information-sharing, decision-making (Brown 2002), innovation (Jaskyte 2012), constructive conflict (Jehn 1999), organizational performance (Ali 2014), and other positive outcomes.

Many nonprofits recognize that a diversity problem exists in the sector and in recent years have started ramping up their efforts toward DE&I. DE&I refers to **diversity, equity, and inclusion**, which are three closely linked values held by many organizations that are working to be supportive of different groups of individuals, including people of different races, ethnicities, religions, abilities, genders, and sexual orientations ("What Is" 2022). The dimension of **diversity** emphasizes the recognition and appreciation of differences and variances in characteristics among individuals, acknowledging the variety of backgrounds, perspectives, and experiences that people bring to an organization ("What Is" 2023). In short, diversity refers to *who* is represented in the workforce.

Staff Diversity

Race

Racial minorities are generally well represented as members of the nonprofit workforce in the United States, with a recent study indicating that 11% of nonprofit workers responding are Latinx/Hispanic; 1% are Native American/ Indigenous; less than 1% are Arab American; 8% are multiracial; 15% are black/African American; 8% are Asian American; and 59% are white (Thomas 2019). Although the ethnic composition of the nonprofit workforce is proportionate with the general population, racial minorities are vastly underrepresented in leadership roles, with just 21% of nonprofit executive leaders identifying as people of color (Faulk 2021).

Ethnic diversity in nonprofit leadership is a widespread issue, with 89% of respondents to a national survey in the United States on nonprofit race and leadership indicating that lack of racial diversity of executive leadership positions in nonprofits as "a big problem" (Thomas 2019). The *Race to Lead* report, derived from the findings of these surveys, confronted long-held beliefs regarding the limited representation of people of color in leadership positions within nonprofit organizations, including the enduring notions that these individuals require additional leadership training and are less inclined than their white counterparts to aspire to high-level leadership roles. The data obtained, however, revealed that individuals of color within the nonprofit sector possess qualifications comparable to those of white participants and exhibit *greater* interest than their white counterparts in pursuing leadership roles within nonprofit organizations (Thomas 2019).

To effectively enact changes aimed at reducing the impact of systemic racial inequalities, nonprofit organizations must expand their DE&I initiatives to encompass more than just talk. Instead, real change requires *action*, such as proactive measures that directly tackle the advantages enjoyed by white individuals prevalent throughout the sector. Nonprofits must also recognize and remove barriers to workplace equity, investing in DE&I efforts as an ongoing process involving the examination of the connections between race and power. This process requires an understanding that change can be disruptive, often uncomfortable, and necessitates pushing beyond existing organizational norms (Thomas 2019).

Gender Diversity

Women tend to be well represented in nonprofit organizations, comprising 60% of the workforce (Smith 2002) and holding the majority (62%) of executive director or CEO positions in the sector (Faulk 2021). Nonprofits provide more opportunities for women in full-time and mission-critical positions than for-profit organizations, even when accounting for the variances in size and hierarchical structure of the agency (Shaiko 1997). Unfortunately, while nonprofits are generally diverse on the basis of gender, a significant gender-based wage gap continues to persist in the sector (Lee 2023; Zhao 2020).

One recent study of executive compensation in private foundations found that the average salary of female leaders was just 84% of the average male salary (Finley 2019). Additional research indicates that the nonprofit executive gender pay gap persists regardless of differences in personal characteristics and organizational and environmental contexts (Schneider 2021). Women executive leaders in nonprofits face challenges, such as implicit barriers which stem from gender biases and stereotypes (Knippen 2018), in establishing themselves as legitimate leaders, which results in less authority and influence within the organization compared to male executives (Brescoll 2010; Main 1995). The intersection of race and gender can produce even worse outcomes, with black women being most likely to feel their race has had a negative impact on their career advancement, according to the *Race to Lead* report (Thomas 2019). Further, nonprofits headed by black women receive notably less funding when compared to those led by white individuals or black men (Dorsey 2023).

These disparities put nonprofits at risk, as studies also find that gender equity in leadership is closely associated with the positive image and performance of the organization (Glass 2018; Liu 2018). Nonprofits that do not achieve pay equity for their executive staff leaders risk reputational damage and decline in organizational performance (Silvera 2021).

Those responsible for hiring in nonprofit organizations should not inadvertently use culture fit in hiring practices to perpetrate implicit bias. Recall from Chapter 4 that culture fit refers to the alignment of values, beliefs, and behaviors between the employee and employer. Rather than focusing on the intended meaning of "culture fit" as alignment with a company's core values, hiring managers often assess whether they would enjoy spending time with a candidate outside of work ("Implicit" 2023). This leads to **implicit bias**, which is a form of bias that occurs automatically and unintentionally but nevertheless affects judgments, decisions, and behaviors, as hiring managers then tend to hire individuals with whom they share similarities ("Implicit" 2023), leading to a lack of diversity.

Addressing the gender pay gap requires concerted efforts by organizational leaders, namely governing boards, toward parity. This includes a shift in culture to one that embraces equity (Lee 2023). Research suggests that diverse nonprofit governing boards with strong representation of women as members contributes to gender equity in executive leadership (Cook 2015). In essence, diverse boards can influence diverse staff leadership. Unfortunately, many nonprofits lack in board diversity and equitable representation, a topic discussed later in this chapter, exacerbating the diversity problem.

Other Identity Groups

Diversity goes beyond race and gender, although these are the two areas most studied in academic research. **Identity groups** refers to social categories or communities of people who share certain characteristics, experiences, or identities. These identities can be based on various factors, including not just race and gender, but also sexual orientation, age, religion, disability, national and immigration status, and others. Identity groups are important for understanding the diverse experiences and perspectives of individuals within society and organizations, and recognizing and respecting the identities of these various groups is essential for promoting DE&I and addressing the unique challenges and needs of these different communities.

LO 15-5: Explain challenges and opportunities nonprofits face around board diversity.

Board Diversity

Nonprofit boards are relatively balanced as a whole in terms of gender composition but are predominantly white (Faulk 2021). Some progress has been made in recent years, however, according to a recent report that showed that boards surveyed in 2019 included a higher percentage of people of color than in the previous study (22% vs. 16% in 2017) ("Reviewing" 2021). Despite this improvement, however, most nonprofit executives and board chairs are dissatisfied with their boards' racial and ethnic diversity, holding the belief that their boards do not adequately represent the communities they serve ("Reviewing" 2021). According to a recent Urban Institute study, nonprofit board member composition includes the following (Faulk 2021):

- 70% have at least one board member of color.
- 16% of nonprofits that primarily serve people of color have all-white boards.
- 58% of rural nonprofits have no board members of color, compared with 15% of urban core nonprofits and 31% of suburban nonprofits.
- 50% of nonprofit board members on average are women.
- 46% of board chairs are female.
- 44% of nonprofits have at least one board member who identifies as LGBTQ+.
- 6% of board chairs identify as LGBTQ+.
- 10% of executive directors identify as LGBTQ+.
- 34% of organizations have at least one board member with a disclosed disability.
- 6% of board chairs have a disclosed disability.
- 9% of executive directors have a disclosed disability.

Just as there are numerous benefits to a diverse workforce, there are specific benefits to diverse boards. Nonprofits with diverse boards have a greater opportunity for transformational change and organizational success (Fredette 2019). Provided that a central function of a nonprofit board is to engage in decision-making, diversity is especially important to avoid blind spots that can negatively impact the board's ability to make the best decisions and plans for the organization ("Reviewing" 2021). Further, as noted above, diverse boards positively influence diversity in the workforce of the nonprofits they lead (Cook 2015).

LO 15-6: Distinguish between diversity, equity, and inclusion.

Equity and Inclusion

While diversity refers to *who* is represented in the workforce, **equity** centers on addressing disparities and ensuring fairness, and **inclusion** emphasizes creating environments where all individuals feel valued and included. These are three distinct yet interconnected concepts that represent approaches organizations take to simultaneously recognize and embrace diverse identities while striving to eliminate disparities, ensure equal opportunities for all, and foster a sense of belonging ("What Is" 2022). Successful organizational DE&I programs result in the creation of environments and systems where all individuals feel valued, respected, and included. Cultivating a diverse workforce is only part of the DE&I challenge. A diverse workforce is ineffectual if those employees do not also share in equal opportunities and are not valued, heard, and included.

LO 15-7: Describe DE&I programs and how they are applied to nonprofits.

DE&I Programs

Diversity, equity, and inclusion programs are increasingly prevalent in the nonprofit sector, with an overwhelming 74% of respondents to the *Race to Lead* survey reporting that their nonprofit is engaged in DE&I initiatives, employing a variety of DE&I activities, with training being the most common (Thomas 2019). While DE&I initiatives are becoming more widespread, they are not necessarily successful in translating to actual results. The heavy reliance on training programs, for instance, is potentially problematic, as research indicates that DE&I training programs are not always effective. The central issue with these programs is whether learning that occurs during training, especially for nonprofit leaders, translates into changes in on-the-job behavior that ultimately make a difference in terms of workplace equity and inclusion (Bernstein 2021).

Another common approach to DE&I is through formalized **diversity statements**, which are formal expressions that outline an organization's commitment to fostering diversity, equity, and inclusion and describe the actions or principles they will uphold to achieve these goals. Diversity statements should go above and beyond basic human resources (HR) policies and be positioned to reflect all stakeholder groups ("Study" 2020). According to one study, a little more than half of responding nonprofit organizations (53%) indicated that they have a formal diversity statement (Lindsay 2023). Research indicates, however, that while policies and procedures can have some impact on diversity, actions are more impactful. For example, encouraging majority-group members to engage in inclusive behaviors is more likely to foster inclusive environments than simply establishing DE&I policies (Fredette 2019).

Ultimately, it is a combination of policy, practice, *and* process that results in meaningful engagement of diverse individuals within nonprofit organizations (Buse 2016). That is why many nonprofit organizations establish **DE&I programs** which are organizational strategies to promote diversity among their workforce, ensure equitable opportunities and treatment for all individuals, and foster inclusive work environments that value and respect the contributions of individuals from diverse backgrounds. Reinforcing the importance and value of diverse boards, data show that nonprofits with boards that include people of color are more likely to have adopted formal DE&I programs than boards that do not include people of color ("Reviewing" 2021).

Takeaways

LO 15-1: NGOs and IGOs are organizations that serve at an international level, typically working to address global issues. Non-governmental organizations (NGOs) are voluntary citizen's groups usually formed as nonprofits, and intergovernmental organizations (IGOs) are entities created by treaty, involving two or more nations.

LO 15-2: International nonprofits address countless global issues, but some common ones include poverty, economic empowerment, education, healthcare, human rights, conservation, and world hunger.

LO 15-3: Given the wide variety of international nonprofits, there are several methods to classify them, and one of the most widely used approaches is the International Classification of Nonprofit Organizations (ICNPO), which uses 12 different major activity groups.

LO 15-4: Like for-profit organizations, nonprofits face several diversity challenges related to the composition of their workforces. While women are well represented as a proportion of both nonprofit employees and executive leadership positions, a significant gender pay gap exists. Regarding diversity of race, minorities are significantly underrepresented in nonprofit executive leadership positions.

LO 15-5: Nonprofit boards are generally balanced in composition of gender but other identity groups, namely people of color, are significantly underrepresented. Nonprofit leaders can enact measures to improve board diversity and to achieve improved organizational outcomes.

LO 15-6: Diversity, equity, and inclusion (DE&I) are related but distinct concepts. Diversity emphasizes the recognition and appreciation of differences and variances in characteristics among individuals; equity centers on addressing disparities and ensuring fairness; and inclusion emphasizes creating environments where all individuals feel valued and included.

LO 15-7: DE&I programs are intended to promote diversity, ensure equitable opportunities, and foster inclusive work environments, and they consist of initiatives such as diversity statements, training programs, policies, and proactive practices to diversify the workforce and board.

Bibliography

"26 Incredible Nonprofit Statistics [2023]: How Many Nonprofits Are in the U.S.?" *Zippia*, 12 May 2023, www.zippia.com/advice/nonprofit-statistics/.

Ali, M., Y.L. Ng, and C.T. Kulik. "Board age and Gender Diversity: A Test of Competing Linear and Curvilinear Predictions." *Journal of Business Ethics*, vol. 125, 2014, pp. 497–512.

Bernstein, Ruth S., Paul F. Salipante, and Ohio Library and Information Network. *Performance through Diversity and Inclusion: Leveraging Organizational Practices for Equity and Results*. Routledge, London, 2021, doi:10.4324/9780367822484.

Brescoll, V.L., E. Dawson, and E.L. Uhlmann. "Hard Won and Easily Lost: The Fragile Status of Leaders in Gender-Stereotype-Incongruent Occupations." *Psychological Science*, vol. 21, no. 11, 2010, pp. 1640–1642. Crossref. PubMed. ISI.

Brown, W.A. "Inclusive Governance Practices in Nonprofit Organizations and Implications for Practice." *Nonprofit Management & Leadership*, vol. 12, 2002, pp. 369–385.

Buse, K., R.S. Bernstein, and D. Bilimoria. "The Influence of Board Diversity, Board Diversity Policies and Practices, and Board Inclusion Behaviors on Nonprofit Governance Practices." *Journal of Business Ethics*, vol. 133, 2016, pp. 179–191.

Cook, A., and C. Glass. "Diversity Begets Diversity? The Effects of Board Composition on the Appointment and Success of Women CEOs." *Social Science Research*, vol. 53, 2015, pp. 137–147. Crossref. PubMed. ISI.

Dorsey, Cheryl, et al. "Racial Equity and Philanthropy." *Echoing Green*, 1 Jan. 2023, www.bridgespan.org/getmedia/05ad1f12-2419-4039-ac67-a45044f940ec/racial-equity-and-philanthropy.pdf. Accessed 3 Sept. 2023.

Faulk, L., M. Kim, T. Derrick-Mills, E. Boris, L. Tomasko, N. Hakizimana, and L. Nath. "Nonprofit Trends and Impacts 2021." 2021, https://www.urban.org/sites/default/files/publication/104889/nonprofit-trends-and-impacts-2021_2.pdf

Finley, A., C.M. Hall, and A. Marino. *Executive Gender Pay Gaps in Nonprofit Organizations*, 5 June 2019. Claremont McKenna College Robert Day School of Economics and Finance Research Paper, Claremont, CA, No. 3385848.

Fredette, Christopher, and Ruth Sessler Bernstein. "Ethno-Racial Diversity on Nonprofit Boards: A Critical Mass Perspective." *Nonprofit and Voluntary Sector Quarterly*, vol. 48, no. 5, 2019, pp. 931–952.

Glass, C., and A. Cook. "Do Women Leaders Promote Positive Change? Analyzing the Effect of Gender on Business Practices and Diversity Initiatives." *Human Resource Management*, vol. 57, no. 4, 2018, pp. 823–837. Crossref.

"Implicit Bias." *National Institute of Health (NIH)*, 2023, diversity.nih.gov/sociocultural-factors/implicit-bias. Accessed 12 Sept. 2023.

"Intergovernmental Organizations (IGOs)." *Harvard Law School*, hls.harvard.edu/bernard-koteen-office-of-public-interest-advising/about-opia/what-is-public-interest-law/public-service-practice-settings/international-public-interest-law-practice-setting/intergovernmental-organizations-igos/. Accessed 5 Sept. 2023.

Jaskyte, K. "Boards of Directors and Innovation in Nonprofit Organizations." *Nonprofit Management and Leadership*, vol. 22, 2012, pp. 439–459.

Jehn, K.A., G.B. Northcraft, and M.A. Neale. "Why Differences Make a Difference: A Field Study of Diversity, Conflict and Performance in Workgroups." *Administrative Science Quarterly*, vol. 44, 1999, pp. 741–763.

Knippen, J.M., J. Palar, and R.J. Gentry. "Breaking the Mold: An Examination of Board Discretion in Female CEO Appointments." *Journal of Business Research*, vol. 84, 2018, pp. 11–23. Crossref.

Lee, Young-joo. "Board Gender Diversity and Nonprofit CEO Compensation: Implications for Gender Pay Gap." *Nonprofit and Voluntary Sector Quarterly*, 2023, pp. 89976402311585.

Leverty, Sally. "NGOs, the UN and APA." *American Psychological Association*, 2008, www.apa.org/international/united-nations/publications. Accessed 11 Sept. 2023.

Lindsay, Drew. "Actions Have Yet to Match Words on DEI, Nonprofit Survey Says." *The Chronicle of Philanthropy*, 18 Jul. 2023, www.philanthropy.com/article/actions-have-yet-to-match-words-on-dei-nonprofit-survey-says. Accessed 10 Sept. 2023.

Liu, C. "Are Women Greener? Corporate Gender Diversity and Environmental Violations." *Journal of Corporate Finance*, vol. 52, 2018, pp. 118–142. Crossref.

Main, B.G., C.A. O'Reilly, and J. Wade. "The CEO, the Board of Directors and Executive Compensation: Economic and Psychological Perspectives." *Industrial and Corporate Change*, vol. 4, no. 2, 1995, 293–332. Crossref.

Mitchell, George E. "The Construct of Organizational Effectiveness: Perspectives from Leaders of International Nonprofits in the United States." *Nonprofit and Voluntary Sector Quarterly*, vol. 42, no. 2, 2013, pp. 324–345.

"Non-Governmental Organizations (NGOs) in the United States." *U.S. Department of State*, 20 Jan. 2021, www.state.gov/non-governmental-organizations-ngos-in-the-united-states/. Accessed 12 Sept. 2023.

"Reviewing the State of Diversity, Equity, and Inclusion on Nonprofit Boards." *Leading with Intent*, 2021, leadingwithintent.org/wp-content/uploads/2021/06/2021-Leading-with-Intent-DEI-Report.pdf?hsCtaTracking=6fea211c-bd59-41a5-bfec-19e4a5e97ee4%257Cbb4b1792-83d8-4942-a949-3794a8ad5554.

Salamon, Lester M., and Helmut K. Anheier. "In Search of the Non-Profit Sector II: The Problem of Classification." *Voluntas (Manchester, England)*, vol. 3, no. 3, 1992, pp. 267–309.

Schneider, M.R., A. Iseke, and K. Pull. "The Gender Pay Gap in European Executive Boards: The Role of Executives' Pathway into the Board." *The International Journal of Human Resource Management*, vol. 32, no. 14, 2021, pp. 2952–2974. Crossref.

Shaiko, R.G. "Female Participation in Association Governance and Political Representation: Women as Executive Directors, Board Members, Lobbyists, and Political Action Committee Members." *Nonprofit Management and Leadership*, vol. 8, no. 2, 1997, 121–139.

Silvera, G.A., and J.R. Clark. "Women at the Helm: Chief Executive Officer Gender and Patient Experience in the Hospital Industry." *Health Care Management Review*, vol. 46, no. 3, 2021, pp. 206–216. Crossref. PubMed.

Smith, T.W., A.L. Kalleberg, and P.V. Marsden. *National Organizations Survey (NOS), 2002*. Chicago: National Opinion Research Center (NORC) [producer], 2003. Computer file

Wiley Online Library, "Study Shows Nonprofits Still Lacking in Diversity Efforts." *Nonprofit Business Advisor*, vol. 2020, no. 365, 2020, pp. 1–3.

"The 15 Biggest NGOs in the World." *Human Rights Careers*, 20 Jan. 2021, www.humanrightscareers.com/issues/biggest-ngos-in-the-world/. Accessed 7 Sept. 2023.

"The UN and Civil Society." *United Nations*, 2023, www.un.org/en/get-involved/un-and-civil-society. Accessed 10 Sept. 2023.

Thomas-Breitfeld, Sean, and Frances Kunreuther. *Race to Lead: Confronting the Nonprofit Racial Leadership Gap*. Building Movement Project, New York, NY, 2019.

"What Is Diversity?" *Workable: Resources for Employers*, 2023, resources.workable.com/hr-terms/diversity-definition. Accessed 4 Sept. 2023.

"What Is Diversity, Equity, and Inclusion?" *McKinsey & Company*, 17 Aug. 2022, www.mckinsey.com/featured-insights/mckinsey-explainers/what-is-diversity-equity-and-inclusion. Accessed 13 Sept. 2023.

Zhao, R. "Are Nonprofits More Equitable Than for-Profits? An Estimate of the Gender Pay Gap in the U.S. Human Services Field." *Human Service Organizations: Management, Leadership & Governance*, vol. 44, no. 4, 2020, pp. 343–361. Crossref.

Cases

Case 1: Controversy at the UGA Alumni Association

The University of Louisville (UofL) Alumni Association is a tax-exempt nonprofit organization in Louisville, Kentucky charged with engaging more than 144,000 UofL alumni around the world. In 2015, then Executive Director Deborah Dietzler resigned from her position when a whistleblower complaint at her former place of employment, the University of Georgia (UGA) Alumni Association, led to a fraud investigation (Seward 2015).

Dietzler was employed at the UGA Alumni Association from 2005–2014, and the whistleblower, Dietzler's employee Sallyanne Barrow, alleged that Dietzler would book hotels and airline tickets to run in marathons around the country for personal gain, and then order staff to find UGA alumni with whom she could meet so she could justify the travel as work-related and receive reimbursement for her trip expenses using funds from the association. Like the UofL Alumni Association, the UGA Alumni Association is a tax-exempt nonprofit organization funded in part by alumni donor contributions. Georgia's state attorney general's office directed the state Board of Regents to investigate the allegations of travel fraud, with the conclusion that Dietzler likely committed crimes, but the school's mishandling of the investigation – including a failure to report Dietzler's conduct to the state – kept her from facing formal criminal charges. "I'm a CPA, and I had a fiduciary duty to report fraud," whistleblower Sallyanne Barrow told an investigative reporter with Atlanta's *Channel 2 Action News* ("The Atlanta" 2016).

1.1 What ethical breach(es) happened in this case? If Dietzler could make a strong case that her travel was legitimately work-related, was her behavior still unethical? Why or why not? Was this a conflict of interest?

1.2 Boards of directors are well known to have a fiduciary responsibility to the nonprofit organizations they serve, but what other stakeholders have this responsibility? Why? Does one need to hold a CPA or accounting credential to have a fiduciary responsibility? Why or why not?

1.3 While Dietzler did not face criminal charges, and therefore there is no clear result on whether her actions were definitively criminal, were they unethical? Why or why not?

1.4 Can an action be legal, but unethical? Can an action be ethical, but illegal? Explain.
1.5 The accusations of Dietzler's unethical behaviors occurred while she was at her former employer, UGA, not her current employer, UofL. Had she not voluntarily resigned from her position at UofL, what actions (if any) do you think leaders at UofL should have taken when the accusations came to light?
1.6 Although the alleged unethical behavior happened at UGA, not UofL, how could this situation possibly negatively impact UofL? If you were a UofL supporter, would this affect your trust in the organization and willingness to continue to donate?
1.7 What ethical guidelines or policies could be put in place to govern this type of situation? The UGA Alumni Association likely *did* have ethical guidelines, and if that is the case, why did they fail? How should organizations monitor and enforce their guidelines?
1.8 Had Barrow not blown the whistle, do you think Dietzler's actions would ever have come to light? Did the UGA Alumni Association board fail here in their fiduciary duty to detect this breach?
1.9 How did the University of Georgia's inaction contribute to this ethical breach and the outcome of it?

Seward, Christopher. "Former UGA Alumni Director Quits Louisville Job amid Georgia probe." *The Atlanta Journal-Constitution*. 20 November 2015. https://www.ajc.com/news/local/former-uga-alumni-director-quits-louisville-job-amid-georgia-probe/lPgJuz9f5tCcjMemGWYa7J/. Accessed 11 July 2023.
The Atlanta Journal-Constitution. "UGA Alumni Director Likely Committed Crimes but Won't Be Charged, Prosecutors Say." *The Atlanta Journal-Constitution*, 18 July 2016. https://www.ajc.com/news/uga-alumni-director-likely-committed-crimes-but-wont-be-charged-prosecutors-say/192415042/. Accessed 11 July 2023.

Case 2: A Culture of Poverty?

There are many ways to describe culture types common to nonprofits, but here's another one. Do nonprofits operate within a culture of *poverty*, with an unstated but very real expectation that staff essentially take a pledge of poverty in exchange for doing work in a nonprofit? That's the very blunt question being addressed by Sean Goode, executive director of Choose 180, a youth diversion nonprofit based in Washington State. In November 2021, Goode took the bold step of confronting head-on what he calls a "culture of poverty" by raising all staff salaries at the agency to a minimum of $70,000 per year. The move resulted in an overall increase of $400,000 to the annual budget, but came with full support of the board, also ready to tackle this issue. In an article in *The Seattle Times*, Goode pointed out that like most organizational change, especially for something as significant as culture, change doesn't come easily, nor does it happen overnight. The Choose 180 pay plan took time to implement, both in execution and attitude change, which included change to the original stance of Goode, who initially balked at the idea. As one of the Choose 180 employees pointed out to sway him, there was a sad hypocrisy in that the very issue at the heart of the agency's mission, helping people escape poverty, was one that it was essentially contributing to by paying employees so poorly (Ishisaka 2021).

2.1 Knowing what you do now about culture, what do you think Goode means when he describes most nonprofits as existing in a "culture of poverty"? Do you agree? Why or why not?
2.2 If Choose 180 states that it values the need to lift people out of poverty, is it hypocritical of them to pay their own staff such low wages? Are their actions in accordance with their stated values?
2.3 Why is it important for the board to agree to such a change, both in terms of direct cost, but also in terms of what is a sort of reorganization since it involves a culture change?
2.4 Other than increasing pay, what are some other measures Choose 180 leaders can take to change their own self-proclaimed "culture of poverty"?
2.5 Is it fair for nonprofit employees to be held to a different standard of pay compared to employees in the for-profit sector? Why or why not?
2.6 While the $70,000 minimum pay represented a significant increase for many Choose 180 employees, a parent in the county in which the agency operates would need a salary of $76,000 to have a living wage. Knowing this, is the $70,000 minimum enough? What else could or should be done?
2.7 Culture change takes time, even for organizations committed to it. Do you think it's possible to make universal change across all nonprofits to stop perpetuating a culture of poverty in their own organizations? Why or why not? What would it take for systemic change?

Ishisaka, Naomi. "A King County Nonprofit Raised All Staff Salaries to $70,000 Minimum. Will More Organizations Follow?" *The Seattle Times*, 16 Nov. 2021, www.seattletimes.com/seattle-news/labor-shortage-or-living-wage-shortage-one-king-county-nonprofit-is-taking-a-different-approach/. Accessed 19 Jun. 2023.

Case 3: Tainted Donations – Removing the Sackler Name

In 2022, Purdue Pharma, a privately-held American pharmaceutical company owned principally by members of the Sackler family, reached a $6 billion legal settlement because of lawsuits filed against the family, alleging wrongdoing in aggressive marketing practices for addictive painkiller drugs that arguably directly led to the opioid crisis in the US (the Sackler family denies wrongdoing). The various lawsuits led to significant global media attention, including more than one documentary highlighting the case, and the Sackler name quickly fell into disrepute. The Sackler family had for years provided substantial financial support to the arts community, making such significant contributions that the family name appeared on plaques, signs, and entire buildings. This now presented a problem for recipient organizations, as they risked their own reputations by retaining the Sackler name prominently in their institutions.

Nonprofit leaders were faced with the ethical dilemma of how to address this situation, and whether to accept future contributions from the family. Not only were the Sacklers tainted donors, but their contributions were arguably from tainted money, earned from unethical means. Eventually, many recipients of Sackler contributions, including Tate Britain, Serpentine Galleries in London, the Metropolitan Museum of Art in New York, and the Musée du Louvre in Paris, removed references to the Sackler name within their institutions. Other museums and institutions, however, still retain the name. The case not only brought the concept of tainted money and tainted donors to national prominence, but it also raised questions for future practices and risks when it comes to using naming rights as a fundraising tool. As an outcome of this case, some nonprofits have begun introducing "morals clauses" within major gifts contracts to allow for the institution to protect itself and remove naming rights should the donor's name become tainted (Seymour 2023).

3.1 If you were an executive director leading a nonprofit that had received Sackler contributions and had named something in your building after them, how would you handle this situation?
3.2 If the Sackler family has never faced criminal charges and deny wrongdoing, why would some organizations remove their name?
3.3 If you were a donor, would you be reluctant to donate to an organization that prominently featured the Sackler name somewhere on or in their facility? Why or why not?
3.4 In your opinion, what rises to the level of a "tainted donation"? Who decides on the standard and how does a leader fairly apply this standard to all donors?
3.5 In deciding how to address this dilemma, what frameworks could a nonprofit leader consult in order to aid their decision-making?
3.6 What measures could nonprofit leaders put in place to avoid this situation from occurring again the future?
3.7 Is it ethical for organizations to still accept contributions from the Sackler family, even if it doesn't include naming rights? Why or why not?
3.8 How can development professionals vet donors before accepting their money and/or providing naming rights in exchange for a contribution? Should they? Why or why not?

Seymour, Tom. "Tainted Gifts: As British Museum and the Met Disavow the Sackler Name, Museums Rethink Donation Deals." *The Art Newspaper*, 28 Mar. 2022. Accessed 11 July 2023.

Case 4: Culture Shock at Wofford County Humane Society

Carla was excited to receive an offer as Adoptions Director from the Wofford County Humane Society, a position that provided her with a better title and a significant pay increase from her current role. She was a superstar at her current position, having played a significant role in expanding pet adoptions throughout the middle-Tennessee region through her expertise in program design, efficiency of adoption processes, robust yet streamlined adopter vetting, and effective program marketing.

After just two months in the new job, however, Carla was at her wit's end. She was frustrated because she had so many innovations to improve adoptions at Wofford but was unable to execute them because her new executive director quickly shot down most of the ideas she brought to him. After getting to know her coworkers and volunteers more, she learned that the organization really valued tradition and the old way of doing things. Change and innovation weren't embraced, but rather were seen as unnecessarily risky and potentially costly. The organizational mindset was "if it ain't broke, don't fix it!" and her coworkers didn't understand why Carla couldn't conform to their way of doing things. They started to perceive her as a troublemaker and, just a few months into the new role, Carla felt alone and isolated, bored by her job, and miserable.

Carla began coming to work late and stopped meeting weekly with the lead volunteer on the adoptions team, resulting in miscommunication and the ultimate resignation of the volunteer, who grew frustrated by the lack of support and direction in managing the adoptions process. As a result of the departure of this key volunteer position, the agency's adoption rate dropped significantly. Carla's key performance measure was "Increase agency adoptions by 5% over the next quarter," and because of this underperformance, she was ultimately reprimanded by the executive director during her 90-day performance evaluation, and, three days later, she quit.

4.1 Given what you know about Carla's job, how would you categorize her staff position (management, administrative, development, and/or program delivery)? Why?

4.2 Why is the volunteer-staff partnership so important, and what lapses occurred in this case? What was the outcome and how could this have been prevented?

4.3 Carla had a strong performance track record, so what contributed to her falling so short of goal in her new role?

4.4 Based on what you know about Carla's goal, what performance evaluation method does Wofford County Humane Society use?
4.5 What withdrawal behaviors did Carla exhibit and what could the executive director have done to intervene?
4.6 What's the term used to describe a scenario like this, when an employee exits the organization within the first year?
4.7 What are the likely costs to the organization (both direct and indirect) of this scenario?
4.8 How would you describe the culture of the Wofford County Humane Society and the culture shock Carla experienced when her own values didn't align with the organization's?
4.9 In hiring the new Adoptions Director to replace Carla, what questions should the hiring team ask to ensure a good culture fit?

Glossary

360-degree appraisal An employee performance evaluation approach that involves gathering feedback on employee performance from a wide array of individuals with whom that employee works.

501(c)(3) organization Nonprofit entities in the US recognized by the Internal Revenue Service (IRS) for their tax-exempt status.

80/20 rule A fundraising concept that signifies that roughly 80% of contributions stem from around 20% of donors.

Accommodating style A conflict resolution approach that involves one party yielding their own needs to the preferences or needs of the other party.

Accountability The obligation of a nonprofit to responsibly use its resources toward its mission and to benefit the community.

Ad hoc advisory boards Advisory boards that are assembled for shorter-term activities or for a special purpose or short-term issue.

Administrative positions Nonprofit staff positions that are generally not directly involved in either development work or program delivery, but rather exist to support those functions.

Advertising Paid media used to communicate with prospective customers including ads in channels such as TV, print, radio, online, and social media, among others.

Advisory board A board of directors that does not have governance oversight, but instead provides expertise, guidance, and recommendations to the organization without decision-making authority.

Advocacy campaigns Activities meant to facilitate grassroots lobbying, such as calling campaigns, online advocacy, petitions, rallies, litigation, and other actions designed to facilitate grassroots lobbying.

Advocacy events Nonprofit non-revenue events organized to support advocacy efforts, such as marches or lobbying days to advocate for policy changes, social justice, or specific causes related to their mission.

Advocacy meetings A form of direct lobbying where nonprofits meet with legislators to lobby for their cause and which may include the constituents they serve in addition to representatives from the nonprofit organization, often staff or advocacy volunteers.

Advocacy organizations Nonprofit organizations that raise public awareness and push for policy reform.

Advocates Members of the community who volunteer to work on behalf of the nonprofit to engage in advocacy efforts to influence decisions that advance the cause.

Affiliate organizations Separate legal nonprofit entities connected to a larger nonprofit organization, referred to as the parent organization or "headquarters." Affiliates share mission, purpose, or goals with the parent organization, but may have distinct operations, governance structures, and sometimes geographic locations.

Agreeableness A personality trait that refers to a person's general concern for social harmony and their degree of warmth, kindness, and cooperativeness in interpersonal relationships.

Agreement A step in the negotiation process under closing, where the parties finalize the terms of their negotiated agreement, outlining responsibilities, timelines, and any specific commitments.

Analysis paralysis Excessive scrutiny or overthinking of options in the decision-making process that ultimately prevents an individual or a group from reaching a decision.

Annual giving The practice of individuals or organizations making regular, yearly charitable donations to support a cause, institution, or nonprofit.

Association of Fundraising Professionals (AFP) A global nonprofit professional association that supports and promotes ethical and effective fundraising and philanthropy.

Association of Fundraising Professionals (AFP) guidelines Ethical guidelines provided by the AFP to nonprofit fundraising professionals to encourage and facilitate ethical fundraising practices.

Avoiding style A conflict resolution approach where conflicting parties choose not to address the conflict directly and instead choose to delay dealing with it or ignore it entirely.

Awareness and networking events Nonprofit non-revenue events such as community picnics, potlucks, or networking mixers that are designed to foster connections among supporters, beneficiaries, and stakeholders.

Awareness campaigns A type of cause marketing campaign that occurs when companies use their marketing channels to raise awareness, rather than funds, for a particular nonprofit or cause.

B Corp certification A designation from the nonprofit B Lab that companies generally use for marketing purposes, which signifies that a business is meeting high standards of verified performance, accountability, and charitable giving.

Balanced partnership A relatively equal and equitable exchange of resources, rewards, and costs between two or more individuals.

Bargaining A stage in the negotiation process where the parties exchange offers and counteroffers, discussing various terms and potential compromises to bridge the gap between their positions.

Barrier to entry Obstacles that prohibit prospective participants from engaging in an event or activity, and often include factors such as cost.

Behavioral segmentation A base of segmentation that divides people into segments based on their actions, such as purchasing behavior, usage patterns, and others.

Behaviorally anchored rating scales (BARS) Measurement tools that assign a numeric value to specific descriptions of employee behavior that are used to evaluate employee performance.

Benefit performances Nonprofit fundraising events such as concerts, performances, or musical events for the purpose of building awareness and raising funds for the cause and in support of their mission, primarily through the sale of admission tickets.

Board development plan A strategic framework used by nonprofit leaders to strategically recruit, train, and retain effective board members who can advance the organizational mission.

Board development The process of systematically enhancing the effectiveness, composition, and performance of a nonprofit organization's governing board of directors.

Board engagement The active participation, commitment, and involvement of board members in the fulfillment of their board obligations, contributing their skills and expertise to advance the organization's mission and goals.

Board nominating process The organized procedure a nonprofit organization follows to identify, evaluate, and select suitable candidates for board of director positions, as detailed in the organization's bylaws.

Board of directors A group of individuals elected or appointed to provide oversight, make strategic decisions, and guide the activities of an organization, ensuring that it operates in accordance with its mission and relevant laws.

Board pipeline The ongoing process of identifying, nurturing, and preparing potential candidates to serve on a nonprofit organization's board of directors in the future.

Board president The individual nonprofit board member elected to lead and preside over the board of directors, who works in partnership with the executive director to collaboratively lead the organization by providing strategic leadership, guiding board discussions, facilitating decision-making, and representing of the organization to external stakeholders.

Board scorecard A board of directors performance evaluation tool that uses a document that details the expectations of board members and measures member performance or contribution to each area. This can include measures such as annual giving expectations, hours of service, meeting attendance, event participation, money raised or solicitations made, and others.

Board secretary An elected board member executive committee position responsible for maintaining accurate records of board meetings, including minutes and official documents, compliance with legal requirements, communication related to board matters, and documentation of the organization's governance.

Board self-assessment (BSA) A board of directors performance evaluation tool that involves a questionnaire sent to individual board members to gather their input and feedback to measure the collective performance of the board.

Board treasurer An elected board member executive committee position responsible for overseeing the financial matters of the organization, including management of financial records, budgets, and financial reporting, for providing guidance on financial decisions, and for ensuring the organization's financial health and accountability.

Board vice president An elected board member executive committee position that serves as deputy to the board president and that may assume the president's responsibilities in their absence, lead specific initiatives or committees, and provide support in various governance and leadership activities.

Bounded rationality The concept that human decision-makers are limited in their ability to fully process information and make fully rational choices due to cognitive constraints and time limitations.

Breach of trust A violation or betrayal of a relationship or duty in which someone fails to fulfill their responsibilities or obligations, often resulting in a loss of confidence or faith in that person or organization.

Business intelligence (BI) dashboards Data visualization tools that present important information like key performance indicators in a visual and easily digestible format.

Bylaws A written set of rules and regulations that outlines the internal structure, governance, and operations of the organization, including details about board composition, decision-making processes, and key policies.

Calling campaigns Grassroots advocacy activities where supporters engage in a coordinated and organized fashion to contact their legislators by phone to express their views on a specific policy issue or piece of legislation of concern to the nonprofit organization.

Calls to action Grassroots advocacy campaigns enacted by nonprofits where they encourage supporters to take immediate and meaningful action in support of a specific advocacy effort.

Capital campaign A time-specific fundraising effort focused on raising significant funds for a specific project.

Cause marketing A company's promotional campaign that not only promotes the company or a specific product, but also benefits a nonprofit organization, either through building awareness or directing a portion of sales of that product to the cause.

Centralized organizations Organizations where power is held centrally by management positions at the top of the hierarchy of authority and where delegation and distribution of power to lower-level positions is rare.

Certified Fund Raising Executive (CFRE) A fundraising credential for development professionals that provides continuing education and bolsters their professional credibility.

Charity A type of nonprofit that engages in activities to assist people in need.

Civil disobedience A form of public awareness campaign where nonprofits use activities such as sit-ins or other nonviolent actions to draw attention to an issue of significant importance.

Closing A stage in the negotiation process where the parties review and confirm the agreed-upon terms, addressing any last-minute concerns or clarifications.

Coalitions A form of grassroots lobbying that involves nonprofits collaborating with other organizations, advocacy groups, and stakeholders to form coalitions to amplify their efforts.

Cocktail parties Nonprofit fundraising events that are generally less formal than galas but follow a similar format, with food, entertainment, auctions, and a mission moment.

Code of ethics A written set of guidelines that provide ethical standards that the organization expects their employees, volunteers, and stakeholders to follow in their decision-making and conduct.

Collaborating style A conflict resolution approach that involves the parties working together to find a mutually beneficial solution and requires open communication, active listening, and a willingness to compromise to meet the needs and interests of all who are involved.

Committees Teams assembled to address specific issues or make decisions around a certain issue, often for a long period of time.

Communications channel A specific medium or method used to transmit information and messages from one party to another, including channels such as websites and newsletters, social media, email, direct mail, telephone, and others.

Community foundations Regional or local organizations that provide grants to nonprofits within a specific geographic area, and often focus on addressing community needs and improving the quality of life in that region.

Community organizing The building of grassroots support and networks within communities to effect change and mobilize supporters to take collective action.

Community-focused culture An organizational culture that prioritizes strong connections with local communities and the beneficiaries served by the organization.

Competing style A conflict resolution approach where one party prioritizes their own interests and goals over those of the other party, and where that person may use authority, power, or assertiveness to win the conflict.

Compromising style A conflict resolution approach that seeks a middle ground where both parties make concessions to reach an agreement, involving negotiation and finding solutions that partially satisfy the interests of each party.

Conflict A disagreement or discord arising from differences in interests, opinions, or perspectives among individuals, groups, or teams, in which those individuals or groups block or thwart one another's attempts to achieve their objectives.

Conflict of interest A situation in which a person or entity has competing or conflicting interests or loyalties that could potentially influence their ability to make fair, unbiased, or impartial decisions.

Conflict of interest policy A formal set of guidelines used to address and manage conflicts of interest that may arise among an organization's stakeholders that outlines the organization's expectations, procedures, and mechanisms for identifying, disclosing, and appropriately addressing these conflicts.

Conflict resolution styles The various approaches or strategies people use to address and resolve conflict.

Conscientiousness A personality trait that describes a person's level of responsibility, organization, self-control, and dependability, and designates that the individual is highly motivated and goal-oriented and therefore more likely to achieve their objectives.

Constructive conflict Disagreement that is directed in a positive and productive manner, leading to positive outcomes such as diversity of perspectives and improved decision-making.

Corporate grants Grants awarded to nonprofits by corporations that have established their own foundations to manage their charitable giving.

Corporate social responsibility (CSR) A company's commitment to conducting its business in an ethical and socially responsible manner, including efforts to contribute positively to society and the environment beyond its profit-making activities, which includes initiatives related to sustainability, community engagement, and philanthropy.

Corporate sponsorship model An approach where companies sponsor a nonprofit's specific programs or events, receiving advertising and other benefits in return.

Customer Relationship Management (CRM) systems Software programs and databases designed to help nonprofits track and manage donor information and interactions to better manage the donor fundraising cycle and relationships with supporters.

Crowdfunding A fundraising method where nonprofits raise funds from a large number of individuals online, leveraging the collective contributions of many donors, each giving relatively small amounts, to support the cause.

Cultivation events Events hosted by a nonprofit for the purpose of engaging with current and prospective donors, where they share information about the agency's mission and impact and build or strengthen relationships among development representatives and potential donors.

Cultivation The process of forming relationships with current and potential donors by providing information, involving them in events and programs, and demonstrating the impact of their potential contributions on the mission of the organization.

Culture fit The alignment of values, beliefs, and behaviors between the employee and employer.

Culture shock The discomfort an individual feels when confronted with unfamiliar work practices, values, and dynamics in a new job or organization.

Customer departmentalization A departmentalization approach that groups people into departments based on the customer segments or types of customers that they serve, allowing departments to tailor products and services to specific customer groups.

DE&I programs Organizational strategies to promote diversity among their workforce, ensure equitable opportunities and treatment for all individuals, and foster inclusive work environments that value and respect the contributions of individuals from diverse backgrounds.

Decentralized organizations Organizations that allow for more delegation of decision-making authority to lower-level positions, rather than concentrating power centrally at the top of the hierarchy of authority.

Decision avoidance A decision-making problem that occurs when an individual avoids making a choice by postponing it or by seeking an easy way out that involves no action or no change.

Decision fatigue A state where the limited reserve of stamina for making decisions becomes drained, potentially leading to impulsive or suboptimal decisions.

Delegating leadership style A leadership style that calls for a leader to empower their followers to take responsibility and independently complete tasks.

Delegation The process of assigning authority, responsibility, and tasks from a higher-level position or manager to a subordinate or lower-level employee.

Democratic leadership style A leadership approach that distributes responsibility among the membership, empowers group members, and aids the group's decision-making process.

Demographic segmentation A base of segmentation that divides a market based on demographic factors such as age, gender, income, education, and other factors.

Departmental teams Functional teams composed of individuals who work within the same department or functional area of the organization.

Departmentalization The process of grouping people, teams, or activities into departments or functions with specific objectives, goals, and outcomes to be achieved. Common approaches include functional, product, geographic, customer, and matrix departmentalization.

Destructive conflict A form of disagreement characterized by hostility and personal attacks that ultimately harms productivity and relationships.

Development positions Nonprofit staff positions that are central in raising funds for the organization and can include not just donor-facing roles, but also fundraising around grants, foundations, and corporate giving.

Diagonal communication Communication that cuts across different levels and functional areas of the hierarchy. Unlike upward and downward communication, diagonal communication involves interactions between those not directly connected by reporting relationships.

Direct corporate donations Financial contributions made from a company to a nonprofit.

Direct lobbying A form of lobbying where nonprofits attempt to influence lawmakers or government officials through direct communication such as meetings, emails, letters, or phone calls.

Direct marketing Direct communication with targeted individuals through methods like email marketing, direct mail, telemarketing, and online advertising.

Direct service agencies Nonprofit organizations that provide programs in local communities or directly to the stakeholders they are intended to serve.

Diversity statements Formal expressions that outline an organization's commitment to fostering diversity, equity, and inclusion and describes the actions or principles they will uphold to achieve these goals.

Diversity The process of recognizing and appreciating the differences and variances in characteristics among individuals, acknowledging the variety of backgrounds, perspectives, and experiences that people bring to an organization.

Diversity, equity, and inclusion (DE&I) Three closely linked values held by many organizations that are working to be supportive of different groups of individuals, including people of different races, ethnicities, religions, abilities, genders, and sexual orientations.

Doers Volunteers who provide hands-on labor in completing tasks, through participation in events, volunteering for programs and services, or completing work needed by the organization.

Donation campaign A type of cause marketing where companies commit to donating a portion of their sales, profits, or a fixed amount for each product sold to a designated nonprofit or cause.

Donation proposal A written document that outlines the details of a donation solicitation, including information about the requested donation amount and need and the intended use of the contribution.

Donor acknowledgment The process of expressing gratitude and formally recognizing a donor's contribution.

Donor agreement A formal document in fundraising that outlines the terms, conditions, and expectations related to a donation and clarifies how the funds will be used, any specific restrictions or conditions attached to the gift, the recognition or naming rights associated with the donation, and the responsibilities of both the donor and the nonprofit.

Donor An individual or entity that contributes funds, goods, or services to support a nonprofit organization's mission and activities.

Donor experience The sum of all touchpoints a donor encounters as they engage with a nonprofit organization.

Donor fundraising cycle The process nonprofits follow to engage potential donors, starting from identification and qualification, cultivating relationships, moving through solicitation, and ultimately looping back to ongoing stewardship and relationship-building to encourage continued support.

Donor impact reports Formal reports produced by nonprofits that account for the donations that a nonprofit received over a certain time period, describe what was accomplished with these funds, and may list the names of donors.

Donor retention A measure of how many donors continue to donate to the organization.

Donor retention rate A key performance indicator that represents the percentage of nonprofit donors who continue to support the organization over time.

Donor-centric culture An organizational culture that prioritizes donors as a stakeholder group.

Door-openers Supporters who are willing to use their personal and professional networks and relationships to "open doors" for the organization to solicit support.

Dotted-line relationship An organizational relationship where two individuals are linked, but neither has direct managerial authority or direct supervision over the other.

Downward communication Communication that originates from management and flows down to lower-level employees.

Duty of care The obligation of a board of directors to "take care" of the organization by ensuring prudent use of all resources, encompassing facilities, personnel, and the nonprofit's reputation.

Duty of loyalty The set of obligations of a board of directors to ensure that no conflicts of interest exist, that the interests of the organization are put ahead of any individual, and that work is always conducted in a manner that advances the mission.

Duty of obedience The obligation of a board of directors to ensure compliance with relevant laws and regulations and assurance that the organization is committed and focused on its mission, vision, and values and adheres to its own stated bylaws.

Educational events Nonprofit non-revenue events designed to educate stakeholders through activities such as conferences, symposia, workshops, and seminars.

Efficiency margin A calculation of the percentage of nonprofit expenses allocated to programs and services compared to administrative and fundraising expenses. The resulting number represents the portion of the organization's budget that goes directly toward fulfilling its mission.

Emotional labor The efforts of employees to understand others, have empathy with their situation, and internalize their feelings.

Empathetic leadership style A leadership style that emphasizes active listening, compassion, and creation of a supportive environment in understanding and addressing the emotions, needs, and perspectives of team members.

Employee giving programs Corporate support of nonprofits that comes from employees of the company, as opposed to the corporation itself.

Employee retention Strategic actions managers use to keep employees motivated and focused, so they elect to remain employed and fully productive for the benefit of the organization.

Employee volunteer programs Corporate programs where companies encourage their employees to volunteer for nonprofits during work hours. This may include providing employees with paid time off for volunteering, or the company organizing structured group volunteer activities for their staff.

Employee-driven fundraising initiatives Activities organized and led by employees within a company to raise funds for nonprofit causes through voluntary participation from their coworkers.

Endowment A substantial donation that is invested and the generated income or interest from that gift is used to support the cause while preserving the initial gift intact.

Endurance events Nonprofit fundraising events where participants raise money by engaging in some sort of physical activity such as walking, running, climbing, or biking.

Entry-level gift An initial or modest donation made by a supporter.

Equity An approach that seeks to address disparities and ensure fair treatment for all.

Equity theory A theory that suggests that motivation at work is driven primarily by the employees' perception of fairness, measured by a comparison of inputs to outcomes.

Escalation of commitment A situation that occurs when individuals continue to invest in a decision or project, even in the face of negative outcomes, to avoid admitting failure or losing face.

Ethical culture An organizational culture that prioritizes ethical and moral standards.

Ethical dilemma A situation where someone must make a choice between two or more conflicting moral principles and values.

Ethical frameworks Structured systems of principles and values that guide individuals in making moral decisions and evaluating right and wrong.

Ethical guidelines Formal documents that provide direction and guidance for ethical conduct.

Event advisory boards An advisory board that exists to lead and execute specific nonprofit events.

Executive committee The leaders of a board of directors that hold distinct responsibilities and have a higher level of authority compared to a general board member position, with their primary role being to streamline decision-making between board meetings, particularly in critical or urgent situations.

Executive director The highest-ranking staff position in a nonprofit organization that is overseen by a board of directors, with shared responsibility for making staffing decisions, engaging in strategic planning, and making crucial determinations to advance the organization's mission.

Expectancy theory A theory that posits that people are motivated to perform when they believe their efforts will lead to successful performance (expectancy), that successful performance will lead to desired outcomes (a term called instrumentality), and that these outcomes are valuable and aligned with their goals (valence).

Exploration A step in the negotiation process under exchange of information where both sides engage in discussions to understand each other's viewpoints, needs, and concerns.

External communication Interactions between an organization and parties outside of it, such as customers, suppliers, stakeholders, and the general public.

Extrinsic rewards Rewards that come from external sources that include tangible benefits and career progression.

Extroversion A personality trait associated with a person's ease in navigating external relationships and situations and enjoyment of socializing with others.

Federal grants Financial awards provided by various federal agencies to support specific functions such as healthcare, education, environmental conservation, and social services.

Fiduciary A legal or ethical relationship of trust and confidence where one party (the fiduciary) is obligated to act in the best interests of another party, putting the other party's needs and interests ahead of their own.

Flat span of control A situation where a manager supervises a relatively large number of subordinates, resulting in a wider organizational hierarchy with fewer management layers.

Form 990 A US Internal Revenue Service document designed to increase financial transparency of nonprofit organizations by requiring disclosure of revenue, expenditure, and income data in addition to information used to assess whether a nonprofit aligns with federal requirements for tax-exempt status.

Formal communication The flow of official information through proper, predefined channels and routes.

Formal groups Groups assembled by leaders to perform a specific task for an organization, such as workgroups or volunteer committees.

Four-component model of ethical decision-making An approach to ethical decision-making that says that, when confronted with a moral dilemma, individuals move through a multistage, interactive sequence of psychological processes: moral awareness, moral judgment, moral intention, and moral action.

Functional departmentalization A departmentalization approach that groups people into departments based on similar job functions or tasks.

Fund a need A nonprofit fundraising auction frequently deployed at galas and generally conducted as a live auction for supporters to "bid" on the mission, rather than an item, experience, or service, as they would in a traditional live auction. Bidders can contribute directly to the organization's mission, receiving nothing in return.

Fundraising advisory boards Advisory boards that assist a nonprofit in fundraising through the development and execution of plans and projects.

Fundraising channels Avenues where supporters can donate to a nonprofit organization, including at events, direct mail, online platforms, social media campaigns, and others.

Fundraising efficiency A key performance indicator that represents the "cost per dollar raised," which is the cost to the nonprofit organization to raise one dollar in donations.

Fundraising return on investment (ROI) A key performance indicator used to assess the effectiveness of nonprofit fundraising campaigns by comparing the amount of money raised to the cost of fundraising activities.

Galas Formal nonprofit fundraising events where guests wear black-tie attire and purchase tickets or sponsor tables in order to attend and enjoy a plated dinner and entertainment.

Gap analysis An assessment in the decision-making process that helps decision-makers identify a problem that involves understanding the difference that exists between current and desired states.

General leadership styles An overarching leadership philosophy that a leader may consistently apply across various situations, including their methods, characteristics, and behaviors when directing their teams.

Geographic departmentalization A departmentalization approach that groups people into departments on the basis of geographic territory.

Geographic segmentation A base of segmentation that divides people into groups based upon their geographic location.

Get one, give one campaigns A type of cause marketing campaign where a company pledges to donate or provide a product or service to a person in need for each product or service sold or acquired.

Gifts of securities The donation of stocks, bonds, or other marketable financial assets to nonprofit organizations.

Giving capacity An individual's potential ability to give based on their discoverable financial resources, such as assets, income, and past giving history.

Giving days Specified days where nonprofits promote and encourage charitable contributions online during a 24-hour period.

Giving society A donor-recognition program used by nonprofit organizations to acknowledge donors based on different giving levels, with each offering various benefits such as exclusive events, recognition in publications, or special access to the organization's activities.

Goal-setting theory A theory that asserts that setting specific and challenging goals leads to increased motivation, effort, and performance as individuals strive to achieve those objectives, aided by clear direction and feedback.

Golf outings Nonprofit fundraising events where sponsors and participants pay to play golf, either as part of a tournament or a less formal golf outing, with proceeds benefiting a nonprofit organization.

Governing board A board of directors that has fiduciary responsibility and authority for overall governance and strategic direction and makes high-level decisions, sets policies, and ensures the organization is fulfilling its mission.

Government grants Financial awards provided by government agencies at the federal, state, or local levels to support various programs or projects that serve the public interest.

Grant proposals Applications submitted by a nonprofit to a grantmaker to submit for potential grant funding that includes information about the project's goals, budget, timeline, and expected outcomes.

Grantmakers Organizations such as government agencies, private or public foundations, or others that provide financial awards to nonprofit organizations.

Grants Financial awards provided to nonprofit organizations by various entities, such as government agencies, private or public foundations, or other organizations.

Grassroots lobbying An indirect form of lobbying that happens when nonprofits encourage their supporters and the public to contact elected officials on their behalf to express their views on specific legislation or policies.

Grassroots organizations Locally based, community-driven initiatives or movements that work to address specific issues from the ground up, and that may later evolve into organizations with broader reach.

Grassroots support Activities that originate from and are driven by community members and local volunteers rather than top-down organizational structures or external authorities.

Groups An assembly of individuals who come together for various reasons, either formally or informally, with independent outcomes and individual accountability.

Groupthink An occurrence where team members conform prematurely to a dominant viewpoint without critical evaluation.

Guest experience The overall impression that individuals have when attending nonprofit events, encompassing aspects such as engagement, satisfaction with the experience, meaningful interactions, and connectedness to the organization's mission and goals.

Head, heart, halo framework A framework commonly used in the nonprofit sector to describe these three central motivations that drive individuals to support charitable organizations: head motivation, heart motivation, and halo motivation.

Halo motivation The social or reputational benefits that motivate a donor to contribute to a nonprofit, such as a desire to be associated with a reputable organization and to be perceived as a caring or generous person.

Head motivation The rational assessment that motivates a donor to contribute to a nonprofit, including logical reasons as to why donating is beneficial, such as impact or tax benefits.

Heart motivation The emotional factors that motivate a donor to contribute to a nonprofit, including a personal connection to the cause or passion around the mission.

Hierarchy of authority The formal structure of levels and positions within an organization that outlines the reporting relationships and the flow of decision-making and communication.

High readiness A situation where an employee is capable, confident, experienced, and needs little direction to complete a task in the workplace.

Horizontal communication Lateral communication which occurs between individuals or departments on the same level in the hierarchy of authority.

Identification A fundraising term that describes the process of uncovering potential donor prospects to a nonprofit organization.

Identity groups Social categories or communities of people who share certain characteristics, experiences, or identities. These identities can be based on various factors, including not just race and gender, but also sexual orientation, age, religion, disability, national and immigration status, and others.

Implementation A stage in the negotiation process where the agreed-upon terms are put into action, and both parties fulfill their commitments as outlined in the agreement.

Implicit bias A form of bias that occurs automatically and unintentionally but nevertheless affects judgments, decisions, and behaviors.

Inclusion The creation of environments where all individuals feel valued and included.

Inclusive culture An organizational culture that emphasizes diversity, equity, and inclusion among all stakeholder groups.

Indirect corporate donations Contributions made from a company to a nonprofit that are not direct financial support from the company itself, including corporate sponsorships, employee giving programs, pro bono work, and cause marketing.

Individual donor A person, rather than a foundation or group of donors, who provides individual and voluntary financial support to a nonprofit organization.

Individual grants Grants awarded to nonprofits by high-net-worth individuals, philanthropists, and donors who choose to direct their personal giving through grant programs in support of specific causes or organizations.

Informal communication The flow of unofficial information throughout an organization, which often moves rapidly and is not confined by predetermined channels or established communication pathways.

Informal groups Groups formed organically around common interests, identities, or social goals.

In-kind gifts Non-monetary contributions of goods or services.

Innovativeness An organization's ability to offer new products and services and to keep abreast of advances in technology and practices.

Intergovernmental organization (IGO) An entity created by treaty, involving two or more nations, to work in good faith on issues of common interest.

Internal communication The exchange of information within an organization.

International Classification of Nonprofit Organizations (ICNPO) A widely used framework that classifies nonprofit organizations worldwide into 12 categories based on their primary activities and purposes.

Intrinsic rewards Rewards derived from internal motivation, such as the satisfaction a person feels in knowing they have done a good job.

Job analysis A process used to investigate and identify the duties, tasks, responsibilities, skills, knowledge, and essential qualifications for a certain job profile.

Job burnout A state of physical or emotional exhaustion that also involves a sense of reduced accomplishment and loss of personal identity.

Job characteristics theory A theory that proposes that jobs designed to include certain characteristics – variety, identity, significance, autonomy, and feedback – can lead to greater motivation, satisfaction, and performance in employees.

Job description A document that outlines the elements of the job established in the job design process, serving as a clear and concise way to convey what the job entails.

Job design The process of defining an individual's responsibilities at work, areas of decision-making responsibility, and expectations and goals, while motivating and rewarding the employee.

Job enlargement A job design approach that seeks to decrease the boredom of performing a redundant task by expanding the scope of a job by quantitatively adding more tasks at a similar skill level.

Job enrichment A job design approach that aims to enhance the depth and complexity of a job by adding qualitative tasks that require more responsibility, autonomy, and skill, making the job more challenging, interesting, and creative.

Job rotation A job design approach where employees rotate through different roles in the organization, which provides them with more variety in their work and allows them to develop new skills.

Key performance indicators (KPIs) Measurable values used to evaluate organizational performance by focusing on the aspects of performance that are the most critical for the current and future success of the organization.

Laissez-faire leadership style A leadership approach that uses a hands-off leadership approach where the leader avoids leadership duties altogether and allows their followers to have the autonomy to make their own decisions and manage their own tasks.

Leadership The use of power and influence to direct the activities of followers toward goal achievement.

Legacy gifts Contributions that individuals include in their wills or estate plans to be donated to a nonprofit after their death.

Lencioni's model of high-performing teams A model that puts forth the idea that high-performing teams prioritize five traits (trust, conflict, commitment, accountability, and results) and work to address any dysfunctions that may hinder their effectiveness.

Litigation Filing lawsuits or other legal actions to challenge existing laws or policies that run counter to a nonprofit organization's mission.

Live auctions Nonprofit fundraising auctions with a live auctioneer who engages guests in auctioning off various items, experiences, or services to the highest bidders, with proceeds going to support a nonprofit organization.

Lobbying Advocacy activities undertaken by nonprofit organizations to influence policies, laws, regulations, and decisions.

Local grants Grants awarded by local governments to nonprofits for projects that address regional needs and priorities.

Low readiness A situation where an employee is unable, unwilling, or too insecure to complete a task in the workplace.

LYBUNT An abbreviation in fundraising pronounced as "lie-bunt" that stands for "Last Year But Unfortunately Not This," referring to donors who gave in the previous year or giving period, but have not given in the current year.

Major gift A substantial and impactful donation from an individual, organization, or entity that significantly supports the organization's mission and programs.

Majority vote The outcome of a vote on a motion where more than half of the votes cast by persons legally entitled to vote are affirmative.

Management by objectives (MBOs) A performance evaluation approach that involves setting clear, measurable goals aligned with the organization's objectives to improve performance and decision-making.

Management positions Nonprofit staff positions that require oversight of other employees and carry a higher level of responsibility.

Market segment A distinct subgroup within a larger market who share one or more common characteristics, lumped together for marketing purposes.

Marketing The strategic process of identifying, creating, promoting, and delivering products or services that fulfill customer needs and generate value for both the business and its target audience.

Matching gifts A component of some employee giving programs where an employer provides a match for employee contributions, enhancing the impact of employee donations and providing an incentive for them to contribute.

Matrix departmentalization A hybrid departmentalization approach in which two or more forms of departmentalization are used together.

Media and communication advocacy A form of public awareness campaigns where nonprofits use various media channels to communicate their messages and engage with the public. This can involve writing op-eds, issuing press releases, conducting interviews with journalists, and other activities.

Meeting minutes Official written records that capture the key discussions, decisions, actions, and outcomes of board meetings or other organizational gatherings.

Memorial gifts Contributions made in memory of someone who has passed away.

Mid-level gift A moderately sized donation that falls between smaller, regular contributions and larger, major gifts, often indicating a higher level of donor engagement and support.

Mission drift What happens when an organization loses focus on its original mission and begins to pursue unrelated activities.

Mission review The process of examining and updating an organization's mission statement to ensure that it aligns with the organization's values, goals, and objectives.

Mission statement An expression of the purpose of the organization that describes how it meets the needs of its stakeholders.

Mission test A simple approach nonprofit decision-makers can use when pressed for a quick decision or when facing an ethical dilemma, which involves simply asking, "Which course of action aligns most effectively with and supports the organizational mission?"

Mission-driven culture An organizational culture that prioritizes mission above all else.

Mobilization The act of not just placing volunteers in various roles to complete tasks, but actively engaging them to make a meaningful impact on the organization's mission and activities.

Moderate high readiness A situation where an employee is capable but not confident in doing a task in the workplace.

Moderate low readiness A situation where an employee is confident, but not willing or able to do a task in the workplace.

Monetary gifts Gifts of cash donations, checks, credit card payments, and electronic funds transfers.

Monthly giving Donations made on a consistent basis each month, providing a consistent source of funding for the nonprofit.

Moral action The actual behavior and outcome of the four-component model approach to decision-making process.

Moral awareness The recognition that a moral issue exists and the ability to discern problematic scenarios with an ethical dilemma; the first step of the four-component model.

Moral disillusionment effect A theory that suggests that nonprofit organizations are judged more harshly than for-profit organizations when ethical breaches or moral transgressions occur within the organization.

Moral intention The desire of a decision-maker to *want* to commit to the moral course of action, meaning that they are willing to prioritize moral values over their personal values.

Moral judgment The evaluation of choices and outcomes decision-makers complete in order to explore which action is morally justified.

Multilateral agencies Member states that provide grant funds to nonprofits for projects that align with their global development goals.

Negotiation A process in which parties with differing interests engage in discussions and exchanges to reach a mutually acceptable agreement or resolution.

Networking The action or process of interacting with others to exchange information and develop professional or social contacts, such as attending networking and social events, joining professional organizations, and asking for introductions.

Neuroticism A personality trait that describes an individual's emotional reactivity and tendency to experience adverse feelings, such as anger, nervousness, or despair, especially in threatening situations and loss.

New hire turnover A measure of the percentage of employees who leave a company during a period of time, typically within the first year on the job.

Non-governmental organizations (NGOs) Nonprofit, voluntary citizen's groups that are organized on a local, national, or international level to address issues in support of the public good. NGOs often serve as grantmakers to fund grants for nonprofits focused on global issues.

Nonpartisan Remaining impartial and not aligned with any political party or group.

Nonprofit advocacy Efforts undertaken by nonprofit organizations to influence public policies, laws, regulations, and public opinion in support of their mission.

Nonprofit auctions Nonprofit fundraising activities in which items, experiences, or services are auctioned off to the highest bidders, with the proceeds going to support a nonprofit organization.

Nonprofit behavioral segments Distinct subgroups within a larger target market who share common behaviors in terms of how they engage with the nonprofit and its products, including donors, service recipients, event attendees, and volunteers.

Nonprofit events Organized activities to gather people for various purposes in support of the organizational mission and objectives of a nonprofit. Unlike programs, which result in the delivery of services, events generally center on activities such as fundraising, community engagement, networking, advocacy, and others.

Nonprofit governance The system of policies, practices, and processes that guide the management and decision-making within a nonprofit organization. It encompasses the structure and mechanisms through which a nonprofit's leadership, including its board of directors, executive leadership, and management, work together to ensure the organization's mission is carried out effectively and ethically.

Nonprofit organization Organizations that advance a social cause for public benefit, are not independently owned, and do not generate a profit for owners or investors.

Nonprofit programs Broad, structured initiatives designed to achieve specific objectives aligned with the nonprofit's mission and strategic plan that encompass a wide range of activities and may involve multiple services or interventions working together toward a common outcome.

Nonprofit services Specific, focused, and practical activities or offerings to meet immediate needs of the agency's constituency or deliver direct assistance to individuals or communities.

Nonprofit-corporate partnership A mutually beneficial relationship between a nonprofit organization and a for-profit entity, where both parties commit resources to work together toward a common objective.

Nonprogrammed decisions Decisions that are difficult to solve that arise when a problem is new, complex, or not recognized.

Non-charitable Nonprofit A nonprofit organization, such as social welfare organizations, trade associations, and recreational clubs, that exists to provide direct services on a not-for-profit basis, but these services are not charitable in nature.

Non-revenue events Nonprofit events that are designed to build awareness, engage supporters in advocacy, recognize supporters, cultivate donors, or educate stakeholders, rather than for the primary purpose of fundraising or delivering programs and services.

Obligation to advocate The obligation of a board of directors to serve as vocal, positive, and passionate ambassadors of the organization and to advocate for legislative policy that advances the nonprofit's mission.

Obligation to fund The obligation of a board of directors to ensure the financial sustainability of the organization, including not just financial policy oversight, but also fundraising responsibilities, both in making direct personal contributions and in raising funds from other sources.

Obligation to lead The obligation of a board of directors to oversee the organization and its strategic direction, including one of its most important responsibilities, which is to hire and set the compensation for the CEO/executive director position and supervise and evaluate that person.

Onboarding A process that goes beyond job training and assists new employees into acclimating into the organization, understanding the agency's culture, people, mission, and expectations.

One-time gift A singular, non-recurring donation made by individuals or organizations to support a cause, institution, or nonprofit.

Online advocacy Grassroots advocacy activities where supporters send emails, tag legislators on social media platforms, write blogs, or contact their representatives via online web forms to express their views on a specific policy issue or piece of legislation of concern to the nonprofit organization.

Online auctions Nonprofit fundraising auctions conducted over the internet.

Opening A step in the negotiation process under exchange of information, where parties present their initial positions, outlining what they hope to achieve and setting the tone for the negotiation.

Openness to experience A personality trait that reflects an individual's willingness to be open to new ideas, experiences, and ways of thinking.

Organizational chart A diagram that shows the structure of an organization and the relationships and relative ranks of its parts and positions/jobs.

Organizational design A step-by-step methodology which involves intentionally shaping various organizational components to align them with the organization's strategy to achieve specific goals and outcomes.

Organizational ethics A form of applied ethics that examines ethical principles and moral or ethical problems that can arise in a business environment.

Organizational restructuring The process of making significant changes to an organization's design, which can include its structure, processes, roles, and sometimes even its culture.

Organizational structure A formal framework that refers to the hierarchy and arrangement of roles, rules, responsibilities, and reporting relationships within an organization.

Organizational trustworthiness A term related to interpersonal trustworthiness that refers to organizations delivering on a set of personal and ethical duties, obligations, and responsibilities.

Participating leadership style A leadership style where leaders share ideas and decisions to gain followers' commitment to the task and foster a sense of mutual understanding and cooperation.

Peer-to-peer (P2P) assessment A board of directors performance evaluation tool that involves a survey that asks board members to evaluate their own performance as well as the performance of their fellow board members, aiming to understand how the overall performance and culture of the entire board are influenced by the individual members' styles and engagement.

Peer-to-peer fundraisers A fundraising approach where attendees use their participation in a nonprofit fundraising activity to solicit sponsorships from their friends, family, and corporate connections to enhance their individual impact.

Performance-based compensation An approach that ties organizational outcomes such as compensation, rewards, and recognition to employee performance.

Personal selling One-on-one interactions between sales representatives and potential customers. In the nonprofit setting, this describes the fundraising work done by development professionals as they progress through the donor fundraising cycle.

Personality An individual's unique and enduring pattern of thoughts, feelings, behaviors, and characteristics that shape their consistent way of interacting with and responding to the world around them.

Petitions Grassroots advocacy activities where supporters create, circulate, and sign petitions as a formal appeal to legislators, urging them to act in alignment with a nonprofit's mission or piece of legislation of concern to the nonprofit organization.

Phone-a-thons Organized phone campaigns where volunteers or staff members call potential donors to request contributions.

Physical withdrawal A withdrawal behavior that happens when individuals physically distance themselves from their work environment, such as frequently and intentionally missing work, consistent tardiness, leaving work early, and taking frequent breaks.

Place The location where customers can buy a product, or where they discover it.

Pledge A commitment made by an individual or organization to contribute a specific amount of money to a cause or nonprofit over a specified period.

Point-of-sale campaigns A type of cause marketing campaign where companies solicit donations from customers for a specific nonprofit upon checkout.

Policy research The systematic process of conducting studies, analyses, and investigations to gather information, data, and evidence relevant to specific policy issues, often with the goal of informing public policy discussions and decisions.

Political campaign activity Organized efforts and actions undertaken by a nonprofit to support or oppose political candidates running for public office during an election or campaign season. There are significant restrictions imposed by the IRS on this activity.

Political nonprofits Nonprofit advocacy organizations that focus on political activities and work to influence legislation.

Positive deviance A deviation from norms that may result from good intentions and even bring about positive results.

Preparation The stage in the negotiation process that is the most important, which occurs when each party identifies their goals, priorities, and potential concessions.

Price The cost that a customer pays for the product.

Primary product The main or core offering sold by an organization, which serves as the central focus of its operations and provides the primary value or benefit to its customers or stakeholders.

Principles Practical and action-oriented expressions of organizational values that reflect the shared behaviors and mindsets of people in the workplace.

Private foundations Nonprofit organizations established exclusively for charitable purposes that derive their financial support from a sole individual, family, or corporation.

Pro bono The voluntary provision of services or expertise by professionals to individuals or organizations in need, typically without charging a fee.

Product departmentalization A departmentalization approach that groups people into departments based on different product lines or categories, allowing specialized focus on each product's development, marketing, and sales.

Product The most visible of the four components of the marketing mix, referring to the tangible or intangible goods, services, or offerings that a company provides to fulfill the needs and wants of its target customers.

Product mix The array of products an organization sells; in the nonprofit sector this includes all areas where the organization generates revenue or receives contributions.

Program advisory boards Advisory boards that exist to lead and execute specific nonprofit programs.

Program delivery positions Nonprofit staff positions that directly provide and deliver programs and services to beneficiaries of the nonprofit organization's mission.

Program evaluation and monitoring Assessment of the impact and effectiveness of nonprofit programs or services through measuring outcomes, collecting data, and seeking feedback from beneficiaries.

Program impact metrics Key performance indicators that assess the impact of a nonprofit's programs, including measures such as the number of beneficiaries served, the percentage of program goals achieved, or beneficiary outcomes like improvements in quality of life for service recipients.

Programmed decisions Decisions that are made automatically with little consideration because of prior knowledge that allow for immediate recognition of the situation and the course of action to be taken.

Projection bias A faulty perception that occurs when decision-makers project their own thoughts, motives, and attitudes onto other people.

Promotion mix The array of promotion activities executed by an organization, including advertising, public relations, personal selling, sales promotion, and direct marketing.

Propensity to give A donor's likelihood of donating.

Prospect research A fundraising term that refers to the research development professionals conduct about prospective donors to determine their giving capacity and propensity to give.

Psychographic segmentation A base of segmentation that divides individuals based on psychological variables such as lifestyle, attitudes, and values.

Psychological withdrawal A withdrawal behavior that occurs when an employee engages in actions that disengage them mentally or emotionally from their work or responsibilities, such as goofing off at work, daydreaming, neglecting responsibilities, and social withdrawal.

Public awareness campaigns Strategic advocacy initiatives used by nonprofits to inform, educate, and raise awareness among stakeholders about the nonprofit and its mission and work and are designed to inspire action and mobilize resources to advance the organizational mission.

Public charities Nonprofit charitable organizations and public foundations that provide direct services to individuals and groups in need.

Public education campaigns A form of public awareness campaign that has a broader educational objective, aiming to provide the audience with detailed information, knowledge, and understanding of a particular issue.

Public relations A nonpaid form of promotion used to manage awareness and the image and reputation of an organization through activities such as media coverage, events, and press releases.

Public testimony A form of direct lobbying where individuals testify at public hearings or legislative sessions, representing the nonprofit and sharing their personal stories of how the organization has positively impacted their lives.

Qualification A fundraising term that describes the process of determining if a donor prospect is capable of making a financial contribution and, if so, in what likely range.

Quality assurance Measures taken by organizations to ensure that the programs and services provided to beneficiaries meet certain quality standards and adhere to ethical guidelines.

Rallies Highly visible, public grassroots advocacy gatherings where stakeholders convene around a shared issue to express their views to raise awareness around that cause, mobilize public support, and advocate for action.

Rational decision-making model A step-by-step approach to the decision-making process that allows decision-makers to use facts and information to maximize outcomes by examining all available alternatives.

Readiness The degree to which employees have the ability and the willingness to accomplish their specific goals.

Recurring gifts Ongoing, scheduled donations made at regular intervals, such as monthly or annually, by individuals or organizations to support a cause, institution, or nonprofit.

Regional advisory boards Advisory boards for chapters or affiliates of a larger nonprofit parent organization that engage leaders in the local communities where the affiliates are located.

Resource allocation The distribution of resources, including staff, volunteers, funding, and materials, to deliver the services within the program.

Restricted gifts Donations made with specific conditions or purposes defined by the donor, dictating how the funds should be used.

Robert's rules of order A framework often used in running nonprofit board meetings that allows groups to have majority rule while allowing minority voices to be heard.

Role ambiguity Confusion that arises when various parties hold conflicting expectations regarding an individual's responsibilities.

Rule-bending An action where an individual circumvents the formally stated obligations by not fully following a rule, requirement, procedure, or specification.

Salary productivity ratio A key performance indicator that measures the efficiency of staff compensation by comparing the total payroll expenses to the organization's overall expenses.

Sales promotion Short-term promotional incentives like discounts, coupons, contests, and giveaways aimed at encouraging immediate purchases or increasing customer loyalty.

Satisficing A decision-making problem where decision-makers select the first acceptable alternative considered.

Secondary products Additional offerings or services provided by an organization that complement its primary product or core offering.

Self-efficacy The belief one has in oneself to achieve specific goals.

Selling leadership style A leadership style where a leader attempts to convince a follower of their ideas by explaining task directions in a persuasive manner, emphasizing the importance of the task and providing step-by-step guidance.

Servant leadership style A leadership style that emphasizes the leader's primary role as a servant to their team or organization, rather than as a traditional authority figure.

Silent auctions Nonprofit fundraising auctions with written bids, online, or mobile bidding, with proceeds going to support a nonprofit organization.

Silo effect The isolated and compartmentalized functioning of different departments or teams within an organization, leading to limited communication and stifled collaboration across the organization.

Situational leadership model A theory that suggests that effective leadership involves adjusting one's leadership style based on each unique situation, including tasks and relationships, to meet the needs of the team or its members.

SMART goals An acronym that means that goals should each be specific, measurable, achievable, relevant, and time-bound.

Social and recreational clubs Non-charitable nonprofits that operate for the benefit of their membership and must be primarily supported by such membership, rather than focusing on charitable activities.

Social enterprise The actions of for-profit organizations not just in prioritizing profits, but doing so while balancing social needs like sustainability and positive social or environmental impact.

Social entrepreneurship Individuals who use their entrepreneurial skills and innovative approaches to solve social needs through the nonprofit sector.

Social welfare organizations Non-charitable nonprofits that primarily focus on the common welfare of a community but that are not necessarily limited to charitable activities.

Solicitation A formal request for a donation, which is often presented with a compelling case for support and explanation of how the donor's contribution will make a difference.

Span of control The number of subordinates or employees that a manager or supervisor can effectively oversee and manage within an organization.

Specialization The division of labor that occurs when workers learn how to perform specific tasks very well rather than focusing on doing many different tasks.

Spheres of influence The network of individuals, such as board members and volunteers, that are connected to a nonprofit or cause and have the potential to influence others to contribute.

Stakeholders Individuals, groups, or entities with an interest in or concern for a particular organization, who can influence or be influenced by the actions and outcomes related to that agency.

Standing advisory boards Advisory boards established for ongoing, major activities that last longer than a year.

State grants Grants awarded by states to nonprofits for projects that address needs and priorities of people and communities in that state.

Stereotyping A faulty perception that happens when assumptions are made about others on the basis of their membership in a social group.

Stewardship The process of thanking donors for their support and continuing to nurture the donor relationship.

Storytelling An approach nonprofits use to connect emotionally with their current and prospective supporters by conveying personal stories and narratives of those positively impacted by the organization and its mission.

Strategic Plan A comprehensive, high-level document that outlines an organization's long-term goals and the methods it intends to use to achieve them.

Strategic planning A broad term that encompasses approaches used to steer decision-making in an organization, with the process resulting in a strategic plan, which is a comprehensive, high-level document that outlines an organization's long-term goals and the methods it intends to use to achieve them.

Succession planning A strategic process that identifies and prepares potential future leaders to assume key roles as they come vacant.

Supporter recognition events Nonprofit non-revenue events designed to recognize, thank, and steward supporters such as volunteers, corporate sponsors, and donors.

SWOT analysis A commonly used method in the early stages of strategic planning that helps leaders analyze an organization's resources and environment across four dimensions: strengths, weaknesses, opportunities, and threats.

SYBUNT An abbreviation in fundraising pronounced as "sigh-bunt" that stands for "Some Year But Unfortunately Not This," referring to donors who have given in some previous year or years, but not in the current or most recent year or giving period.

Tainted donor A contribution received by a donor with a questionable reputation, which may be entirely unrelated to the gift's manner or means.

Tainted money Donations of questionable origin, such as money derived from illegal or unethical activities.

Tall span of control A situation where a manager supervises a small number of subordinates, leading to a narrow organizational hierarchy of authority with more management layers.

Target market A specific group of potential customers or consumers that an organization aims to reach with its products, services, or marketing efforts.

Teams Groups of individuals who work collaboratively to achieve shared goals, which requires interdependence, collective accountability, and a collaborative purpose.

Telling leadership style A leadership style that involves a leader directly telling a follower what to do, with specific instruction and close supervision.

Term limits The predetermined maximum length of time that individuals can serve on the board of directors before they are required to step down from their positions.

Three D's framework A framework commonly used in the nonprofit sector to describe the attributes of the ideal volunteer, representing doers, donors, and door-openers, as a way of categorizing volunteers based on their level of engagement and commitment.

Three T's framework A framework commonly used in the nonprofit sector to describe the attributes of what is contributed by the ideal volunteer, representing time, talent, and treasure.

Trade associations Non-charitable nonprofits that represent the interests of businesses, professional groups, or even entire industries rather than focusing on charitable activities.

Training The process of equipping newly hired individuals with the necessary skills, knowledge, and information to perform their job roles effectively.

Transactional leadership style A leadership style where leaders generally establish clear expectations, monitor performance closely, and provide rewards in exchange for employees meeting goals or outcomes.

Transformational leadership style A leadership style where leaders motivate their teams by establishing an inspiring vision and promoting individual development.

Transparency The practice of openness, honesty, and disclosure in the actions, decisions, and operations of an organization.

Tribute gifts Contributions made in honor of someone or to commemorate a special occasion.

Trustworthiness The quality or characteristic of being relied upon, dependable, and honest.

Turnover A measure of the number of employees who leave an organization during a specified period, typically in one year.

Unrestricted gifts Donations made without specific conditions, providing the receiving nonprofit organization the flexibility to allocate the funds where they are most needed without specific donor-imposed restrictions.

Unrestricted grants Financial grants awarded to nonprofits by grantmakers without restriction and not for a specified purpose, allowing agencies the flexibility to allocate funds where they are most needed.

Upward communication Communication that flows from employees at a lower level on the organization's hierarchy of authority up to higher-level management.

Value proposition A description of the benefits and value that a product, service, or offer provides to its target customers.

Values The stated convictions of an organization that represent the foundation of its culture and direct the actions and decision-making of people in the organization.

Vision statement A statement that outlines the long-term aspirations and goals of an organization, describes the desired future state of the organization, and provides a clear picture of what the organization hopes to achieve in the long run.

Volunteer burnout A state of physical or emotional exhaustion of volunteers that often results in diminished participation or organizational exit.

Volunteer chair A volunteer leader of a designated nonprofit team, committee, or advisory board.

Volunteer communications The practice of reaching out to volunteers and potential volunteers to educate them about a nonprofit organization and volunteer opportunities, activate and inspire them to get involved, learn more about them and their experiences, and build lasting relationships.

Volunteer contracts Formal but not legally binding written agreements between a nonprofit organization and its volunteers that outline the terms, expectations, and commitments for both parties involved in the volunteer engagement.

Volunteer engagement An organizational strategy that encourages collaboration between staff and volunteers to develop meaningful volunteer opportunities that positively impact the organization and the community.

Volunteer engagement cycle Stages through which individuals progress when becoming and remaining involved as volunteers in a nonprofit organization.

Volunteer management platform (VMP) A digital tool or software program designed to streamline and enhance the process of recruiting, organizing, and coordinating volunteers for nonprofit organizations.

Volunteer program A structured and organized initiative within a nonprofit organization that outlines strategies to recruit, supervise, and engage individuals who offer their time, skills, and services willingly and without financial compensation.

Volunteer retention A key performance indicator that measures the percentage of volunteers who continue to volunteer with a nonprofit over time.

Volunteer turnover The rate at which volunteers discontinue their involvement with a nonprofit organization, whether due to completing their assignments, transitioning to other commitments, or other reasons.

Volunteer-staff partnership The collaborative relationship between volunteers and paid staff within a nonprofit organization that involves the parties working together harmoniously to achieve shared goals, utilizing their respective skills, expertise, and resources to enhance the organization's impact and effectiveness.

Whistleblowing The act of reporting or disclosing information about illegal, unethical, or wrongful activities within an organization.

Withdrawal behavior The actions or behaviors that employees exhibit as a way of mentally or emotionally distancing themselves from their work responsibilities, which often signal dissatisfaction, disengagement, or burnout.

Workplace giving campaigns Charitable giving programs facilitated by employers in which employees can donate a portion of their salary or wages through payroll deduction directly to a nonprofit organization of their choice.

Young professional (YP) advisory boards Advisory boards comprised of young professionals with the purpose of nurturing upcoming board members and stakeholders for an organization, serving as a valuable introduction to the nonprofit and a critical part of an organization's board pipeline.

Index

Page numbers in **bold** and *italics* refer to tables and figures